GCSE Science for OCR Gateway

Homework and Summary Book

for OCR GCSE B, Additional B and Separate Sciences

Colin Bell
Gurinder Chadha
Pam Large

Collins

William Collins' dream of knowledge for all began with the publication of his first book in 1819. A self-educated mill worker, he not only enriched millions of lives, but also founded a flourishing publishing house. Today, staying true to this spirit, Collins books are packed with inspiration, innovation and practical expertise. They place you at the centre of a world of possibility and give you exactly what you need to explore it.

Collins. Freedom to teach.

Published by Collins
An imprint of HarperCollins*Publishers*
77–85 Fulham Palace Road
Hammersmith
London
W6 8JB

Browse the complete Collins catalogue at
www.collinseducation.com

10 9 8 7 6 5 4 3 2 1

ISBN-13 978 0 00 721639 0
ISBN-10 0 00 721639 4

British Library Cataloguing in Publication Data
A Catalogue record for this publication is available from the British Library

Commissioned by Cassandra Birmingham

Publishing Manager Michael Cotter

Project managed by Nicola Tidman

Edited by Anita Clark

Proofread by Lynn Watkins

Cover artwork by Bob Lea

Cover design by Starfish

Internal design and page make-up by JPD

Illustrations by JPD, Peter Harper, Mark Walker and IFADesign Ltd

Production by Natasha Buckland

Printed and bound by the Bath Press, Glasgow and Bath

Acknowledgements
The Publishers gratefully acknowledge the following for permission to reproduce photographs. Whilst every effort has been made to trace the copyright holders, in cases where this has been unsuccessful or if any have been inadvertently overlooked, the Publishers will be pleased to make the necessary arrangements at the first opportunity.

p6 istockphoto; p8 Eye of Science / Science Photo Library; p9 Pasieka / Science Photo Library; Biophoto Associate / Science Photo Library; p12 Colin Bell; p16 © 2006 JupiterImages Corporation; p22 istockphoto; p23 Cordelia Molloy / Science Photo Library; p33 Paul Rapson / Science Photo Library; p36 Martin Bond / Science Photo Library; Philippe Psaila / Science Photo Library; p44 © 2006 JupiterImages Corporation; p46 istockphoto; p47 © 2006 JupiterImages Corporation; p55 Andrew Lambert Photography / Science Photo Library; p58 David Taylor / Science Photo Library; p61 Peter Bowater / Science Photo Library; p62 Carlos Dominguez / Science Photo Library; p63 Laguna Design / Science Photo Library; p67 Kairos, Latin Stock / Science Photo Library; p68 © 2006 JupiterImages Corporation; p69 © 2006 JupiterImages Corporation; p71 istockphoto; p73 Sheila Terry / Science Photo Library; p75 CC Studio / Science Photo Library; p76 N. Feather / Science Photo Library; p77 istockphoto; p78 istockphoto; p81 istockphoto; p83 istockphoto; p86 © 2006 JupiterImages Corporation; p88 Ian Hooton / Science Photo Library; p95 © 2006 JupiterImages Corporation; p98 Martyn F. Chillmaid / Science Photo Library; p102 istockphoto; p104 istockphoto; p107 istockphoto; p108 Gregory K. Scott / Science Photo Library; p114 Science Photo Library

Contents

Introduction

Welcome to Collins GCSE Science!

This Homework and Summary book is designed to help you get the most out of your GCSE Science studies. It covers GCSE Science, GCSE Additional Science, and GCSE Biology, Chemistry, Physics, all in one handy book!

There are several sections within the book. Here's how they work.

Summary content and Now Try This

This book is structured into topics which summarise the content you will learn on your course. The panels of summary points break all of the content down into short handy chunks to help you remember the key ideas. Any summary points that are Higher tier are shown in italics. For more details, references to the relevant Collins Science textbook are also provided.

Within each summary panel there is a Now Try This box with practice questions. These questions are provided to help you check your own progress and understanding. Answers are provided at the back of the book.

At the top right of each page you will notice three circles. These are for you to mark in how well you feel you have understood everything on that page. For example:

 I have started this section but I don't completely understand or remember it all yet.

 I am getting better, but I have not yet been able to complete the Now Try This exercises correctly.

 I completely understand this section, and can complete all of the Now Try This exercises correctly.

Homework questions

Homework questions are provided for every topic. Your teacher will suggest which homework you should do.

Exam practice

The Exam-style questions pages will let you really prove you understand the Science, and will help you get ready for the exams. Note that these sample exam questions may cover content from more than one topic. This will help keep the key ideas you have learned fresh in your mind.

Model exam question answers

The Model answers are provided so you can see how questions should be answered.

We hope you find this Homework and Summary book useful. Good luck with your studies!

Your name ____________________

Class ____________________

Fitness and diet

AEROBIC/ANAEROBIC RESPIRATION

- Fitness is linked to physical activity.
- Exercise raises breathing and pulse rates.
- Aerobic respiration uses oxygen to release energy from food: glucose + oxygen → carbon dioxide + water (+energy).
- *The symbol equation for aerobic respiration is:*

$$C_6H_{12}O_6 + 6O_2 \rightarrow 6CO_2 + 6H_2O.$$

- During hard exercise the oxygen demand is too high so anaerobic respiration takes place (oxygen debt).
- Anaerobic respiration does not use oxygen:
glucose → lactic acid (+ energy).
It produces less energy and much lactic acid causing muscle pain and fatigue.

TOP TIP Breathing means exchange of gases. Respiration is using oxygen to release energy from food.

Now try this

a Complete these sentences.

Cassie walks to school. She uses ________________ respiration. This releases ________________ for her muscles to contract. The main source of energy is $C_6H_{12}O_6$ which is ________________.

In a PE lesson she plays netball. During hard exercise she uses ________________ respiration. Her muscles will be short of ____________ and will contain a lot of ____________ which causes them to ache.

Homework

1 Write down and remember the word equations for aerobic and anaerobic respiration.
2 Use a search engine to find out about warming up and warming down when training.
3 Name **three** activities using aerobic respiration and **three** activities using anaerobic.

BLOOD PRESSURE

- The contraction of heart muscles puts blood under pressure.
- Blood in arteries is under pressure.
- Blood is under pressure so it can reach all body parts.
- Blood pressure is measured in mmHg (millimetres of mercury).
- Diastolic and systolic measurements are used.
- The systolic pressure is written first, then the diastolic.
- Age and lifestyle affect blood pressure.
- *High blood pressure can cause strokes and kidney damage.*
- *Low blood pressure can cause dizziness and poor circulation.*

Now try this

b Answer the following questions.

Nikki's blood pressure is 150/90 mmHg. Which number is the systolic measurement?

____

What does mmHg mean?

____

Her blood pressure is high. What are the dangers of high blood pressure?

____

What lifestyle changes can she make to reduce her blood pressure? ____________

____

Homework

4 Complete a blood pressure questionnaire (see the student book, page 17).
5 What lifestyle changes could you make to keep your blood pressure at normal levels?
6 Use a search engine (or visit a Health Centre) to find out about cardio-vascular efficiency.

DIET

- A balanced diet contains carbohydrates, fats, proteins, minerals, vitamins, fibre and water. The amounts of substances required depends on gender, activity and age.
- Carbohydrates, fats and proteins provide energy.
- High levels of protein are needed for growth.
- Protein deficiency (kwashiorkor) is common in developing countries.
- Obesity is linked to increased health risks for arthritis, heart disease, diabetes and breast cancer.
- The Body Mass Index (BMI) can be calculated:

$$\frac{\text{mass in kg}}{(\text{height in m})^2}$$

- The recommended daily average (RDA) for protein intake is $0.75 \times$ body mass in grams.

Now try this

c Circle the correct answers.

Which one of the following is a food?

calcium carbohydrate vitamin C

You need a lot of protein when:

growing resting running

An obese person is:

very overweight underweight growing old

A vegetarian does not eat:

fibre meat plants protein

Homework

7 Work out your BMI. Plot the information on a chart like the one on page 19 in your student book.

8 Work out your RDA of protein. Use food labels to check your actual protein intake.

9 Use a search engine to find out the countries where protein deficiency is common.

DIGESTION

- Digestion is the breakdown of food.
- Digestion makes food soluble.
- Physical digestion by teeth breaks down food into smaller pieces.
- Chemical digestion uses enzymes to break down food into smaller molecules.
- Different enzymes need different conditions. For example, protease needs acid conditions.

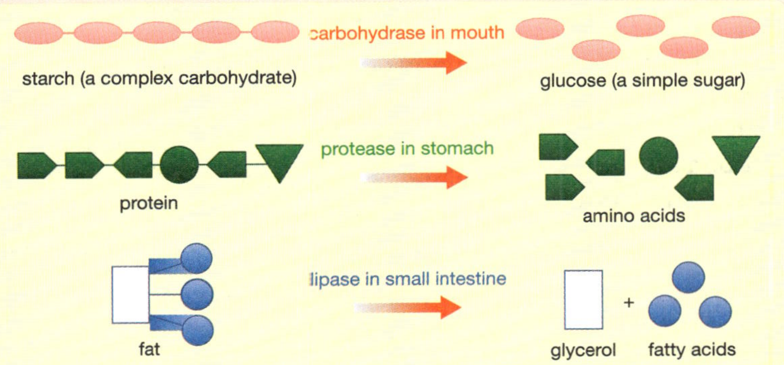

Now try this

d Link each food type to the correct enzyme and product.

Food	Enzyme	Product
Carbohydrate	protease	amino acids
Protein	carbohydrase	fatty acids
Fat	lipase	glucose

TOP TIP Protease enzymes break down proteins.

Homework

10 Your gall bladder makes bile. Find out how it helps digestion.

11 List the different sugars (their names end in -ose) found in fruit drinks.

12 Explain why fruit drinks will supply a quick energy source.

Disease and the nervous system

DISEASE

- Microorganisms that cause disease are called pathogens.
- Pathogens cause infectious diseases.
- Athletes foot is caused by a fungus, flu by a virus, cholera by a bacterium and dysentery by a protozoan.
- Scurvy is caused by a vitamin deficiency, anaemia by a mineral deficiency, diabetes by a body disorder and red-green colour deficiency is inherited.
- Vectors such as the mosquito spread diseases.
- The body resists entry of pathogens by blood clotting, mucous membranes, stomach acid and the skin covering.
- *Benign tumours grow slowly and are harmless.*
- *Malignant tumours grow quickly and can be fatal.*

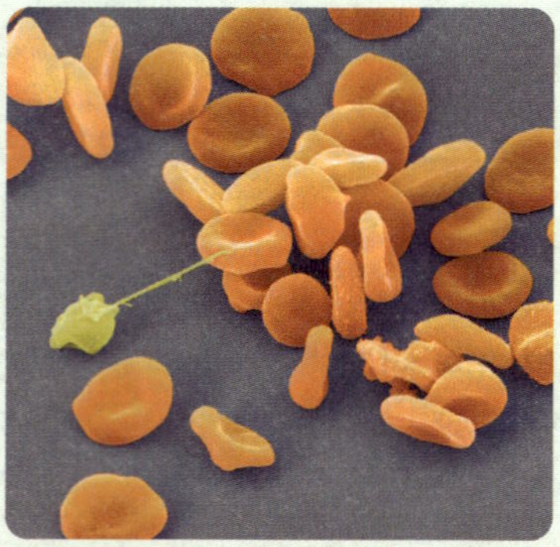

Now try this

a Answer the following questions.

Name two infectious diseases.

____________ ____________

Name two non-infectious diseases.

____________ ____________

What is a pathogen?

____

What does the stomach make to protect us from pathogens?

____

Which of the following is a way to control malaria?

eating a balanced diet
killing flies   killing mosquitoes

A mosquito is which of the following?

parasite   prey   vector

Homework

1 Make a list of diseases you know then find out what causes them.
2 Use a search engine to find in which areas of the world you can get malaria.
3 Find out which mineral deficiency causes anaemia.

IMMUNITY

- White blood cells make antibodies that kill pathogens.
- Pathogens have different antigens on their surface.
- *The correct antigen locks on to the matching antigen.*
- Antibodies give immunity to some diseases.
- Active immunity comes from white blood cells.
- Passive immunity comes from injected antibodies.
- Passive immunity is fast-acting but only lasts a short time.
- Immunisation protects against specific diseases.
- Drugs called antibiotics only kill bacteria and fungi.

TOP TIP White blood cells and antibiotics kill pathogens, not the disease.

Now try this

b Complete these sentences.

Antibodies are made by our ____________. This is called ____________ immunity. Antibodies lock onto ____________ on the surface of a ____________. Immunisation uses ____________ immunity. Antibiotics do not kill pathogens such as ____________.

Homework

4 Find out which diseases you have been immunised against.
5 Use a search engine to find out about MMR.
6 Explain the use of placebos in drug testing.

THE NERVOUS SYSTEM AND REFLEXES

- The brain and spinal cord form the central nervous system (CNS).
- Spinal and cranial nerves form the peripheral nervous system.
- The nerve cells are called neurones.
- The axon of a neurone carries the electrical impulse.
- Reflex actions (for example, knee jerk, pupil reflex) are fast, automatic and protective.
- The reflex arc involves sensory neurones (from a receptor) and a motor neurone (to an effector).
- Reflex actions do not involve the brain and thought.
- *A synapse is the gap between two neurones.*
- *A transmitter substance diffuses across a synapse.*

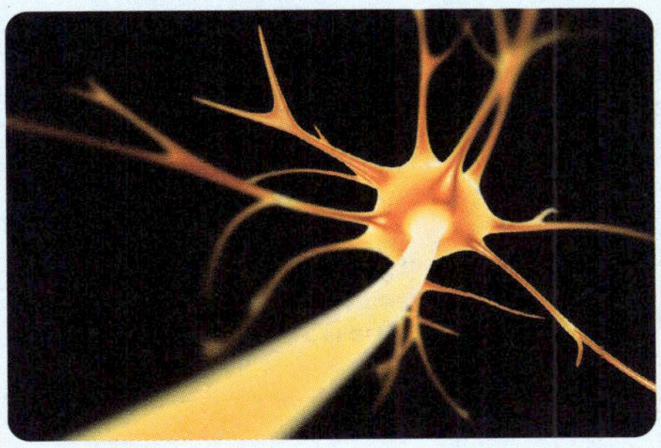

Now try this

c Are the following statements true (T) or false (F)?

Neurones are cells in the nervous system.	______
Sensory neurones carry impulses to an effector.	______
Muscles are an example of an effector.	______
Reflex actions are fast and automatic.	______
Reflex actions involve the brain.	______
An electric impulse crosses a synapse.	______
A neurone has an insulating sheath.	______

Homework

7 List **three** reflex actions and explain how they are protective.

8 Find out how some reflexes can be controlled (conditioned).

9 Draw and label a diagram to show an example of a reflex arc.

VISION

- The eye is a receptor; it reacts to light.
- The skin, tongue and ears are also receptors.
- Rays of light are refracted (bent) by the lens and cornea.
- Light rays are focused to form an image on the retina.
- Using both eyes gives binocular vision to judge distance.
- Red-green colour deficiency is inherited.
- Long and short sight is when the eyeball or the lens is the wrong shape.
- *The suspensory ligaments and ciliary muscles alter the shape of the lens.*
- *The eye accommodates by altering the shape of the lens.*
- *Long and short sight can be corrected by glasses, contact lenses or laser surgery.*

Now try this

d Match the parts of the eye to the correct function.

Cornea	focuses light
Iris	controls amount of light into eye
Lens	refracts light
Retina	carries nerve impulses
Optic nerve	reacts to light

TOP TIP The bending of light is refraction not reflection.

Homework

10 Draw a labelled diagram to show the structure of the eye.

11 Find out why the image on the retina is upside down.

12 Use a search engine to find out more about laser surgery on the cornea.

Homeostasis, drugs and genes

HOMEOSTASIS

- Keeping the inside of our body at steady levels automatically is called homeostasis.
- Temperature, water and carbon dioxide levels are kept steady.
- Our body temperature (approximately 37 °C) can be measured in various places (ear, mouth, finger, anus).
- The body is cooled by evaporation of sweat.
- *Vasoconstriction reduces heat loss.*
- High temperatures can cause heat stroke; low temperatures can cause hypothermia.
- Hormones are made in endocrine glands and carried in the blood.
- The pancreas makes insulin; the ovary and testes make testosterone, oestrogen and progesterone.
- Insulin controls blood sugar levels. A lack of it causes diabetes.
- Oestrogen and progesterone control the menstrual cycle.

Now try this

a Answer the following questions.

Why do we sweat?

to lose heat   to gain heat
to make hormones

Name two conditions in the body that are kept steady.

________ ________

Diabetes is caused by a lack of which hormone? ________

What is vasoconstriction? ________

Which two hormones control the menstrual cycle? ________ ________

Homework

1. Draw an outline of the human body and put in the endocrine glands.
2. Use a search engine to make a time line about discoveries to understand diabetes.
3. Find out how negative feedback mechanisms work.

DRUGS

- Drugs can be useful or harmful.
- Harmful drugs are classified A, B or C according to how dangerous they are.
- Drugs can be depressants (alcohol), pain killers (aspirin), stimulants (nicotine, ecstasy), hallucinogens (cannabis) or performance enhancers (anabolic steroids).
- *Depressants and stimulants affect synapses.*
- Cigarette smoke contains carbon monoxide, nicotine (addictive), tars (cancer-causing) and particulates.
- Smoking increases the risk of lung cancer, heart disease and low birth weight.
- Alcohol has quick effects (poor judgement and muscle control) and also damages the brain and liver.

Now try this

b Complete the following.

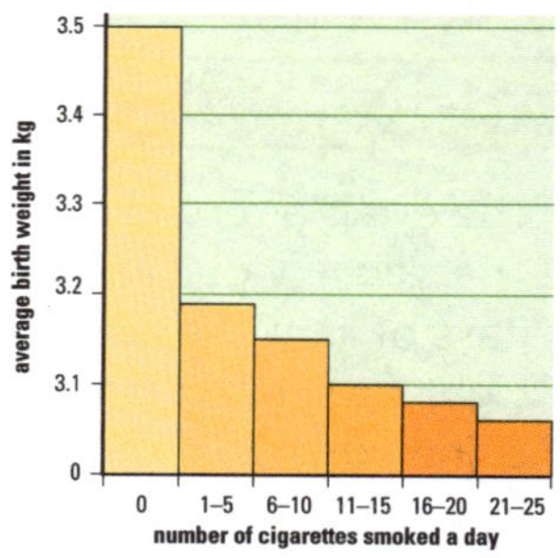

What is the average birth weight if you smoke no cigarettes a day? ________

What is the average birth weight if you smoke 20 cigarettes a day? ________

The more cigarettes you smoke when pregnant the ________ the baby's birth weight.

Homework

4. Find out about drug testing in sports such as football.
5. Find out about the legal limits of alcohol in the blood for drivers.
6. Use a search engine to find data on the dangers of cannabis.

See pages 32–47 of Collins GCSE Science

CHROMOSOMES AND GENES

- Asexual reproduction only involves one parent and produces clones that are identical.
- Sexual reproduction involves two parents and results in a unique individual with some characteristics from each parent.
- Gametes contain only half the number of chromosomes in body cells.
- Human body cells contain 23 pairs of chromosomes.
- Chromosomes carry genetic information and are in matching pairs.
- The genetic information is the genetic code.
- Genes are sections of a chromosome and contain DNA.
- DNA has four different bases.
- *The bases are A, T, G and C.*
- Each gene contains a different sequence of bases.
- *DNA controls protein synthesis such as enzymes.*
- *Some genes in a specialised cell are switched off.*

Now try this

c Fill in the missing words.

Sexual reproduction results in the fusion of male and female _______. These only contain _______ the number of chromosomes in body cells. Body cells contain _______ pairs of chromosomes. DNA has _______ different bases. The sequence of bases is the _______ code. DNA controls body characteristics by making certain _______.

TOP TIP Remember to look carefully at the words asexual and sexual.

Homework

7 Read the book 'The double helix' or use a search engine to find out about Watson and Crick.
8 Work out why gametes have only half the number of chromosomes in body cells.
9 Understand why all genes are switched on in unspecialised cells.

INHERITANCE AND MUTATIONS

- Characteristics can have environmental or genetic causes.
- Inherited characteristics are either dominant or recessive.
- Inherited diseases are caused by faulty genes.
- Gender in mammals is controlled by sex chromosomes.
- A male has XY sex chromosomes.
- A female has XX sex chromosomes.
- Mutations are sudden changes in genes or chromosomes.
- *Alleles are different versions of the same gene.*
- *Recessive alleles are only expressed in the absence of dominant alleles.*
- *A heterozygote has both versions of the same gene.*
- *A homozygote has the same version of a gene.*

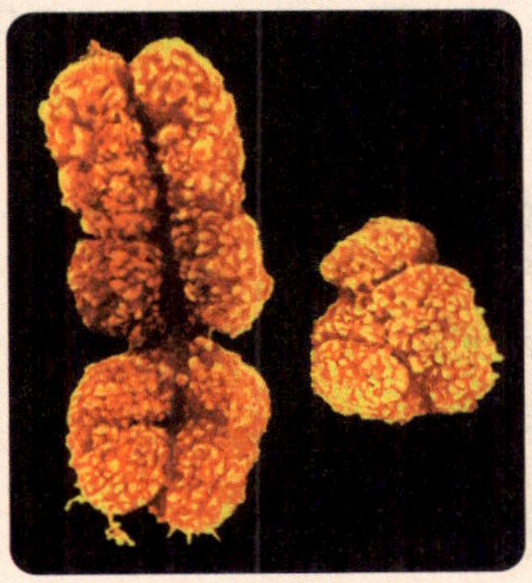

Now try this

d Complete the following.

Are the following characteristics environmental (E) or genetic (G)?

ear lobe shape _______

eye colour _______

scar _______

Circle the inherited condition:

cholera   cystic fibrosis   flu

Which gametes will contain XY chromosomes? _______

If B is for brown eyes and b for blue eyes, what eye colour is Bb? _______

What eye colour is bb? _______

Is Bb a homozygote or a heterozygote? _______

Homework

10 Use text books and a search engine to list human dominant characteristics.
11 Use text books and a search engine to list human recessive characteristics.
12 Draw a genetic diagram to show the inheritance of gender.

Ecosystems, respiration and photosynthesis

SAMPLING AND IDENTIFYING ORGANISMS

- Population size and distribution of plants and animals can be estimated by sampling.
- Plants and animals are collected using pooters, nets, pitfall traps and quadrats.
- Keys are used to identify plants and animals.
- *A small sample size will give an inaccurate estimate.*
- Most organisms are classified as plants or animals.
- Animals are either invertebrates (no backbone) or vertebrates (with a backbone).
- Fish, amphibians, reptiles, birds and mammals are all vertebrates.
- A binomial system is used to name species.
- An organism will only breed successfully with the same species.
- *A hybrid is a result of a cross between two species.*
- *It is difficult to classify some organisms like Euglena and hybrids such as mules.*

Now try this

a Match each class with the correct characteristic.

Fish	moist skin
Amphibians	gills
Reptiles	fur
Birds	feathers
Mammals	dry scales

TOP TIP A species has two names. (*Homo sapiens* is you!)

Homework

1 Find out what types of animals would be found in a pit fall trap in a garden.
2 Use a search engine to find out about the work of John Ray and Carl Linnaeus in classification.
3 Find out how to calculate a population size by sampling.

ECOSYSTEMS

- An ecosystem describes living things and where they live.
- A community is the plants and animals living there.
- A habitat is where the plants and animals live.
- Ecosystems can be natural (a lake) or artificial (aquarium).
- Some ecosystems (deep oceans) are unexplored.
- *Weed killers, pesticides and fertilisers are used in artificial ecosystems.*
- *Artificial ecosystems have a limited variety of organisms (smaller biodiversity).*

Now try this

b Complete the following.

community ecosystem habitat

_______________ Living things and where they live
→ _______________ Plants and animals
→ _______________ Where they live

Artificial ecosystems have a _______________ biodiversity because _______________ are used there.

Homework

4 Select a natural ecosystem and list **five** plants and **five** animals living there.
5 Select an artificial ecosystem and list **five** plants and **five** animals living there.
6 Explain how artificial ecosystems are different from natural ecosystems.

See pages 54–65 of Collins GCSE Science

PHOTOSYNTHESIS

- Plants make their own food by photosynthesis.
- They use light energy, carbon dioxide and water to make glucose and oxygen.
- Photosynthesis takes place in the chlorophyll molecule.
- The word equation is:

  carbon dioxide + water $\xrightarrow[\text{(chlorophyll)}]{\text{(light energy)}}$ glucose + oxygen
- *The balanced symbol equation is:*

  $6CO_2 + 6H_2O \rightarrow C_6H_{12}O_6 + 6O_2$.
- Glucose is used to provide energy from respiration.
- Glucose can be turned into insoluble starch for storage.
- Glucose can be turned into protein for growth.

TOP TIP 'Photo' means light, 'synthesis' means to make.

Now try this

c Answer these questions.

Which gas is used in photosynthesis? ________

Which gas is produced by photosynthesis? ________

Which form of energy is used in photosynthesis? ________

In which molecule does photosynthesis take place? ________

As what can glucose be stored? ________

Why is glucose not stored? ________

Homework

7 Find out why animals depend on plants for their food.
8 Find out why fungi such as mushrooms can be grown in the dark.
9 Learn the word and symbol equations for photosynthesis.

PHOTOSYNTHESIS AND RESPIRATION

- Green plants photosynthesise faster in warm, light conditions with plenty of carbon dioxide.
- *The rate of photosynthesis can be limited by carbon dioxide levels, light and temperature.*
- Plants, like all living things, respire at all times.
- During daytime, green plants will take in carbon dioxide and give out oxygen in photosynthesis.
- Respiration in plants will only be noticed at night when the plants are not photosynthesising.

TOP TIP The equation for photosynthesis is the reverse of respiration.

Now try this

d Are the following statements true (T) or false (F)?

Respiration takes place only at night. ________

Photosynthesis takes place only during the light. ________

Green plants use up carbon dioxide for respiration. ________

Green plants use up carbon dioxide in photosynthesis. ________

Light, carbon dioxide and temperature can be limiting factors in photosynthesis. ________

Homework

10 Find out how the rate of photosynthesis can be measured.
11 Explain why heating a greenhouse by burning a fuel can have **two** advantages.
12 Produce a table to show similarities and differences between photosynthesis and respiration.

Competition, adaptations and survival

COMPETITION

- Organisms compete to survive and breed.
- Animals compete for food, water, shelter and mates.
- Plants compete for light, water and minerals.
- *Similar animals in the same habitat are in close competition.*
- *An organism's role in an ecosystem is its ecological niche.*

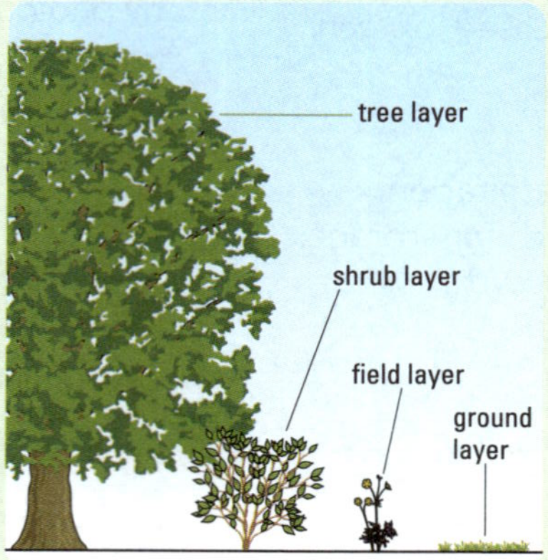

Now try this

a Complete the following.

Above ground, plants compete for __________.

Below ground plants compete for __________ and __________.

Organisms compete to __________.

Red and grey squirrels are in close __________ because they occupy the same __________ __________.

Homework

1 Explain why animals and plants compete for different things.

2 Use your text book to find out why the number of lemmings fluctuates.

3 Use a search engine to find out the changes in distribution of red and grey squirrels.

ANIMAL RELATIONSHIPS

- A predator (for example, a badger) hunts and eats its prey (for example, shrews).
- The populations of predator and prey fluctuate.
- In mutualism, organisms depend on other organisms (for example, oxpecker birds remove fleas from buffalo).
- *Another example of mutualism is bacteria living in root nodules of leguminous plants.*
- In parasitism, one organism lives on or in another organism so only one organism benefits.
- Fleas and tapeworms are parasites on and in their human hosts.

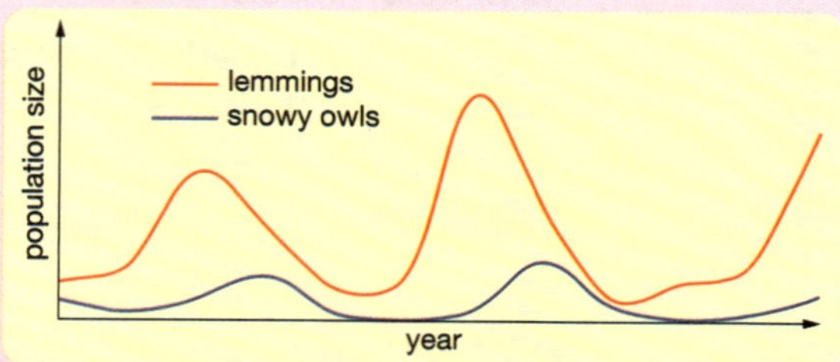

Now try this

b Complete these sentences.

The badger is a ______________ when it eats shrews. The shrew is its ______________.

The shrew is a ______________ when it eats caterpillars. The caterpillar is its ______________.

Tapeworms are ______________ inside humans. Humans are their ______________.

______________ is when two organisms depend on each other.

Homework

4 Name **five** different predators and their main prey.

5 Find out **two** other examples of parasitism.

6 Write a short explanation of how mutualism differs from parasitism.

See pages 66–69 and 72–75 of Collins GCSE Science

ADAPTATIONS TO ENVIRONMENT – ANIMALS

- Animals are adapted to different habitats such as in water, under ground or in the air.
- Animals adapted to their environment are better able to compete and survive.
- Predators show adaptations such as binocular vision, sharp teeth and claws and camouflage.
- Some animals are adapted to avoid predators by having a wide field of view, having stings and living in groups.
- Polar bears are adapted to cold conditions by having thick fur, a thick layer of fat and large surface area to volume ratio.
- Camels are adapted to dry desert conditions by having large feet, nostrils that can close and a fatty hump.

Now try this

c Complete the following.

Match up the correct words.

Vision	**Field of vision**	**Type of animal**
Mainly binocular	wide	predator
Mainly monocular	narrow	prey

A polar bear's thick fur will ________ its body against heat loss.

A camel's large feet will help it to __________ its weight.

TOP TIP When describing an adaptation remember to explain how it helps survival.

Homework

7 Use a search engine to plot the distribution of camel species on a world map.
8 Choose a named bird and list its adaptations to flight.
9 Explain why a polar bear would not survive in a desert.

ADAPTATION TO ENVIRONMENT – PLANTS

- Plants are adapted to different environments such as hot dry deserts.
- Plants that are adapted to their environment are better able to compete and survive.
- *Cacti are adapted to hot dry conditions by having a thick cuticle, reduced leaves and means of storing water.*
- *Some plants are adapted for wind pollination by having feathery stigmas and small light pollen.*
- *Some plants are adapted for insect pollination by having colourful petals, sugary nectar and sticky pollen.*

Now try this

d Complete these sentences.

Well adapted plants will _________ and _________.

A plant with reduced leaves will lose less _________.

A plant with light pollen will be pollinated by _________.

Pollination is the transfer of _________.

Colourful petals will attract _________ for _________.

Homework

10 Write a full explanation of the adaptations of a cactus to desert life.
11 Use a reference book to name **five** plants showing insect pollination.
12 Use a reference book to name **five** plants showing wind pollination.

Evolution, natural selection and extinction

FOSSILS

- Fossils can be formed by impregnation, casts or preserved in amber, peat or ice.
- Fossils provide evidence of evolution.
- Older fossils are found in older and usually lower layers of rock.
- Fossil records are incomplete because fossilisation rarely happened and soft body parts are not fossilised.
- *Fossil records can be interpreted in different ways.*

Now try this

a Answer the following questions.

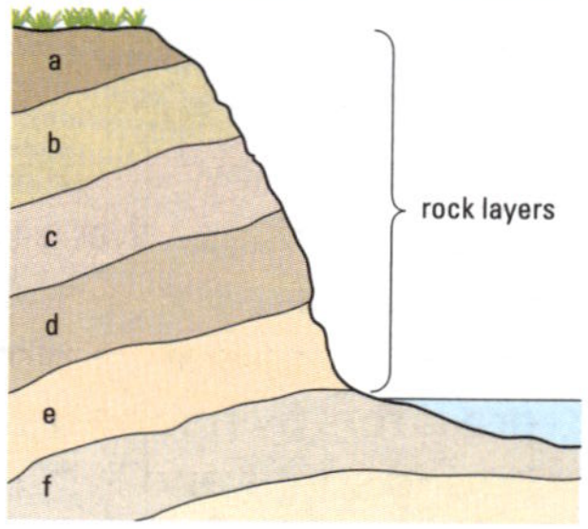

Which rock layer will have the oldest fossils?

____

Which rock layer will have the youngest fossils? _______________

Fossils of the same organism are slightly different in each layer. What does this show?

____

Homework

1 Write a short description of how a dinosaur became fossilised.
2 Use a search engine to trace the fossil record of an animal.
3 Find out which types of rock are likely to contain fossils.

VARIATION AND NATURAL SELECTION

- Organisms of the same species show variation.
- Natural Selection is when less well adapted organisms do not survive and breed.
- The characteristics which result in variation will be inherited in genes.
- Examples of Natural Selection are the survival of dark or pale forms of moths, antibiotic-resistant bacteria and warfarin-resistant rats.
- *Darwin's theory of natural selection depends on variation, competition, 'survival of the fittest' and inheritance of successful adaptations.*
- *Lamarck's theory of evolution depends on characteristics developed in a life time being 'acquired' and inherited.*

TOP TIP Remember Natural Selection is a theory to explain evolution.

Now try this

b Complete these sentences.

Organisms of the same species show _______________ from each other. They _______________ with each other for food. Some are better _______________ than others. Better adapted organisms survive and _______________. Their characteristics are _______________ by their offspring. This is an example of _______________ _______________.

Homework

4 Write a short explanation about the survival of dark moths in industrial areas.
5 How does Darwin's theory explain the giraffe's long neck?
6 How does Lamarck's theory explain the giraffe's long neck?

POPULATIONS

- The human population is increasing exponentially (increasing at an increasing rate).
- An increasing population increases use of resources.
- An increasing population increases pollution.
- Pollution causes global warming (from carbon dioxide), ozone depletion (from CFCs) and acid rain (from sulfur dioxide).
- Absence of indicator species shows pollution.
- Absence of blood worms and waterlouse shows water pollution.
- Absence of lichens shows air pollution.
- *Exponential population growth will have many consequences (more pollution, overcrowding, exhaustion of resources).*

Now try this

c Match the sources to the correct chemicals and results, then complete the sentence below.

Source	Chemical	Result
Burning fossil fuel	carbon dioxide	ozone depletion
Old fridges	sulfur dioxide	acid rain
Burning fossil fuel	CFCs	global warming

Lichens are an ____________ species for ____________ ____________.

TOP TIP Remember that pollution occurs when the environment cannot cope with the high level of pollutant.

Homework

7 Write a short description of global warming and its consequences.

8 Write an explanation of how acid rain is formed.

9 Use a search engine to find different predictions of human population growth.

ENDANGERED SPECIES AND EXTINCTION

- Endangered species are in danger of becoming extinct.
- The red squirrel and osprey are endangered in the UK.
- The mammoth and dodo are recently extinct animals.
- Animals become endangered or extinct due to climate change, habitat destruction, pollution or hunting.
- They can be protected by laws, captive breeding programmes and protected habitats.
- Some whale species are endangered.
- Many people object to keeping whales in zoos.
- Sustainable resources such as fish will continue only if few are used.
- *Conservation programmes protect our food supply, maintain food chains, and allow for future medical use.*

TOP TIP Extinction means there are none of that species alive in the world, not just the UK.

Now try this

d Complete these sentences.

Fish stocks in the North Sea are very low. This has been caused by ____________. The fish can be protected by ____________ and ____________ ____________.

Red squirrels are endangered because they are in competition with ____________ ____________.

Pandas are endangered due to ____________ ____________ and ____________. Zoos often exchange pandas for ____________ ____________ programmes.

Homework

10 What is the difference between being endangered and being extinct?

11 Use a search engine to find a list of endangered animals in the UK.

12 List reasons for and against keeping whales in captivity.

Carbon chemistry 1

COOKING

- Food is cooked by boiling, steaming, grilling, frying, heating with microwaves or baking/roasting in ovens.
- Cooking kills microbes, improves the taste, flavour and texture, and makes food easier to digest.
- Cooking is a chemical change because new substances are made, it is irreversible and energy is absorbed.
- *Cooked potato feels softer and its carbohydrates are easier to digest because heat destroys cell walls.*
- *Proteins change shape irreversibly/denature as meat browns and egg white solidifies.*
- Baking powder gives off CO_2 and trapped gas bubbles expand during cooking to make cakes rise.
- *Sodium hydrogen carbonate in baking soda decomposes when heated.*

  $$2NaHCO_3 \rightarrow Na_2CO_3 + H_2O + CO_2$$
- Carbon dioxide turns limewater cloudy.

Now try this

a Match the substances on the left with what happens when they are heated. Each substance matches up with more than one effect.

Potato	releases carbon dioxide
	proteins denatured
	cell walls destroyed
Meat	decomposes
	absorbs heat energy
	changes chemically
Sodium hydrogen carbonate	flavour improves
	gets softer

TOP TIP Eggs and meat are good sources of proteins.

Homework

1 Find 'before' and 'after' pictures to show how foods change when they cook.
2 How could you prove that sodium hydrogen carbonate decomposes?
3 Prepare a presentation on reactions that occur when food cooks.

FOOD ADDITIVES

- All food is made from chemicals but some additives can be harmful to certain individuals.
- Food additives include colours, flavour enhancers, emulsifiers and antioxidants.
- Antioxidants stop food spoiling due to oxidation, for example, ascorbic acid in tinned fruit and cereals.
- Emulsions contain immiscible liquids, for example, mayonnaise has oil drops dispersed in water.
- Emulsifiers stop them separating into layers.
- They have hydrophobic and hydrophilic ends.
- *The 'water hating' ends stick into the oil and the 'water loving' ends face outwards, so drops of oil are suspended in the water.*

Now try this

b Match the key words with the definitions.

Oxidation	water loving
Emulsify	cannot be mixed
Emulsifier	disperse one substance in another
Hydrophilic	stops emulsions separating
Antioxidant	a reaction with oxygen
Hydrophobic	water hating – attracted to oil
Immiscible	stops food reacting with O_2

Homework

4 Print or copy a mayonnaise recipe and highlight the oil, water and emulsifier.
5 Find images of emulsions and add labels to explain how they form.
6 Dirty washing-up water is an emulsion – explain why.

See pages 94–105 of Collins GCSE Science

PACKAGING

- Water lets bacteria and moulds grow.
- Active packaging can reduce the need for antioxidants and preservatives in food.
- *Active packaging changes the gas composition around food so its shelf life is extended, for example, by scavenging oxygen or removing water vapour.*
- Intelligent packaging uses sensors and indicators to show how fresh the food is.
- Self-heating/cooling cans have chemicals in them which release/absorb heat when they react.

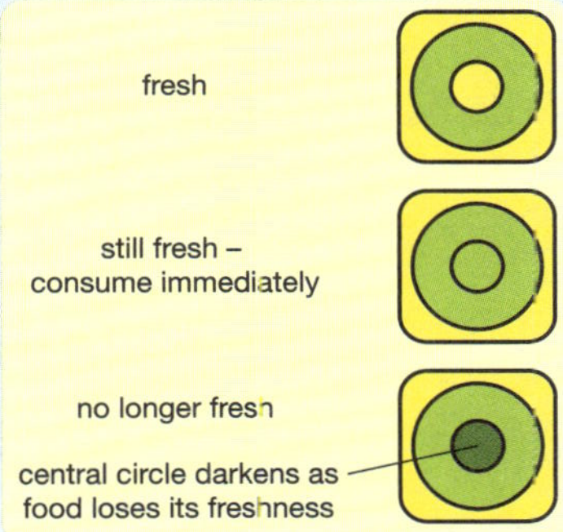

TOP TIP Active packaging changes the contents. Intelligent packing shows the changes.

Now try this

c Decide if each package is **intelligent (I), active (A)** or **neither (N).**

Goes green when fruit is ripe	______
Stops air getting in	______
Absorbs oxygen	______
Produces antioxidants	______
Absorbs water	______
Keeps out water	______
Warms up	______
Displays warning sign if bacteria start to grow	______

Homework

7 Design a modern crisp bag that is active and intelligent.
8 Prepare a presentation to explain why food spoils.
9 Research the advantages of smart packaging.

SMELLS

- Some cosmetics are made from natural chemicals, for example, lavender oil.
- Synthetic perfumes contain esters.
- Perfume must be non-toxic, non-irritant, insoluble in water, unreactive with water and volatile.
- Volatile liquids evaporate, stimulating sense cells in the nose to create a smell.
- *Weak attractive forces between their particles let the most energetic molecules escape.*
- A solution is a stable mixture of solvent and solute, for example, nail varnish remover is a solvent for nail varnish.
- Animal testing ensures products are safe, but some people argue it is unethical and unreliable.

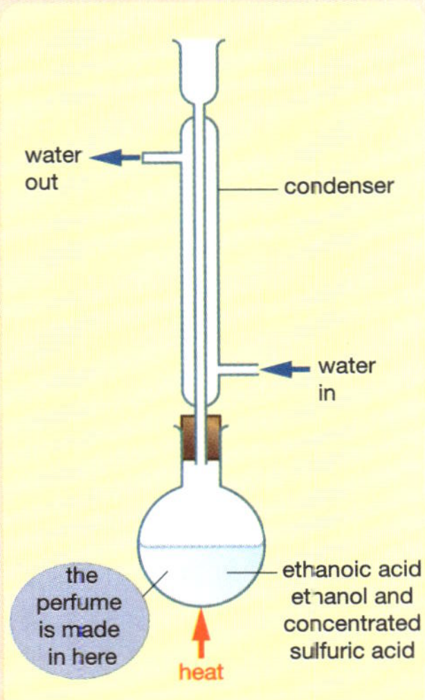

Now try this

d Decide if each description matches an **organic acid (O), alcohol (A)** or **ester (E).**

Makes esters	______
Fruity smell	______
Reacts with alcohols	______
Weak intermolecular forces	______
Reacts with organic acids	______
Good solvent	______
Volatile	______

TOP TIP Esters have pleasant fruity smells and make good solvents.

Homework

10 Explain why perfumes need to be volatile.
11 Produce a list of esters and say what they are found in.
12 Use particle pictures to explain why nail varnish remover works.

Carbon chemistry 2

DISTILLATION

- Crude oil, coal and gas are non-renewable fossil fuels which cannot be replaced.
- *Few countries have large oil reserves. Political instability can limit supplies.*
- Spills during transport cause oil slicks and damage wildlife and beaches.
- *Large alkanes have strong intermolecular forces and high boiling points (b.p.).*
- During fractional distillation:
  - the mixture of hydrocarbons in oil is heated
  - bitumen (high b.p.) sinks to the bottom
  - gases (low b.p.) leave from the top
  - fractions with similar b.p. are collected: LPG (propane + butane), petrol, diesel, paraffin, heating oil, fuel oils and bitumen.

Now try this

a Decide whether the alkane described is very **short (S)**, **long (L)** or **either (E)**.

Leaves the top of a fractionating column	______
Has a high boiling point	______
Is found in crude oil	______
Is hard to remove after spills	______
Has weak intermolecular forces	______
Collects at the bottom during distillation	______

Homework

1 Prepare a presentation to show how fractional distillation works.

2 Find out how oil came to be trapped in sedimentary rocks.

3 Research environmental problems caused by oil spills.

CRACKING

- *Demand for petrol is met by cracking.*
- Cracking uses high temperatures and a catalyst (in the absence of oxygen) to break covalent bonds between carbon atoms.
- It turns large unwanted alkanes into smaller alkanes, and alkenes for polymer formation.
- These are separated by fractional distillation.

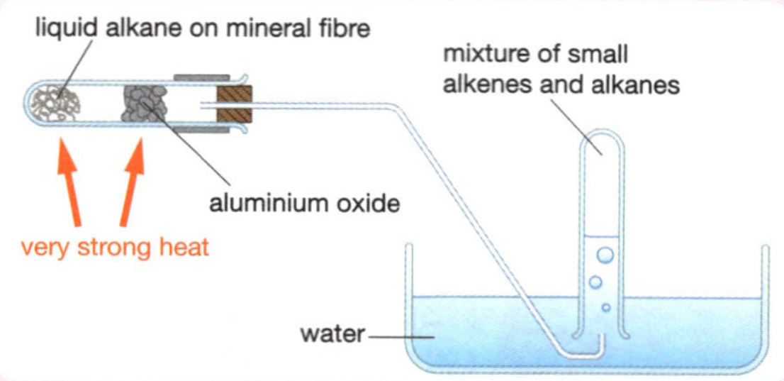

Now try this

b Match each key word to the relevant description(s).

Covalent bonds	link non-metal atoms
Alkene	overcome by boiling
Cracking	broken by cracking
Alkane	alkane or alkene
Hydrocarbon	decomposition of alkanes
Catalyst	used to make polymers
High temperature	found in oil
Liquid paraffin	promotes cracking
Intermolecular forces	a long-chain alkane

TOP TIP Alkanes crack when they are heated – not when they burn.

Homework

4 Find out what ethene and propene are used for.

5 Compare the percentage of each fraction in oil with the demand for each fraction.

6 Research the industrial cracking of hydrocarbons and explain why it is useful.

See pages 106–115 of Collins GCSE Science

ALKANES AND ALKENES

- Carbon atoms make four bonds and can form chains.
- Each bond is a shared pair of electrons.
- The simplest carbon compounds are hydrocarbons.
- Alkanes like methane, ethane, propane and butane contain single covalent bonds and are useful fuels.
- Alkenes like ethene and propene have a C=C bond.
- *Double bonds make alkenes unsaturated.*
- *Bromine water turns colourless with alkenes, because it adds to C=C double bonds.*
- *Alkanes have no double bonds – they are saturated.*

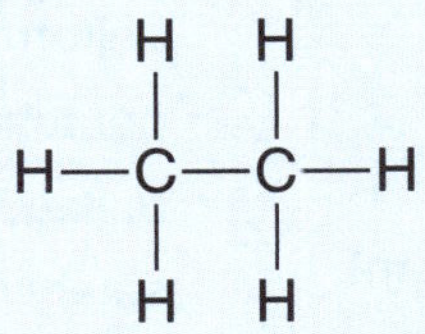

ethane C_2H_6

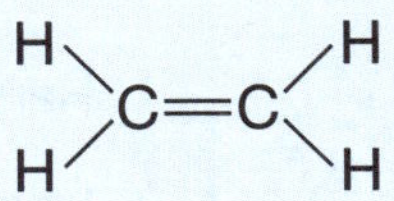

ethene C_2H_4

Now try this

c Match each hydrocarbon to its name.

C_2H_6	methane
CH_4	propane
C_3H_6	butane
C_3H_8	ethane
C_4H_{10}	propene

TOP TIP: Count the bonds around each carbon – there must be four. A double counts as two.

Homework

7 Draw these hydrocarbons and say which are alkanes: C_6H_{14}, C_5H_{10}, C_7H_{16}, C_8H_{16}.

8 Suppose butane splits in two. Draw **two** hydrocarbons made from butane's atoms.

9 Find out how isomers differ and draw the **two** isomers of butane.

PLASTICS

- Plastics contain very large polymer molecules.
- *Addition polymers form when C=C bonds break and unsaturated monomers link up to form saturated polymers with only single C-C bonds*, for example, propene makes polypropene.
- The reaction requires high pressure and a catalyst.
- To draw polymers: turn the C=C to $-(C-C)_n-$ then add the atoms attached to these carbons.
- To draw monomers: turn the $-(C-C)_n-$ to C=C then add the atoms attached to these carbons.

Now try this

d Match each monomer to its polymer.

Styrene	polypropene
Ethene	PVC
C_4H_8	polyethene
C_2H_4	polybutene
C_3H_6	polystyrene
Vinyl chloride	

TOP TIP: When polymers form, only the carbons from the double bond form part of the chain. Any others form side groups.

Homework

10 Prepare a presentation to explain how monomers become polymers.

11 Draw displayed formula to show how ethene and vinyl chloride polymerise.

12 Find out how the chains differ in high density and low density polyethene.

Carbon chemistry 3

DESIGN POLYMERS: PROPERTIES AND USES

- Polymers are designed with properties to suit their uses:
  - polystyrene in shock-absorbent packaging
  - polyester in crease-resistant clothing.
- Strong covalent bonds hold polymer molecules together.
- Weak intermolecular forces let the molecules slide to give a stretchy plastic with a low melting point.
- Strong forces, or cross-links, between polymer chains give a rigid plastic with a high melting point.
- Nylon is tough, lightweight, waterproof and blocks UV, but traps water vapour – so sweat condenses on it.
- In GORE-TEX®, tough nylon is laminated over a fragile waterproof layer of PTFE/polyurethane to protect it.
- PTFE lets vapour escape but keeps out rain drops.

Now try this

a Some polymers have more than one useful property. Find a use for each of Kevlar®'s properties.

Withstands tension	glass workers' gloves
Resists impacts	fire fighters' uniform
Lightweight	parachute ropes
Hard wearing	bullet-proof vests
Flame-resistant	safety helmets
Cut-resistant	run-flat tyres

Homework

1 Design a leaflet or presentation to show why it is worth paying extra for GORE-TEX.
2 Use diagrams to explain the difference between inter- and intramolecular forces.
3 Find out what plasticisers do to polymers like PVC.

DESIGN POLYMERS: DISPOSAL

- The oil that polymers are made from is non-renewable.
- They are difficult to sort and recycle.
- Plastics are coded to make sorting easier.
- Most polymers are non-biodegradable.
- Microbes cannot decompose them.
- They are often left as litter.
- Any disposal method is a waste of resources.
- Burning polymers makes toxic gases and landfill wastes valuable land, so biodegradable polymers are useful.

TOP TIP Biodegradable polymers contain starch.

Now try this

b Tick the statements that are true.

- Recycling codes can be used to identify plastics. ☐
- Plastics break down quickly in landfill sites. ☐
- Some polymers release toxic fumes when burned. ☐
- Most polymers are made from oil products ☐
- Microbes decompose biodegradable polymers. ☐
- Polymers are easily recycled because they are coded. ☐
- Recycling polymers wastes valuable resources. ☐

Homework

4 Find out what the numbers 1–6 mean on plastic recycling codes.
5 Research ways of sorting plastics to make recycling them easier.
6 Find out what is special about the polymer used for hospital laundry bags.

USING CARBON FUELS

- Fuels release energy when they react with oxygen.
- Fossil fuel use increases with the demand for energy.
- Useful fuels:
  - burn completely, producing no soot or ash
  - give out maximum heat energy per gram
  - are readily available and easy to store
  - have low toxicity and produce little pollution
  - are inexpensive and easy to use.
- Complete combustion makes CO_2 and H_2O.
- Incomplete combustion in faulty heaters/yellow flames:
  - gives sooty deposits of carbon (C)
  - releases toxic carbon monoxide (CO)
  - supplies less energy.
- Gas appliances need regular servicing to prevent this.
- CO reduces the blood's ability to carry oxygen.

Now try this

c Finish the following equations.

methane + oxygen → ____________

$CH_4 + 2O_2 \rightarrow 2H_2O +$ ______

methane + less oxygen → ____________

$CH_4 + 1\frac{1}{2}O_2 \rightarrow 2H_2O +$ ______

methane + much less oxygen → ____________

$CH_4 + O_2 \rightarrow 2H_2O +$ ______

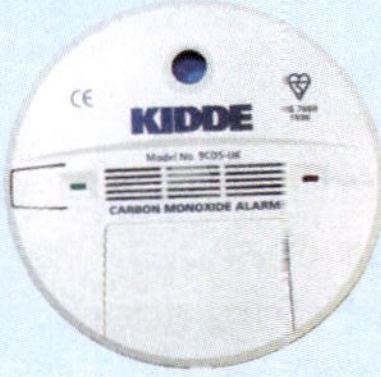

TOP TIP Hydrocarbon fuels usually make water vapour and CO_2. Oxygen shortages produce CO or soot instead.

Homework

7 Explain how a Bunsen's air hole setting affects the burning of methane.
8 Design a safety leaflet to warn gas boiler owners about carbon monoxide.
9 Animate a PowerPoint slide to show methane reacting with oxygen molecules.

ENERGY

- Reactions can release heat, light, sound or electricity.
- Bond breaking is endothermic – heat energy is absorbed.
- Bond making is exothermic – heat energy is released.
- *If the bond making releases more energy than bond breaking takes in, the reaction is exothermic.* For example, $2H_2 + O_2 \rightarrow H_2O$ (and any other fuel burning).
- *If the bond making releases less energy than bond breaking takes in, the reaction is endothermic.*
- The energy transferred per gram of fuel can be found by:
  - burning the fuel in a spirit burner
  - measuring the mass lost
  - heating water in a copper calorimeter
  - measuring the temperature change.
- Energy transferred (J) = mass of water heated (g) × 4.2 × temperature change (°C)
- Energy per gram = energy supplied (J) ÷ fuel burnt (g).

Now try this

d Are the following reactions exothermic (EX) or endothermic (EN)?

A burning fuel	______
Bond formation	______
Used in fireworks	______
Used in cold packs	______
The reactants explode	______
Needs continual heating	______
Product has stronger bonds	______
Used in self-heating cans	______
The reactants lose energy	______
Causes a temperature drop	______
The reactants gain energy	______

Homework

10 Classify photosynthesis and respiration as exo- or endothermic. Give reasons.
11 Make a presentation to explain what bonds have to do with energy changes.
12 Calculate a fuel's energy per gram if 10 g of fuel makes 500 g of water 20 °C hotter.

Rocks and metals 1

PAINTS AND PIGMENTS

- *Colloids have tiny particles of one material dispersed in another and do not separate.*
- Paints are a colloid of pigment particles dispersed in a binding medium like oil.
- Solvents can be used to thin paint.
- Paints dry when the solvent evaporates and the binding medium sticks the pigment in place.
- *Oil paints also react with oxygen as they dry.*
- Thermochromic pigments change with temperature.
- Acrylic paints can enhance their colour changes.
- Phosphorescent pigments absorb and store energy and release it as light over a period of time.
- *They are safer than radioactive paints.*

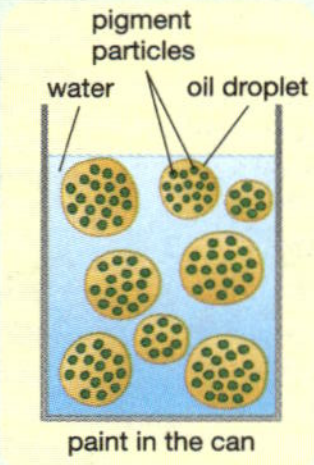

Now try this

a Match each key word with its definition.

Pigment	particles of one thing dispersed in another
Emulsion	hardens oil paints
Phosphorescent	its colour depends on the temperature
Binding medium	coloured chemical
Thermochromic	sticks pigments to surfaces
Colloid	drops of one liquid suspended in another
Oxidation	glows in the dark

Homework

1 Explain the differences between solutions, colloids and emulsions.
2 Find the names of some pigments used in oil paints.
3 Research **three** uses of thermochromic paints.

CONSTRUCTION MATERIALS

- Construction materials include glass from sand, aluminium and iron from ores, and brick from clay.
- Removing rocks from the ground destroys the landscape and increases noise, traffic and dust.
- Limestone and marble contain calcium carbonate.
- Thermal decomposition breaks limestone up.
- *Calcium carbonate → calcium oxide + carbon dioxide.*
  $CaCO_3 \rightarrow CaO + CO_2$.
- *Limestone is a soft sedimentary rock.*
- *High pressures and temperatures turn it into a harder metamorphic rock – marble.*
- Roasting a limestone/clay mixture makes cement.
- Mixing cement, gravel and water makes concrete.
- *Reinforced concrete combines the hardness of concrete with steel's flexibility and strength.*
- *Granite is an igneous rock – the hardest type.*

Now try this

b Do the following characteristics belong to **limestone (L)**, **marble (M)** and/or **granite (G)**?

Igneous ______
Decomposed by heat ______
Sedimentary ______
Hard ______
Calcium carbonate ______
Metamorphic ______
Used to make cement ______

TOP TIP Limestone loses mass when heated, so it must decompose and release a gas.

Homework

4 Prepare a presentation on the uses of building products made from limestone.
5 How could you prove that roasted limestone releases CO_2 when it decomposes?
6 Annotate an image of a quarry to show the environmental problems that are caused.

See pages 134–145 of Collins GCSE Science

IGNEUS ROCKS

- Igneous rock forms when lava or magma cools.
- Lava is molten rock erupted from a volcano.
- Magma is molten rock beneath the surface.
- Magma's low density makes it rise through the crust.
- *It can be runny iron-rich basalt or dangerously explosive silica-rich rhyolite, which makes ash and pumice.*
- *Eruptions can be predicted, but not with certainty.*
- *Their study reveals details of the Earth's structure.*
- Basalt and rhyolite cool quickly and have small crystals.
- Gabbro and granite cool slowly and have large crystals.

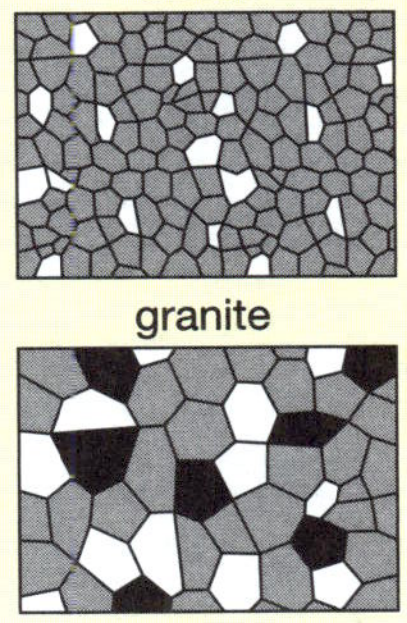

TOP TIP Volcanic soil is fertile so many people live in volcanic areas.

Now try this

c Are the following characteristics of **basalt (B)**, **granite (G)** or **both (Bo)**?

Igneous rock ______

Iron-rich ______

Small crystals ______

Cooled rapidly along a mid-ocean ridge ______

Cooled slowly from molten magma ______

Large crystals ______

Silica-rich ______

Homework

7 Annotate images of basalt, rhyolite, gabbro and granite to show their differences.
8 Label a tectonic plate diagram to show where new rock is pushing plates apart.
9 Find out what pumice, volcanic bombs and graded bedding are.

TECTONICS

- The Earth has a thin crust, mantle and iron core.
- The lithosphere (crust and upper mantle) is divided into plates which float on the denser mantle.
- Tectonics explains why the shapes of continental coastlines match.
- *They were once part of one big continent.*
- *Convection currents in the mantle move them.*
- *Symmetrical bands of younger rocks around mid-ocean ridges support the theory.*
- The mantle is rigid just below the crust but a hot fluid where energy transfers from the core.
- *The denser oceanic plates are subducted, and partially remelted, when they collide with continental plates.*
- Molten rock (magma) is less dense than the crust so it rises through it causing volcanic eruptions.

Now try this

d Are these **causes (Ca)** or **consequences (Co)** of plate tectonics?

Matching coastlines ______

Convection currents ______

Young rocks in the middle of the ocean ______

Energy transfer from the core ______

Fluid magma ______

The crust divides into moving plates ______

Earthquakes and volcanoes occur ______

TOP TIP Earthquakes and volcanoes form where oceanic plates are subducted below continental plates.

Homework

10 Annotate images of a subduction zone and oceanic ridge to show their differences.
11 Label a tectonic plate diagram to show where new rock is pushing plates apart.
12 What are seismometers and what are they used for?

Rocks and metals 2

METALS AND ALLOYS

- Alloys are mixtures of elements, one of which is a metal, for example, brass, bronze.
- They can be different from the metals they are made from, for example, mercury amalgam for fillings.
- *Smart alloys change shape in response to a stimulus, for example, nitinol – an alloy of nickel and titanium.*
- Copper is extracted by heating its ore with carbon, and purified by electrolysis.
- *The impure copper anode (positive) dissolves.*
- *The electrolyte is copper sulfate.*
- *Copper is attracted to a negative cathode made from pure copper, but impurities are left behind.*
- *Pure copper deposits at the negative cathode.*
- Recycling conserves energy, and the ore itself, but is difficult when the metal is mixed with other materials.

Now try this

a Decide if the following refer to the **anode (A)**, **cathode (C)** or **electrolyte (E)** used for copper purification.

Made from impure copper ______
Copper deposits here ______
Negatively charged ______
Copper dissolves here ______
Attracts copper ______
Impurities left here ______
Made from pure copper ______
Copper sulfate ______

Homework

1 Use diagrams to explain how copper is purified.
2 Compare the properties of lead, tin and solder.
3 Find some uses of smart alloys.

CARS FOR SCRAP

- Aluminium and iron are both malleable conductors. Iron is magnetic, denser, and rusts more easily.
- Alloys are more useful than the pure metal, for example, steel is harder, stronger and less likely to corrode than iron.
- *Rusting is oxidation of iron by water and oxygen.*

  iron + oxygen + water → hydrated iron(III) oxide
- Salt water and acid rain accelerate rusting.
- Cars contain glass, plastics, fibres, steel, aluminium and copper. By EU law, 85% of the material must be recycled. This saves energy and raw materials and reduces environmental damage, but is difficult and expensive.
- *Aluminium car bodies are lighter and corrode less so give better fuel economy and last longer*, but they are more expensive.

TOP TIP Aluminium is covered with a tough protective layer of aluminium oxide, so it does not corrode.

Now try this

b Do the following relate to **aluminium (A)**, **iron (I)** or **both (B)**?

Rusts ______
Magnetic ______
Has a low density ______
Will oxidise completely ______
Good conductor ______
Corrodes ______
Hard and strong ______
Malleable ______
More expensive ______
Main component of steel ______

Homework

4 Assess the advantages and disadvantages of making new car bodies from plastic.
5 Research the methods used to prevent cars with steel bodies from rusting.
6 Compare key physical properties of iron, aluminium and their alloys.

See pages 146–159 of Collins GCSE Science

CLEAN AIR: OUR ATMOSPHERE

- Air contains: N_2 (78%), O_2 (21%), CO_2 (0.035%).
- Respiration/combustion increase CO_2 and reduce O_2.
- Photosynthesis decreases CO_2 and increases O_2.
- Pollution includes:
  - *poisonous carbon monoxide from incomplete combustion, which could be converted to CO_2 by catalytic converters:* $2CO + 2NO \rightarrow N_2 + 2CO_2$
  - oxides of nitrogen from car engines which cause photochemical smog and acid rain
  - sulfur dioxide from burning sulfur impurities which causes acid rain, kills plants and aquatic life, erodes stonework and corrodes metals.

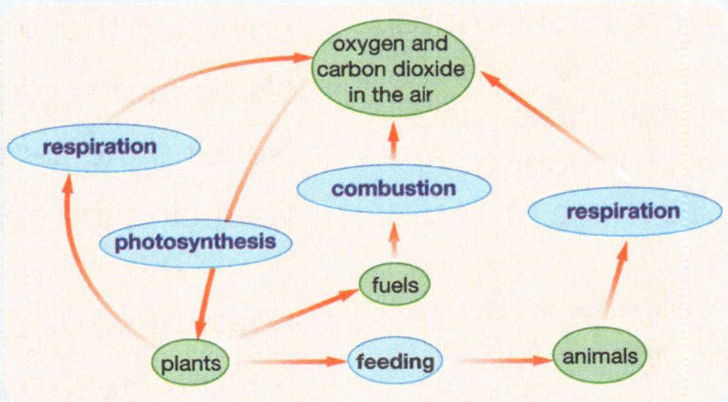

Now try this

c Do the following **increase (I)** or **decrease (D)** atmospheric CO_2?

Photosynthesis ______
Deforestation ______
Drought ______
Forest fires ______
Burning petrol ______
Insulating homes ______
Growing populations ______
Using renewable fuels ______
Coal-fired power stations ______
Catalytic converters ______

Homework

7 Design a leaflet to explain how catalytic converters work.
8 Prepare a presentation on where atmospheric pollutants come from.
9 Describe an experiment to find the percentage of oxygen and n trogen in dry air.

CLEAN AIR: LONG-TERM CHANGES

- Our atmosphere has changed since Earth formed:
  - volcanoes degassed carbon dioxide (CO_2), steam and ammonia from the centre of the Earth
  - oceans condensed and CO_2 dissolved in them
  - photosynthesis released oxygen (O_2)
  - O_2 released inert nitrogen (N_2) from ammonia
  - *O_2 and N_2 increased to their present levels.*
- *Average temperatures and CO_2 levels are rising due to deforestation, burning more fossil fuels, and increased respiration as the population increases.*

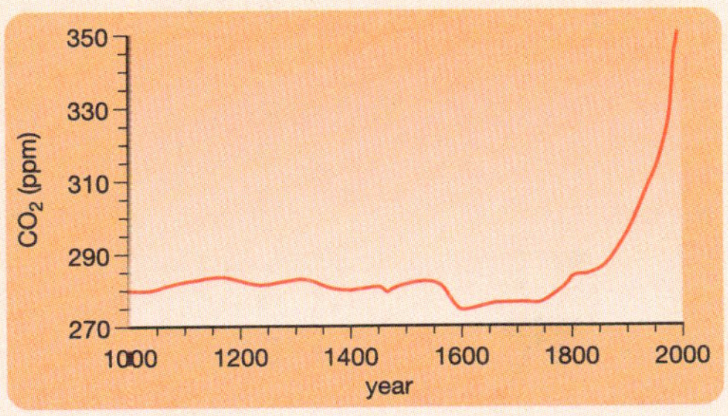

Now try this

d Match each key word to the correct description(s).

Volcanoes
Oxygen
Ammonia
Steam
Nitrogen
Carbon dioxide

oxidised to N_2 and H_2O
condensed to form oceans
dissolved in the first oceans
source of the first atmosphere
in the first atmosphere
made by photosynthesis
an inert gas
an increasing percentage of the air
essential for respiration

Homework

10 Prepare a presentation on how the Earth's atmosphere has changed.
11 Research the possible consequences of rising carbon dioxide levels.
12 Plan how Mars could be 'terraformed' to get an atmosphere like the Earth's.

Rocks and metals 3

TEMPERATURE/CONCENTRATION

- Reactions take place when particles collide.
- The rate of reaction increases with:
  - the collision frequency of the reacting particles
  - *the percentage of collisions that transfer enough energy to lead to a reaction.*
- Higher concentrations or pressures make collisions more frequent because the particles are more crowded, so reaction rates rise, for example, sodium thiosulfate gets cloudy faster with more concentrated hydrochloric acid.
- At higher temperatures reactant particles move faster, so they have more energy.
- *They collide more frequently and more violently, so a larger percentage of the collisions are successful*, for example, sodium thiosulfate gets cloudy faster when it is heated before acid is added.

Now try this

a Will the following make the reaction between magnesium and acid faster (F), slower (S) or neither (N).

Adding water to the acid ______

Lowering the temperature ______

Using more concentrated acid ______

Reusing the same acid ______

Reducing the collision frequency ______

Using more acid ______

Raising the temperature ______

Homework

1 Make a list of ways you can measure the rates of reactions.

2 Explain these cooking times: chips 3 min, boiled potatoes 20 min.

3 Explain why global warming and acid rain make limestone wear away faster.

INTERPRETING RESULTS 1

- Reaction rates vary, for example, rusting is quite slow; explosions are extremely fast.
- The total amount of product formed depends on the amounts of reactants used.
- Gas syringes can monitor gas production.
- Light sensors detect cloudiness/colour change.
- The fastest reactions take least time.
- When the amount of reactant or product is plotted against time on a graph:
  - the steepest part shows the fastest reaction
  - the flat part shows when the reaction stops
- Reactions stop when one reactant is used up.

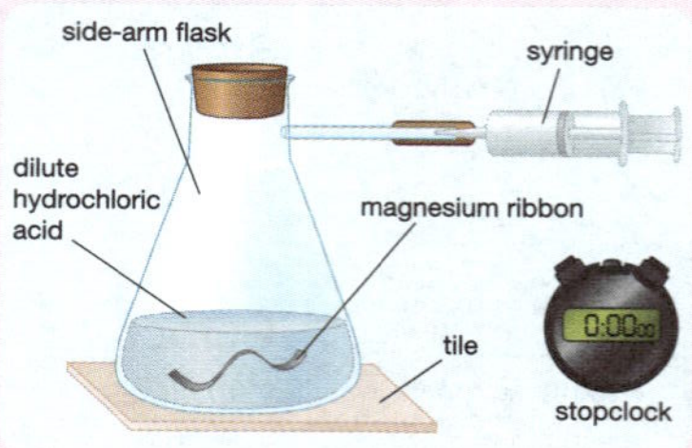

Now try this

b 8 cm of magnesium reacted with excess 0.2 M HCl at 20 °C. It took 160 s and made 100 cm^3 of H_2. Choose the nearest time and H_2 volume for each combination of reactants.

1 8 cm Mg, 0.4M HCl, 20 °C

2 4 cm Mg, 0.2 M HCl, 20 °C

3 8 cm Mg, 0.2 M HCl, 10 °C

i 40 s
ii 160 s
iii 210 s

iv 100 cm^3 of H_2
v 50 cm^3 of H_2
vi 200 cm^3 of H_2

Homework

4 Sketch graphs to show concentration and temperature changing reaction rates.

5 Explain why the rate of reaction between Mg and HCl slows as it nears the end.

6 Draw labelled diagrams for **two** ways of measuring the volume of gas produced.

CATALYSTS

- *Increasing surface area, by cutting solids into pieces, makes collisions more frequent.*
- More atoms are exposed to the other reactant, for example, powders have larger surface areas than lumps.
- Sparks can make fine particles of flour explode.
- Catalysts increase reaction rates by reducing the energy a collision needs to supply.
- *They are specific to particular reactions.*
- They are unchanged at the end of reactions and can be reused, so only small amounts are needed.

Now try this

c Fill in the missing words.

Powders have a much larger ________ ________ than solid lumps so collisions with the reactant take place more ________ and the reaction is ________.

A catalyst allows less energetic ________ to start reactions. They are expensive but are not ________ ________ during reactions so very ________ is needed.

Homework

7 Explain these cooking times: chips 3 min, crisps 30 s.

8 Find a diagram of a catalytic converter and explain its design.

9 Use what you know about surface area to explain how to start a bonfire.

INTERPRETING RESULTS 2

- Hydrogen, custard powder, dynamite and TNT burn explosively and release hot gases.
- Balances can detect loss of a gas by reactions that release carbon dioxide but hydrogen is too light to allow accurate readings.
- If excess marble chips are used, equal amounts of acid should release the same mass of carbon dioxide, whatever the rate.
- Straight line graphs can be extrapolated or interpolated to find missing values.

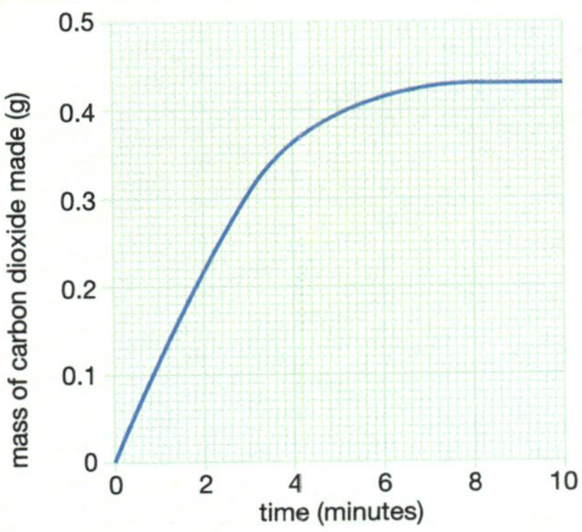

Now try this

d These volumes of gas were collected:

Time (s)	10	20	40	60	80
Volume (cm^3)	2	4	8	10	10

The reaction was over at ______ s

The volume at 30 s was ______ cm^3

The volume at 100 s was ______ cm^3

The graph would be a straight line from 0 to ______ s

TOP TIP Always draw a line of best fit or a smooth curve through the points on a graph.

Homework

10 If 0.60 g of magnesium reacts in 30 s, what is the reaction rate?

11 Make a presentation to show why cutting solids up increases reaction rates.

12 Sketch graphs of HCl reacting with equal masses of powdered and solid zinc.

Homes and insulation

HEATING HOUSES

- Temperature is measured with a thermometer.
- Temperature is measured in degrees Celsius (°C).
- The temperature of a body is a measure of its 'hotness'.
- Heat is a form of energy. It is measured in joules (J).
- Heat always flows from a warm body to a cooler body.
- Energy or heat is required to melt a solid at its melting point.
- Energy or heat is required to boil a liquid at its boiling point.
- During melting or boiling, the temperature of the material remains the same.
- This is what happens to ice when it is heated:

Temperature of ICE increases.

↓

ICE melts into WATER at 0°C. The temperature remains constant.

↓

Temperature of WATER increases.

↓

WATER changes into STEAM at 100°C. The temperature remains constant.

- The energy needed to change the temperature of a material depends on its mass, the type of material and the temperature change.
- *energy transferred = mass × specific heat capacity × temperature change*
- Specific heat capacity of a substance is the amount of energy needed to change the temperature of 1 kg of the substance by 1 °C.
- Specific heat capacity is measured in J/kg°C.
- *When a substance changes state from solid to liquid or liquid to gas, energy is needed to break molecular bonds. This is why there is no change in temperature.*
- *During a change in state:*

  energy transferred = mass × specific latent heat
- Specific latent heat is measured in J/kg.

Now try this

a Are the following statements **true (T)** or **false (F)**?

Heat and temperature are the same. ______

The temperature of a substance does not change during a change of state. ______

An object at –20 °C is warmer than an object at –50 °C. ______

Specific latent heat is measured in J/kg °C. ______

TOP TIP Different substances have different values for specific heat capacity and specific latent heat.

Homework

1. Describe the difference between temperature and heat.
2. Write a short paragraph on specific heat capacity and specific latent heat.
3. Make a list of the different measurements related to temperature and heat, and their units.

See pages 174–185 of Collins GCSE Science

INSULATING HOMES

- Air is an excellent insulator and a poor thermal conductor.
- Insulating a home reduces energy loss to the outside.
- Insulating a house saves you money!
- Many insulators in the home contain trapped air (for example, loft insulation or fibreglass, double glazing in windows and cavity-wall insulation foam).
- Draft-proofing doors and windows can reduce heat loss from homes.
- Energy can be transferred by conduction, convection and radiation.
- Solids (metals, brick walls, etc) are good thermal conductors.
- *In conduction, the kinetic energy is transferred between atoms.*
- A vacuum is a perfect insulator because there are no atoms.
- In convection, energy transfer occurs due to the movement of a fluid (air or liquid).
- In convection, hot air rises and is replaced by falling colder air.
- Hot air rises because it is less dense than cold air.
- *Trapped air in the foam of cavity-wall insulation prevents loss of energy by convection.*
- Shiny surfaces reflect infrared radiation.
- Having shiny reflective foil in or on walls reduces energy loss by radiation.
- *Infrared radiation does not require a medium.*
- *efficiency* = $\frac{\textit{useful energy output}}{\textit{total energy input}}$
- payback time = $\frac{\text{cost of insulation}}{\text{annual saving}}$

Now try this

b Circle the correct answers.

Air is a good:
conductor   insulator.

Trapped air in foam prevents:
conduction   convection.

Solids are good conductors of heat because the particles are:
close together   far apart.

Shiny foil between walls reduces energy transfer by:
convection   radiation   conduction.

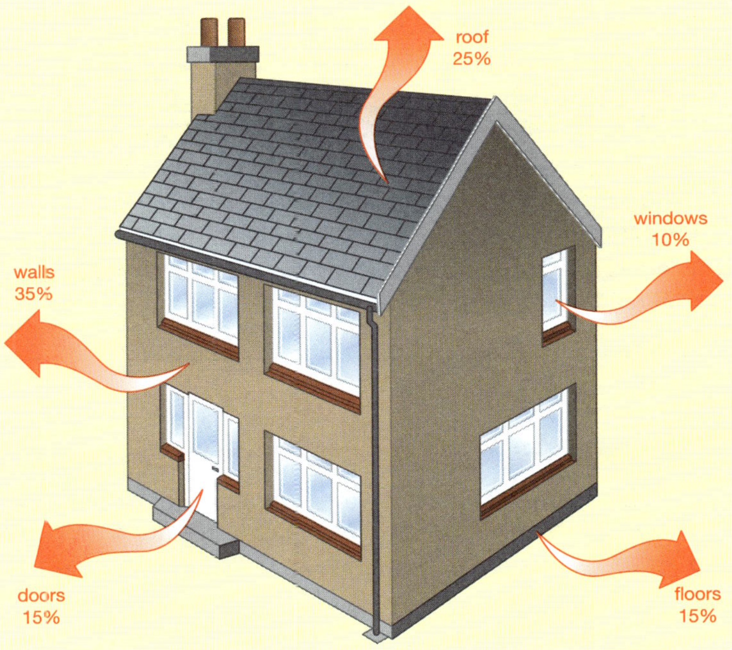

TOP TIP Good insulators are poor conductors.

Homework

4 Make a list of all the insulations used in your home.
5 Use pages 178 to 185 to make a list of all the methods used to insulate our homes.
6 Write a short paragraph on conduction, convection and radiation.

Waves and signals

COOKING WITH WAVES

- Infrared waves and microwaves are both electromagnetic waves.
- Hotter objects emit more infrared radiations.
- Dull black surfaces are good absorbers and emitters of infrared waves.
- Shiny surfaces are poor absorbers of infrared waves.
- Microwaves and infrared waves can both be used to cook food.
- Infrared waves transfer more energy than the microwaves because they have shorter wavelength.
- Infrared waves do not penetrate too deep and only heat the surface of food.
- *Infrared waves increase the kinetic energy of food particles. The energy is then passed to the rest of the food by conduction.*
- *Microwaves penetrate the outer layers of food.*
- *Microwaves increase the vibrational kinetic energy of water and fatty molecules. The energy is then passed to the rest of the food by conduction or convection.*
- There is some evidence that microwaves from mobile phones can warm the brain.

Now try this

a Complete the sentences.

Microwaves are ________________ waves. They have a ________________ wavelength than the infrared waves. Microwaves heat food by making the water and fatty molecules ________________ more. Microwaves are used to heat food in a microwave ________________.

TOP TIP Infrared waves and microwaves are both electromagnetic waves.

Homework

1 Heat a potato in a microwave oven for two minutes. Carefully cut it in half. Describe how the temperature varies from the centre to the surface.

2 Use the Internet to research and write about the process of conduction.

3 Use the Internet to find the power of a microwave transmitted by a mobile phone. Discuss how it compares with the power of a typical microwave oven.

INFRARED SIGNALS

- Infrared radiation is used in remote controls.
- Signals can either be digital (1s and 0s) or analogue.
- An analogue signal can have any value between two levels.
- Analogue signals are affected by external interference.
- *Digital signals are not easily affected by external interference.*
- *Multiplexing is a technique of sending several digital signals along the same path.*
- Digital signals can be sent along flexible optical fibres.
- Optical fibres are used in endoscopes, which enable doctors to see inside the body.

Now try this

b Are the following statements **true** (T) or **false** (F)?

An output from a microphone is analogue. ______

An example of a digital signal is 123456789. ______

A TV remote control sends microwave signals. ______

Optical fibres can be used to send a pulse of light (digital signals). ______

Homework

4 Use an infrared remote control at home to investigate the items (newspaper, walls, curtains, etc) that will reflect the infrared signals. Make a list of these items.

5 Make a list of digital and analogue items in your home.

WIRELESS SIGNALS

- Wireless technology (radio, mobile phones, laptop computers, etc) use either radio waves or microwaves.
- Radio waves and microwaves are transmitted and received by aerials.
- Radio waves and microwaves can be reflected, refracted and diffracted.
- Long wavelength radio waves are easily diffracted by gaps between buildings and hills.
- *Radio waves are reflected from the ionosphere – this enables long distance communication.*
- Short wavelength microwaves travel in straight lines.
- Microwaves are used for satellite communications and mobile phones.

TOP TIP Diffraction is more noticeable when the wavelength is about the size of the gap causing diffraction.

Now try this

c Tick the statements that are correct.

Diffraction and refraction are the same. ☐

Ionosphere is a region of charged particles surrounding the Earth. ☐

Microwaves travel in straight lines. ☐

Radio waves are easily diffracted and reflected by hills. ☐

Homework

6 Write a short paragraph on reflection, refraction and diffraction.

7 Research and write a paragraph on the ionosphere.

Light waves and seismic waves

UNDERSTANDING WAVES

- All waves carry energy from one place to another.
- There are two types of waves: longitudinal and transverse.
- A longitudinal wave has vibrations parallel to the direction of the wave velocity.
- A transverse wave has vibrations at 90° to the direction of the wave velocity.
- Examples of transverse waves are: ripples on the surface of water, all electromagnetic waves (for example, light) and earthquake (seismic) S-waves.
- Examples of longitudinal waves are: sound, ultrasound and seismic P-waves.
- The amplitude of a wave is the maximum distance of the wave from its undisturbed position. Amplitude is measured in metres (m).
- The frequency of a wave is the number of waves produced per unit time. Frequency is measured in hertz (Hz).
- The wavelength of a wave is the distance between two neighbouring peaks or troughs. Wavelength is measured in metres (m).
- The wave speed (v) of the wave is related to its frequency (f) and the wavelength (λ) by the equation: $v = f\lambda$. The speed is measured in metres per second (m/s).

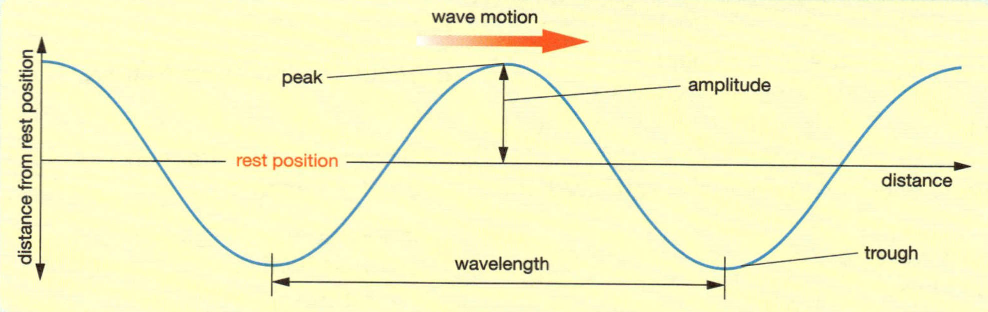

Now try this

a **Circle the correct answer.**

The speed of a wave is measured in:

m m/s Hz.

Wavelength and amplitude can be measured in:

m m/s Hz.

Frequency is measured in:

m m/s Hz.

Amplitude of a wave is measured in:

m m/s Hz.

Homework

1. Draw a mind map for transverse waves and longitudinal waves.
2. Use the Internet to find the minimum and maximum frequencies of sound we can hear. Use this information to determine the range of wavelengths of sound we can hear.

See pages 200–207 of Collins GCSE Science

REFLECTION, REFRACTION AND TIR

- Refraction is the bending of a wave as it travels between mediums.
- Refraction occurs because the wave's speed changes as it travels.
- When a ray of light travels from glass (or water) into air:
  - at small angles: the ray is refracted and reflected at the boundary
  - at an incidence angle equal to the critical angle: the ray is refracted along the boundary and there is a weak reflection
  - at angles greater than the critical angle: there is no refraction but a strong total internal reflection (TIR) takes place.
- TIR is used in prisms, periscopes and optical fibres (endoscope).
- Light has been used for communicating in Morse code.
- Lasers produce beams of light capable of cutting, vaporising and burning materials.
- *Light from a laser has the same frequency and phase.*
- *Lasers are used to 'read' the digital information stored on CDs.*

Now try this

b Are the following statements **true (T)** or **false (F)**?

During refraction, the speed of the wave changes. ☐

At the critical angle, a ray of light shows no refraction. ☐

The light in an optical fibre shows total internal reflection. ☐

The bending of light is called reflection. ☐

TOP TIP TIR cannot occur if light travels into an optically denser medium (for example, from air into glass).

Homework

3 Draw **three** diagrams to illustrate refraction, critical angle and total internal reflection.

4 Describe how an endoscope works.

EARTHQUAKE WAVES

- Earthquakes produce shock waves that are detectable by seismograph.
- The two types of seismic waves are longitudinal P-waves and transverse S-waves.
- *P-waves can travel through liquids and solids. S-waves are slower and only travel through solids.*
- Ultraviolet radiation can cause sunburn and skin cancer. High-factor sun blocks reduce the damage.
- *The ozone layer protects us from ultraviolet radiation.*
- The main contributors of global warming are CO_2 emissions and deforestation.
- Dust from factories reflects radiation back to the Earth causing heating. Dust from volcanoes reflects radiation from the Sun leading to cooling.

Now try this

c Fill in the missing words.

The ______________ layer protects us from excessive exposure to ultraviolet radiation. Ultraviolet radiation can cause skin ______________ and ______________. We can protect ourselves from skin damage by using sun ______________.

Homework

5 Use the information on page 205 to make a list of key points about the structure of the Earth.

6 Describe how dust from volcanoes and factories affect the climate.

Solar power and generating electricity

ENERGY FROM THE SUN

- The Sun is a source of both light and heat (infrared waves).
- The Sun is a renewable source of energy.
- A photocell or a solar cell transfers light into electrical energy, produces a direct current (DC) and can operate in remote locations.
- *A silicon photocell uses light to release electrons from its crystal. These electrons produce a direct current in a circuit.*
- *The power of a photocell can be increased by using a larger surface area or by connecting them in series.*
- Photocells do not require fuel or power cables and do not produce polluting waste. They have long life and low maintenance.
- The Sun is responsible for convection currents or wind.
- A wind turbine changes the kinetic energy of the wind into electrical energy. *It does not produce pollution but can be an eyesore. It requires lots of space and its electrical power depends on wind speed.*
- Curved mirrors can be used to reflect and focus light for heating purposes.
- With passive solar heating, the Sun warms the floor and walls during the day and then the energy is radiated back into the room from the walls and the floor at night.

TOP TIP A solar cell is really a photocell that changes sunlight into electricity.

Now try this

a Circle the correct answer for each statement.

A photocell changes light energy into:

heat light electrical.

The size of a direct current can change but its direction:

does does not change.

The wind on the Earth is produced by the:

Sun Moon.

Homework

1 Write a paragraph to describe how the energy from the Sun is used for heating and for producing electricity.

2 Describe how the Sun is responsible for wind on the Earth.

3 Write a paragraph to describe how a wind turbine produces energy.

GENERATING ELECTRICITY

- A dynamo is a small electrical generator.
- In a dynamo or a generator, an electric current is induced in a circuit by moving a coil near a magnet or by moving a magnet near a coil.
- A generator produces an alternating current (AC). Batteries produce a direct current (DC).
- Rotating the magnet faster, using a stronger magnet or increasing the number of turns on the coil can increase the size of the induced voltage across a dynamo.
- The frequency of the AC from a dynamo is increased when it is spun faster.
- *Frequency is the number of cycles per second and is measured in hertz (Hz).*
- A generator in a power station consists of a coil of wire rotating between the poles of a magnet. The coil cuts the magnetic field lines and this induces a voltage.
- The National Grid uses transmission cables to distribute electricity between power stations and homes or factories.
- In a power station, fossil fuel is burned to heat water to produce high-pressured steam. The steam is used to spin the turbines which turn the generators and this produces electricity.
- The voltage from the generator is stepped up from 25 kV to about 400 kV using transformers.
- *Electricity is transmitted at high voltage to reduce heat loss in the transmission cables.*
- Before the electricity can be used in our homes it has to be stepped down to 240 V using transformers.
- *fuel energy input = waste energy output + electrical energy output*
- *efficiency of power station* $= \dfrac{\textit{electrical energy output}}{\textit{fuel energy input}}$

Now try this

b Match the beginnings and endings to make complete sentences.

Beginning	Ending
A generator produces an	stationary coil.
To induce a current in a wire you have to move it in a	frequency of the current.
In a dynamo the magnet rotates near a stationary	magnetic field.
Rotating the coil of a dynamo faster increases the	alternating current.

TOP TIP A dynamo or a generator changes kinetic energy into electrical energy.

Homework

4 Describe how a generator produces electricity.

5 Draw a block diagram to show the stages in the production of electricity in a coal-burning power station.

6 Use the Internet and the information on page 220 to write a short paragraph on transformers.

Fuels and nuclear radiations

FUEL FOR POWER STATIONS

- Non-renewable energy resources (for example, coal, natural gas, crude oil) will run out.
- Renewable biomass resources (for example, wood, straw, manure) will not run out as long as chopped-down trees are replaced.
- Some power stations use uranium as fuel. Uranium is non-renewable.
- Uranium fuel rods release energy as heat.
- Power is the rate of energy produced. Power is measured in watts (W).
- *power = voltage × current*
- Electrical energy supplied to homes is given in kilowatt hours (kWh).
- *energy used in kilowatts = power in kilowatts × time in hours*
- cost = energy in kWh × cost per kWh

Now try this

a Are the following fuels **renewable (R)** or **non-renewable (NR)**?

Coal ____________

Uranium ____________

Straw ____________

Manure ____________

Crude oil ____________

TOP TIP To convert power in watts to kilowatts, just divide by 1000.

Homework

1 List all the non-renewable and renewable resources used by power stations.

2 Ask your parents for a recent domestic electricity bill. On the bill, highlight the amount of kWh of energy used and the cost per kWh. Does it all add up?

NUCLEAR WASTE

- Nuclear power stations do not produce greenhouse gases like carbon dioxide so do not contribute to global warming. They do produce radioactive waste that can be active for thousands of years.
- Radiation from radioactive sources causes ionisation.
- *In ionisation, the radiation changes the structure of the atoms.*
- Ionising radiations from radioactive waste can destroy healthy cells. They can also damage the DNA that can lead to mutation of cells and cancer.
- Plutonium is a waste product from nuclear power stations.
- Plutonium can be used to make nuclear bombs.

Now try this

b Find the following key words in this word search.

cancer waste bomb mutate cells

A	N	I	T	U	P	A	P
N	C	T	C	E	L	L	S
T	E	I	A	T	S	T	F
U	T	J	N	B	O	M	B
K	A	I	C	B	L	L	D
A	T	N	E	T	S	A	W
V	U	A	R	W	S	T	D
A	M	N	P	E	T	E	I

Homework

3 Explain why radioactive waste is dangerous to humans.

4 Use the Internet to research and write about the storage and disposal of radioactive waste.

See pages 222–229 of Collins GCSE Science

NUCLEAR RADIATIONS

- The natural sources of background radiation are the Sun, outer space, rocks and food.
- The artificial sources of background radiation are nuclear power stations, fallout from nuclear explosions or accidents and waste from hospitals.
- The three main types of ionising radiation emitted from unstable nuclei are alpha (α), beta (β) and gamma (γ).
- Alpha radiation can be stopped by a thin piece of paper.
- Beta radiation can be stopped by a few millimetres of aluminium.
- Gamma radiation can be stopped by a few centimetres of lead.
- Domestic smoke alarms use an alpha-emitting source.
- The thickness of paper can be measured using beta radiation.
- Gamma rays are emitted by radioactive nuclei (for example, cobalt-60).
- Gamma rays are used to sterilise bandages, syringes and other hospital instruments.
- Gamma radiation kills off dangerous bacteria like staphylococcus.
- In radiotherapy, several gamma ray sources are directed towards cancerous tissues to destroy the cancers cells.
- The function of some vital organs can be diagnosed using a radioactive tracer.

Now try this

c Fill in the missing words.

All ionising radiations destroy healthy ________ and can potentially cause ________. Gamma radiation will penetrate through both ________ and ________ but can be stopped by a thick piece of ________. Gamma rays can be used to ________ hospital equipment.

Homework

5 Draw a mind map for **three** ionising radiations.
6 Make a list of all the uses of ionising radiations.
7 Describe how gamma radiation is used in hospitals.

Earth and space

THE EARTH'S MAGNETIC FIELD

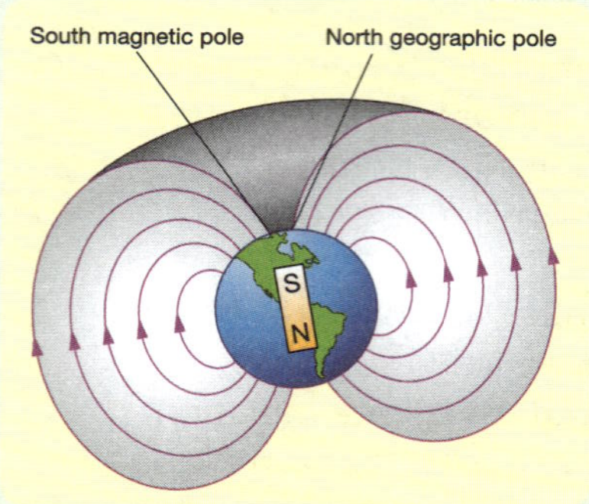

- The Earth has its own magnetic field, with North and South poles.
- The Earth's magnetic field is similar to that created by a coil of wire carrying a current.
- *Cosmic rays are ionising particles from space and the Sun. They spiral around the Earth's magnetic field.*
- *The Sun's solar flares interfere with communications, electricity distribution and artificial satellites.*
- Artificial satellites are used for telecommunications, weather predictions, spying and navigation systems (GPS).
- The Earth-Moon system was the result of two planets colliding many billions of years ago.

Now try this

a Circle the correct answer for each statement.

The Earth has a magnetic:

field   charge.

Cosmic rays are particles from outer space and the:

Sun   Moon.

The Earth and Moon were formed from:

two planets   stars colliding.

TOP TIP *Moving charges create a magnetic field.*

Homework

1 Draw a mind map for the Earth's magnetic field.

2 Describe the similarities between the Earth's magnetic field pattern and that created by a current-carrying coil of wire.

SOLAR SYSTEM

- The universe consists of stars, planets, comets, meteors, black holes and galaxies.
- Manned spacecraft require food, water and oxygen.
- Unmanned spacecrafts can withstand conditions that are lethal to humans.
- The planets in order of increasing distance from the Sun are: Mercury, Venus, Earth, Mars, Jupiter, Saturn, Uranus, Neptune and Pluto.
- Gravitational force between planets and the Sun keeps them in orbit.
- *Gravity provides the centripetal force for orbital motion of the planets round the Sun.*
- *Distances to the stars is measured in light years. One light year is the distance travelled by light in one year.*

Now try this

b Arrange the following in order of increasing distance from the Earth:

Sun   Stars   Mars   Galaxies
Moon   Pluto

____

____

____

____

____

____

Homework

3 Use the information given on page 237 to list the planets in order of increasing size.

4 Describe the advantages and disadvantages of manned spacecrafts.

5 Use the Internet to find the distances in light years from Earth to some of our nearest stars.

See pages 232–247 of Collins GCSE Science

THREATS TO THE EARTH

- Most asteroids orbit between Mars and Jupiter.
- Large asteroids have collided with the Earth in the past.
- Asteroid collisions with the Earth create large craters, can eject dust into the atmosphere, can lead to climate change and may have led to the extinction of the dinosaurs.
- Comets are made from ice and dust. They have highly elliptical orbits. *Their speed increases as they get closer to the Sun.*
- A Near-Earth object (NEO) is an asteroid or comet on a possible collision course with the Earth.

Now try this

c Are the following statements **true** (T) or **false** (F)?

Comets have tails. _______

Asteroids are really large rocks. _______

Asteroids orbit between the Earth and Mars. _______

The speed of a comet does not change in its orbit. _______

Homework

6 Describe the evidence that objects from space have hit the Earth.

7 Research and write about the composition of comets and their motion round the Sun.

THE BIG BANG

- The universe began from a sudden expansion of space 15 billion years ago, known as the Big Bang.
- Evidence of the universe's expansion comes from the observation that all galaxies are moving away from each other and the existence of cosmic microwaves radiation.
- The spectrum of light from all galaxies moving away from us shows red shift.
- *Stars are formed from interstellar dust and hydrogen clouds. Gravitational forces pull them together (this is known as gravitational collapse). This increases the temperature.*
- *Thermonuclear fusion reactions between hydrogen nuclei start when temperatures become too high.*
- A medium-mass star like our Sun will become a red giant, then a planetary nebula and a white dwarf.
- A heavy-mass star will become a red giant, then a supernova and either a neutron star or black hole.
- *A black hole has very high density and an intense gravitational field from which even light cannot escape.*

Now try this

d Are the following statements **true** (T) or **false** (F)?

Most stars will eventually become red giants. _______

Light cannot escape from a red giant. _______

A black hole is denser than our Sun. _______

In fusion reactions energy is released. _______

Homework

8 Draw a mind map to show the end of a star like our Sun and one that is much more massive.

9 Research and write a few sentences about red giants, supernovas and black holes.

DNA, diffusion and circulation

CELLS AND DNA

- A cell has a nucleus, cell membrane and cytoplasm containing mitochondria.
- Chromosomes in the nucleus carry coded information in the form of genes made from DNA. A person's DNA is unique.
- DNA is a double helix with cross links of two bases.
- DNA controls protein synthesis (which can be enzymes). Each gene codes for a protein.
- *DNA has four bases. A–T and G–C are complementary base pairs.*
- *DNA replicates by unzipping and rebuilding by base pairings.*
- The base sequence determines the amino acid sequence and the protein produced.
- Three bases code for one amino acid.

Now try this

a Complete the following.

Match the cell structures to the jobs they do, then complete the sentences below.

Cell structure	Job
Nucleus	for chemical reactions
Cell membrane	controls entry and exit of chemicals
Cytoplasm	genetic information

DNA has __________ bases. They are arranged as __________ __________ __________.

Homework

1 Write a short description of the structure of DNA.

2 Use a search engine to find out about DNA 'fingerprints'.

3 Make a flow diagram to show how an enzyme is produced.

ENZYME ACTION

- Enzymes are proteins.
- Enzymes are biological catalysts. They speed up chemical reactions in respiration and photosynthesis.
- Enzymes are specific. They each act on only one substrate.
- Enzyme action is changed by pH and temperature.
- The best conditions are called optimum conditions.
- *Each protein (and enzyme) has a different shape resulting in different functions.*
- *Enzymes work as a 'lock and key' mechanism.*
- *Enzymes are denatured by a change in their molecular shape caused by extremes of pH and temperature.*

TOP TIP Enzymes are not living organisms so they cannot be killed.

Now try this

b Are the following statements **true** (T) or **false** (F)?

Enzymes are denatured by high temperatures. ______

Enzymes work best at their optimum temperature and pH. ______

Enzymes work on any substrate. ______

Enzymes are proteins. ______

Enzymes are only needed in small amounts. ______

Every protein has the same shape. ______

Protein shape is altered by high temperatures. ______

Homework

4 Find out why some washing powders contain enzymes.

5 Find out what link there is between body temperature and optimum enzyme temperature.

6 Draw diagrams to explain a lock and key mechanism.

DIFFUSION

- Diffusion is the random movement of a substance from a high to a low concentration.
- Oxygen enters and carbon dioxide leaves the blood by diffusion.
- Digested food enters the blood from the small intestine by diffusion.
- Dissolved food, oxygen and carbon dioxide diffuse across the placenta.
- Carbon dioxide, oxygen and water vapour diffuse in and out of plant leaves.
- *The rate of diffusion is increased by a greater concentration difference, a shorter distance to travel and a greater surface area.*
- *Alveoli, the small intestine and plant leaves are adapted for efficient diffusion.*

TOP TIP Remember that when two gases meet, they can each diffuse in a different direction.

Now try this

c **Complete these sentences.**

In the alveoli, oxygen ____________ into the blood capillaries. This is because of a ____________ concentration of ____________ in the blood. There is a ____________ concentration of carbon dioxide in the blood so it will ____________ out and into the ____________. Alveoli are adapted for efficient diffusion by being moist, permeable and having a ____________ ____________ ____________.

Homework

7 Explain how perfume spreads.

8 How does diffusion help a developing foetus?

9 Draw a labelled diagram to explain how the small intestine is adapted for efficient diffusion.

BLOOD CIRCULATION

- Blood is made from red blood cells, white blood cells, plasma and platelets.
- Arteries carry blood away from the heart.
- Veins carry blood towards the heart.
- Arteries and veins are joined by capillaries.
- Cholesterol can block arteries.
- The heart pumps blood around the body.
- Two atria receive blood and two ventricles pump blood out.
- Heart valves prevent back flow of blood.
- A heart can be transplanted or have a mechanical replacement.
- *Mammals have a double circulatory system.*
- *A heart pacemaker can help to regulate heart beat.*

TOP TIP The heart is always drawn as if you are looking at it, so the left and right sides are reversed.

Now try this

d **Label the diagram of the heart and complete the sentence below.**

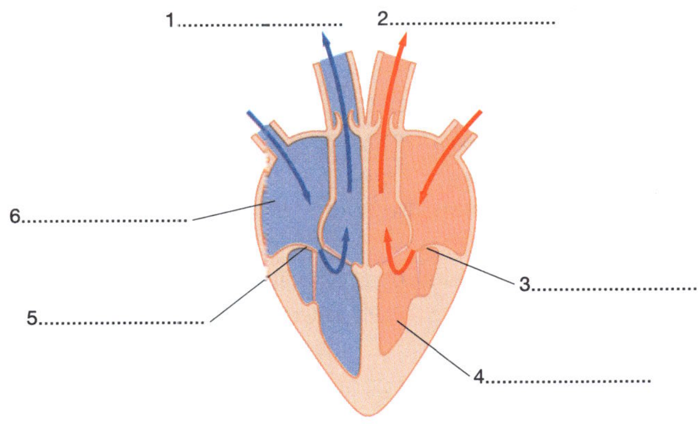

The ______ ______ has the thickest walls because it pumps blood ______ ______ ______ ______.

Homework

10 Make a table to show differences between arteries, veins and capillaries.

11 Use a search engine to find out about heart transplants.

12 Explain how a poor diet can cause poor circulation.

Growth and reproduction

MITOSIS AND GROWTH

- Cells divide so the organism can grow and replace or repair damaged cells.
- This type of cell division is called mitosis.
- Mitosis makes identical new cells containing the diploid number of chromosomes.
- Multi-cellular organisms can be large and complex with different cells.
- Being multi-cellular is better than having one large cell because it will have a better surface area to volume ratio.
- *In mitosis, the chromosomes are copied to produce genetically identical cells.*
- *In mitosis, the chromosomes divide and go to opposite ends of the cell.*

Now try this

a Fill in the missing words.

Mitosis is a type of cell __________. Mitosis produces __________ new cells. It produces cells with the __________ number of chromosomes. The size of a cell is limited because if it gets too big, not enough __________ will get in or out. It is better if a larger organism is __________ rather than one cell. In mitosis, __________ divide and go to opposite __________ of the cell.

Homework

1 Write down the names of **three** single-celled and **three** multi-celled organisms.
2 Write a short paragraph about chromosomes.

MEIOSIS AND REPRODUCTION

- In sexual reproduction, a female gamete (egg) is fertilised by a male gamete (sperm).
- Many sperm are made to ensure fertilisation.
- Sperm have many mitochondria (to release energy) and an acrosome with enzymes to dissolve the egg membrane.
- The egg is larger than the sperm since it has much food.
- The gametes are made by a cell division called meiosis.
- Each gamete has only a half set of chromosomes; this is called haploid.
- Since chromosomes and genes are mixed up in meiosis, the process results in variation.
- *In meiosis, pairs of chromosomes separate to go to opposite ends of the cell.*
- *A second division takes place when the chromosomes divide.*

Now try this

b The diagram shows changes in chromosome number in meiosis.

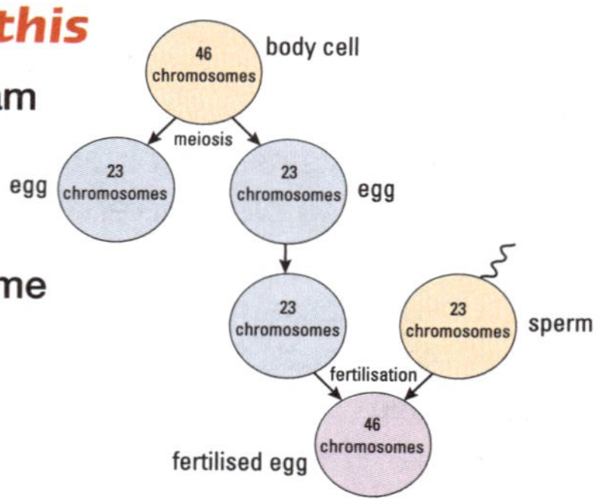

Name two gametes. ______ ______

How many chromosomes are in a human body cell? ______

Which type of cell is diploid? ______

Which type of cell is haploid? ______

Homework

3 Write a short description of the adaptations of a sperm.
4 Use a table to compare and contrast mitosis and meiosis

CELLS AND GROWTH

- A plant cell is different from an animal cell since it has chloroplasts, a cell wall and large vacuoles.
- Plant cells are supported by the cellulose cell wall and pressure from the cell sap in the vacuole.
- Growth in plants and animals needs cell division and cell differentiation (specialised cells).
- Unspecialised cells are called stem cells.
- Plants grow continuously but animals stop growing at maturity.
- *Plant cell growth is different from that in animals because it relies more on cell enlargement, cell division is mainly in the tips and most cells are capable of differentiation.*

Now try this

c **Label the diagrams of a plant cell and an animal cell.**

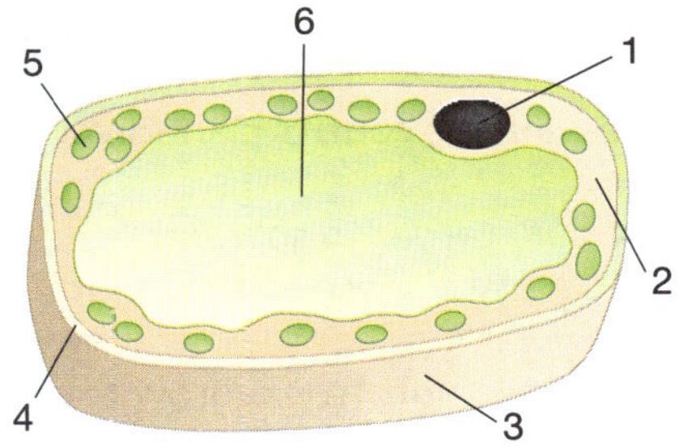

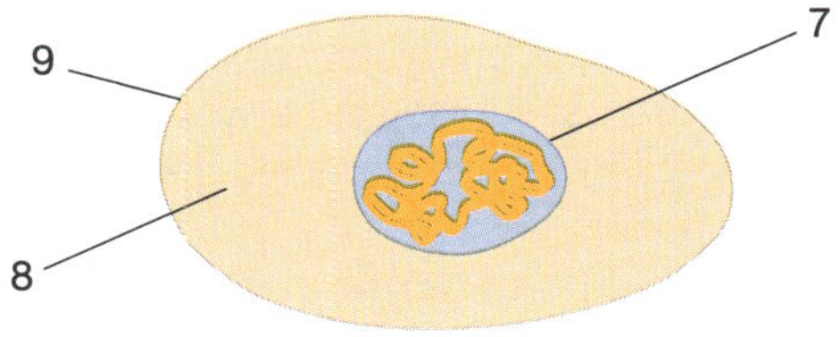

Homework

5 Write down **four** specialised human cells and **four** specialised plant cells.
6 Use a search engine to research Robert Hooke's discoveries about cells.
7 Use a table to show differences between the growth of plants and animals.

HUMAN GROWTH

- There are stages in human growth (infancy, childhood, puberty, maturity and old age).
- The gestation period (time for baby's development) is linked to animal size.
- Different parts of the foetus grow at different rates.
- *Recordings are made of a baby's weight and head size.*

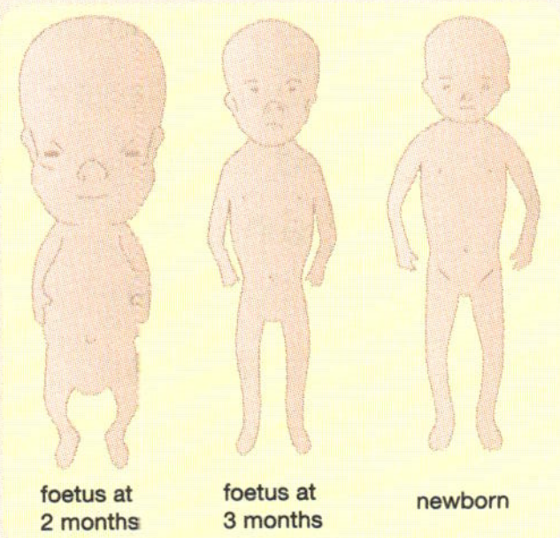

Now try this

d **Answer the following questions.**

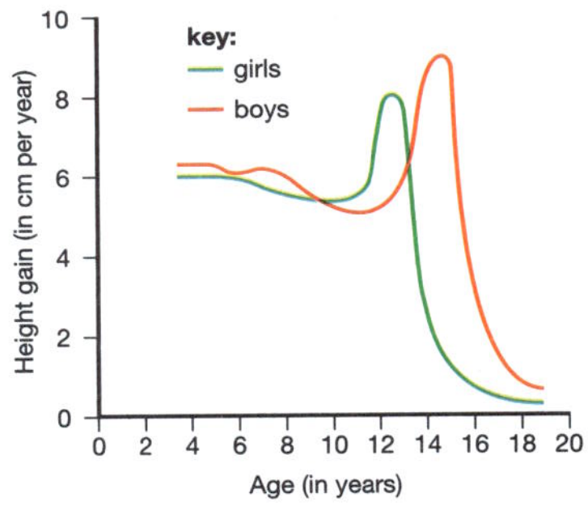

Between which ages are girls growing faster than boys? ______

What is the greatest height gain in boys? ______

What is the greatest height gain in girls? ______

At what age does growth finally stop in boys? ______

At what age does growth finally stop in girls? ______

In a foetus, which part of the body grows fastest? ______

Homework

8 Ask your parent/guardian if they still have your height and weight recordings as a baby.
9 Use a search engine to find out about gestation periods in different mammals.
10 Write a short description about the gestation period.

Hormone and gene control

PLANT HORMONES

- Plant hormones (auxins) control plant growth, flowering and fruit ripening.
- Plant hormones are carried in solution.
- Phototropism is a plant's response to light.
- Geotropism is a plant's response to gravity.
- Shoots are positively phototropic (grow towards light) and roots are negatively phototropic (grow away from light).
- Shoots are negatively geotropic (grow away from the effect of gravity) and roots are positively geotropic (grow towards gravity).
- Plant hormones are used in selective weed killers, rooting powder, fruit-ripening sprays and seed germination.
- *Plant tips make auxins.*
- *The unequal distribution of auxins in a shoot causes it to grow towards light.*

Now try this

a **Are the following statements true (T) or false (F)?**

Plant hormones dissolve in water.	______
Shoots are positively geotropic.	______
Shoots are positively phototropic.	______
Phototropism is a plant's response to light.	______
Geotropism is a plant's response to water.	______

Homework

1 Why should plants on a window sill be turned around?
2 Explain why it is better for roots to grow downwards.
3 Draw diagrams of auxin concentration in a shoot to explain phototropism.

MUTATIONS AND SELECTIVE BREEDING

- Mutations are changes to genes or chromosomes.
- Mutations are mainly harmful; a few are beneficial.
- Mutations can be natural or caused by radiation.
- Selective breeding selects for useful characteristics over many generations.
- Selective breeding increases agricultural yields.
- Selectively bred animals are often cross-bred.

Jersey cattle
Small quantity of very creamy milk

Friesian cattle
Large quantity of slightly creamy milk

What will cross-breeds produce?

Now try this

b **Cows are selectively bred. Tick those characteristics that a farmer will select.**

Grow quickly	☐
Need a lot of grass	☐
Well developed muscles	☐
Produce large quantities of milk	☐
Prone to disease	☐
Breed easily	☐
Large horns	☐
Usually produce twins	☐
Short life span	☐
Well behaved and docile	☐

Homework

4 Write a short description of selective breeding.
5 Write a paragraph about mutations.
6 Use a search engine to find out about Queen Victoria and haemophilia, which is caused by a mutation.

GENETIC ENGINEERING

- The transfer of genes from one organism to another is called genetic engineering or genetic modification (GM).
- Examples of genetic engineering are: inserting a gene into bacteria to produce human insulin, inserting a carrot gene into rice to make vitamin A and producing herbicide resistant crops.
- Genetic engineering produces organisms with new features but can have unexpected results.

- *Genetic engineering raises many ethical and moral issues, for example, unknown consequences, 'playing god'.*
- *Selective breeding reduces the gene pool, reduces variation and accumulates recessive characteristics.*

Now try this

c Fill in the missing words.

GM stands for ____________ ____________. Genetic engineering transfers ____________ ____________ from one ______ to another. When a herbicide-resistant crop is sprayed with herbicide the ____________ die but the ____________ does not. Bacteria with an inserted insulin gene can make lots of ____________ which can be harvested and used to control ____________ in humans.

Homework

7 Use a search engine to find out when GM crops were first used.
8 Write down **two** advantages and **two** disadvantages of using genetic modifications.
9 Use a search engine to find out about the dangers of GM crops.

CLONING

- Cloning is an example of asexual reproduction and produces genetically identical copies.
- Cloned embryos are implanted into surrogate mothers.
- Cloning occurs naturally to produce twins, new strawberry plants and potato plants.
- Cloned plants will have the same colour, taste, smell and crop yield and be easily mass produced.
- Cloned plants will be prone to disease or unable to survive changing conditions due to lack of variation.
- *Dolly was made by removing the nucleus from an egg cell, inserting a nucleus from a body cell and implanting the cell into another sheep to develop into a baby.*
- *Plant cloning cultures small pieces of tissue using aseptic techniques and a suitable growth medium.*

TOP TIP Plants are easier than animals to clone because many of their cells remain unspecialised.

Now try this

d Complete these sentences.

Cloning is an example of __________ reproduction. Clones are __________ copies. Cloned plants are useful because they are all __________. Cloned plants are at a disadvantage if the __________ change or a __________ infects them. Dolly was made by removing the __________ from an __________. Another __________ from a __________ cell was implanted inside.

Homework

10 Describe how cuttings can be used to produce more plants.
11 Use a text book or search engine to find out about the life of Dolly.
12 Use a search engine to find out about aseptic techniques in plant cloning.

Plant processes

LEAVES AND PHOTOSYNTHESIS

- A leaf has an upper and lower epidermis covered with a waxy cuticle.
- The spongy mesophyll and palisade cells contain chloroplasts.
- Guard cells surround stomata.
- Leaves are adapted for efficient photosynthesis by having a large surface area, being thin and having veins.
- Photosynthesis occurs mainly in the leaves.
- Water enters the root hairs by osmosis.
- Carbon dioxide enters and oxygen leaves by diffusion through stomata.
- *The leaf is very efficient in photosynthesising because it has a large internal surface area, internal air spaces and many chloroplasts in the palisade layer.*

Now try this

a Fill in the missing words.

The outer waxy cuticle keeps the leaf ______________. In plants, light energy is absorbed by green ______________. These structures are found in ______________ cells, ______________ cells and ______________ cells. The energy is used to make ______________. Gases enter and exit the leaf through small holes called ______________. The leaf is very efficient as it has many ______________ to absorb a lot of light and a large internal area for rapid ______________ of gases.

Homework

1 Write down a word equation for photosynthesis.

2 Draw and label the inside structure of a leaf.

PLANTS AND WATER

- Plant cells are supported by their cell walls and turgor pressure in the cell sap.
- Water enters the root hairs by osmosis.
- Osmosis is the movement of water from a high concentration to a low concentration through a semi-permeable membrane.
- A semi-permeable membrane only allows movement of small molecules.
- Osmosis is a type of diffusion.
- A plant must balance its water uptake and water loss.
- Water is needed for photosynthesis, cooling and transport.
- A leaf is adapted to reduce water loss.
- *Leaves lose water because a leaf is adapted for photosynthesis.*

Now try this

b Complete the explanation of diffusion.

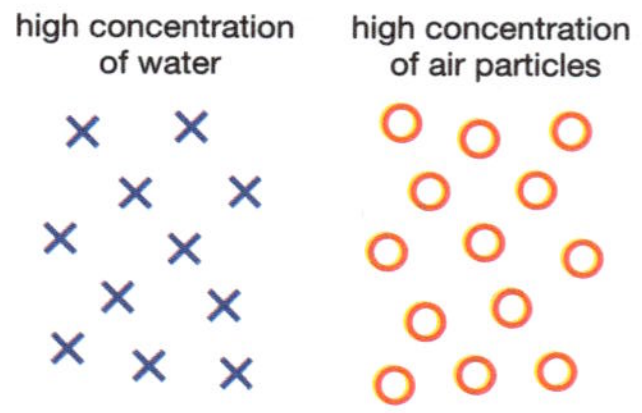

Complete the explanation of osmosis.

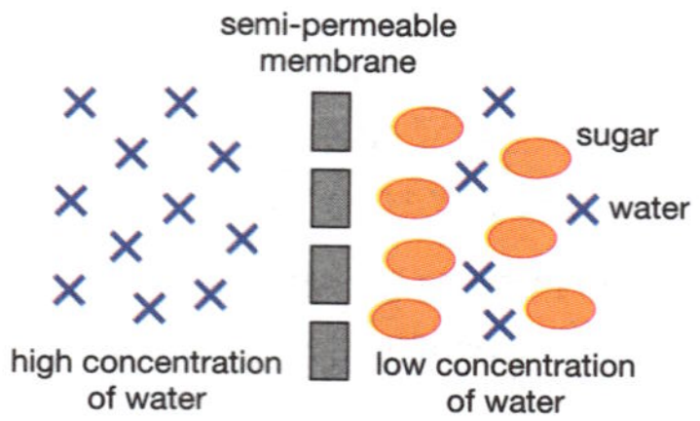

Homework

3 Write a short description of osmosis.

4 Explain why a leaf is adapted to reduce the rate of transpiration.

TRANSPIRATION

- Water loss from a plant is called transpiration.
- The water evaporates and exits the leaves by diffusion.
- Water travels from the roots, through the stem to the leaves in xylem cells.
- Dissolved food travels downwards in phloem cells.
- The rate of transpiration is speeded up by a higher temperature, more wind, a low humidity and more light.
- *More light will increase the transpiration rate because the stomata will be open.*
- *A higher temperature will increase the transpiration rate by increasing the diffusion rate.*
- *A low humidity will allow more water vapour to diffuse out of the leaves.*
- *Xylem cells are dead because they have extra lignin thickening.*

Now try this

c Complete these sentences.

Transpiration is the loss of ________________. Xylem carries ________________ and ________________. Phloem carries ________________ such as ________________. Transpiration is speeded up by a high ________________, more ________________ and ________________ and a low ________________. In bright light, the ________________ will be open. This causes more ________________ to escape from leaves by ________________.

Homework

5 Describe the passage of water from the soil to cells in a leaf.

6 Write a short description of transpiration.

7 Explain why plants living in a hot desert need to be adapted to reduce transpiration.

FERTILISERS AND PLANT GROWTH

- Plants need minerals in fertilisers such as nitrates, phosphates, potassium and magnesium compounds.
- Minerals are needed only in small quantities.
- Nitrates are needed to make proteins for growth.
- Phosphates are needed for root growth.
- Potassium is needed for flower formation.
- Magnesium is needed to make chlorophyll.
- If minerals are missing from the soil water, the plant shows that it is mineral-deficient.
- *Minerals are taken up from the soil water by active transport.*
- *Minerals are taken up against a concentration gradient.*
- *Active transport uses energy.*

Now try this

d Match up the correct boxes.

Element	Absorbed as	Use
Nitrogen	phosphates	chlorophyll
Phosphorus	nitrates	flower formation
Potassium	magnesium compounds	root growth
Magnesium	potassium compounds	proteins

TOP TIP An NPK fertiliser contains nitrogen (N), phosphorus (P) and potassium (K).

Homework

8 Write down **two** advantages and **two** disadvantages of using artificial fertilisers.

9 Use a search engine to find out about the history of fertilisers.

10 Draw a diagram to explain active transport.

Biomass, farming and decay

BIOMASS

- Energy enters food chains in photosynthesis.
- Plants are producers because they produce food.
- Animals are consumers.
- A pyramid of numbers shows the number of organisms in each link (trophic level) in a food chain.
- A pyramid of biomass shows the mass of living material in each link (trophic level) in a food chain.
- Energy is transferred along a food chain or food web.
- Some energy is transferred into less useful forms such as heat or body waste.
- Biomass fuels are wood (by burning), alcohol (by fermentation) and biogas (from decay).
- *Biomass fuels are renewable, produce less pollution and are energy self-reliant.*

Now try this

a Complete the following. Look at the food chain.

1 oak tree → 1000 caterpillars → 100 shrews → 10 badgers

Name the producer. ______

What is the source of energy? ______

Which pyramid of numbers is correct? ______

A B C

Homework

1 Draw a food web of plants and animals in a garden.

2 Explain the difference between a producer and a consumer.

3 Why are biofuels becoming more important?

INTENSIVE AND ORGANIC FARMING

- Intensive farming uses pesticides (insecticide and fungicide) to kill pests and herbicides to kill weeds.
- Intensive farming produces more food but also causes problems such as pesticide accumulation in food chains.
- Fish farming, glasshouses, hydroponics and battery farming are examples of intensive farming.
- Organic farming does not use artificial fertilisers, herbicides or pesticides.
- Organic farming uses animal manure, crop rotation, hand-weeding and biological control of pests.
- *Intensive farming improves the efficiency of energy transfer in food chains.*
- *Hydroponics gives better control of fertilisers and diseases.*

Now try this

b Are the following statements true (T) or false (F)?

Intensive farming uses pesticides. ______

Insecticides kill weeds. ______

Intensive farming produces less food. ______

Organic farming uses artificial fertilisers. ______

Hydroponics is an example of organic farming. ______

Organic farming uses biological control of pests. ______

Homework

4 Write a short description of organic farming.

5 Use a table to list the advantages and disadvantages of intensive farming.

DECAY AND FOOD PRESERVATION

- Decomposers such as fungi and bacteria cause decay.
- Decay breaks down sewage and compost.
- Decay is affected by temperature and the amount of oxygen and water.
- Detritivores are animals that feed on dead and decaying material.
- Earthworms, maggots and woodlice are detritivores .
- *Saprophytes are plants that live on dead and decaying material.*
- Food can be preserved by stopping or reducing decay.
- Food preservation methods include canning, freezing, drying and adding salt, sugar or vinegar.

Now try this

c Complete these sentences.

Decay is cause by microorganisms such as ________________ and ________________. Decay is slowed down by a ________________ temperature. Decay is useful when it breaks down ________________. An example of a detritivore is a ________________. Food preservation works by stopping or reducing ________________. Drying foods will ________________ them and stop them ________________.

Homework

6 Write a short paragraph about the right conditions to compost kitchen waste.

7 Use a search engine to research the history of food preservation.

8 Write an explanation of saprophytic nutrition.

RECYCLING OF NITROGEN AND CARBON

- When plants and animals die, their chemicals, such as nitrogen and carbon, are recycled.
- Plants remove carbon from the air by photosynthesis.
- Respiration and the burning of fossil fuels releases carbon in the form of carbon dioxide.
- *Carbon is recycled through marine shells, limestone and eventual weathering.*
- There is a lot of nitrogen (78%) in the air but it is unreactive.
- Plants take in nitrogen as nitrates.
- Dead bodies decay, releasing nitrates.
- *Decomposers convert proteins and urea into ammonia.*
- *Ammonia is converted into nitrates by nitrifying bacteria.*
- *Some nitrates are converted into nitrogen by denitrifying bacteria.*
- *Nitrogen-fixing bacteria in the soil and root nodules fix atmospheric nitrogen.*

Now try this

d Name the processes in the carbon cycle.

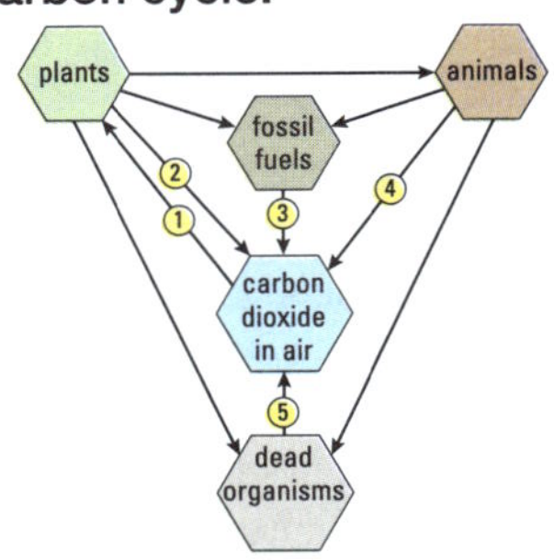

1 ________________

2 ________________

3 ________________

4 ________________

5 ________________

Homework

9 Write a short 'life history' of a carbon molecule.

10 Explain why it is important for chemicals to be recycled.

11 Draw a labelled diagram of the nitrogen cycle.

The periodic table 1

WHAT ARE ATOMS LIKE?

- There are over 100 elements which:
  - contain the same type of atom
  - cannot be broken down chemically
  - combine chemically to make compounds.
- Inside atoms, negative electrons orbit a nucleus, made from positive protons and neutral neutrons.
- The elements are arranged in ascending order of atomic number in the periodic table.
- Each element has a different atomic number, which shows the number of protons.
- In a neutral atom, electrons = protons.
- Positive protons and neutral neutrons both have a relative mass of 1.
- Their total gives the atom's mass number.
- Isotopes have different numbers of neutrons so they have different mass numbers.

Now try this

a Match the statements on the right to the particles on the left.

Proton	negative
	around the outside of an atom
	mass almost zero
	in the nucleus
Neutron	neutral
	number different for every element
	mass 1
Electron	positive

TOP TIP: electrons = protons = atomic number
neutrons = mass number – atomic number

Homework

1 How many protons, neutrons and electrons are there in H, B, Na, Al, K and Ca?
2 Design a test to cover everything in the revision focus.
3 Prepare a presentation to show what atoms are like.

ELECTRONS

- Electrons have a charge of –1 and almost no mass (0.0005).
- They orbit in shells.
- The first shell holds two and the next two hold eight.
- The periodic table reflects these shells.
- The first shell holds two like the first row.
- The second shell holds eight like the second row.
- *Electronic configurations show the electrons in each shell, for example, C 2.4 has two in the first shell, four in the second.*

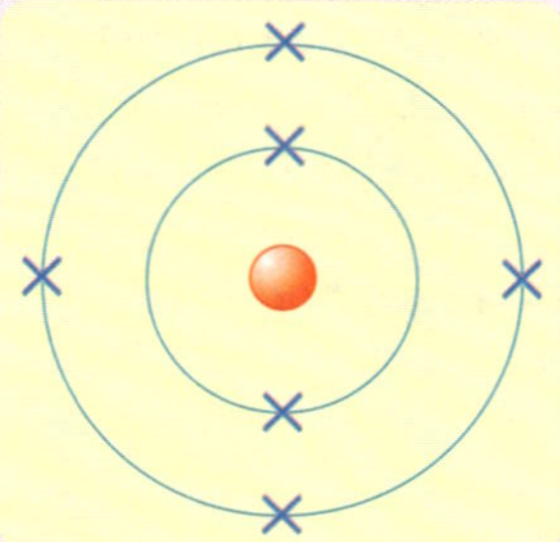

TOP TIP: Group number = electrons in outer shell, and this determines an element's properties.

Now try this

b Write electron configurations for the following.

B ______
N ______
Ne ______
Mg ______
Cl ______
Ca ______
Al ______
P ______

Homework

4 Compile a 10-question quiz on the periodic table with answers on the back.
5 Find images of **five** elements with less than 20 protons and draw their atoms.
6 Write everything you can tell about K, Cl and Ne from the periodic table.

HOW ATOMS COMBINE – IONIC BONDING

- Ions are charged atoms or groups of atoms.
- In reactions, metals become positive ions because they lose negative electrons, for example, $Na_{(2.8.1)}$ – 1 electron → $Na^{+}_{(2.8)}$.
- The electrons are given to non-metals, for example, $Cl_{(2.8.7)}$ + 1 electron → $Cl^{-}_{(2.8.8)}$.
- *In compounds, ionic charges cancel out, for example, $2Na^+$ with 1 O^{2-} makes Na_2O.*
- *Ions like OH^- and NO_3^- may need brackets. for example, Mg^{2+} with $2OH^-$ makes $Mg(OH)_2$ Mg^{2+} with $2NO_3^-$ makes $Mg(NO_3)_2$*
- *The + and – ions are strongly attracted, so melting and boiling points are high, but some (for example, NaCl) can dissolve in water.*

TOP TIP Molten or dissolved ions move around, so they conduct electricity but solid ionic compounds do not.

Now try this

c **Predict the formulae of the following compounds.**

Potassium(K^+) oxide(O^{2-}) = ______

Calcium(Ca^{2+}) chloride(Cl^-) = ______

Sodium(Na^+) iodide(I^-) = ______

Calcium(Ca^{2+}) hydroxide(OH^-) = ______

Calcium(Ca^{2+}) oxide(O^{2-}) = ______

Potassium(K^+) sulfide(S^{2-}) = ______

Calcium(Ca^{2+}) nitrate(NO_3^-) = ______

Sodium(Na^+) sulfate(SO_4^{2-}) = ______

Magnesium(Mg^{2+}) iodide(I^-) = ______

Lithium(Li^-) oxide(O^{2-}) = ______

Homework

7 Draw dot and cross diagrams for NaCl, MgO, $MgCl_2$ and Na_2O.
8 Find images of giant ionic structures and explain why ions form crystals.
9 Research what happens to the ions when compounds like NaCl dissolve.

COVALENT BONDING

- Molecules are groups of non-metal atoms.
- They share electrons to get full outer shells.
- *Electrons in covalent bonds can be shown as dots and crosses – one from each atom.*
- *Bonds are very strong, but the forces between molecules like CO_2 and H_2O are weak, so their boiling points are low and they tend to be gases.*
- Small molecules like CO_2 have no delocalised electrons or ions, so they never conduct electricity.

TOP TIP Only non-metals can bond covalently.

Now try this

d **Draw dots and crosses to show the outer electrons of the atoms in the following molecules.**

H_2	H	H	
H_2O	H	O	H
CO_2	O	C	O
		H	
CH_4	H	C	H
		H	

Homework

10 Use group 7 elements to explain how size affects the forces between molecules.
11 Find out how sand (SiO_2) is bonded, and explain why it is so different from CO_2.
12 Find 3D images of H_2O, CO_2 and CH_4 and explain the shapes of their molecules.

The periodic table 2

COVALENT BONDING AND THE PERIODIC TABLE

- Vertical columns in the periodic table are called groups.
- Elements in the same group have similar properties, because they have the same number of outer electrons.
- The horizontal rows in the periodic table are periods.
- The period shows the number of occupied shells.

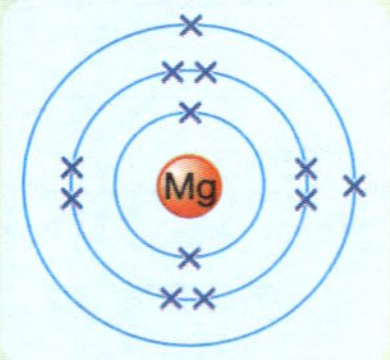

TOP TIP The number of elements in a period is the same as the number of electrons the corresponding shell can hold.

Now try this

a Give the group and period shown by each electron configuration.

2.1 __________

2.8.7 __________

2.8.8.1 __________

2.7 __________

2.8.8 __________

2.8.1 __________

2.8 __________

2 __________

Homework

1. Label a periodic table to show electron configurations up to calcium.
2. Explain the connection between electrons and the periodic table.
3. How can you tell if two elements are joined by ionic or covalent bonds?

THE GROUP 1 ELEMENTS

- To identify group 1 metals, use a flame test.
- Dip moist nichrome wire in the solid and hold it in a blue flame. Observe the colour: Na (yellow), K (lilac), Li (crimson).
- The alkali metals in group 1 are very reactive.
- They are kept under oil to stop them reacting with O_2.
- They all react with water exothermically:
  sodium + water → sodium hydroxide + hydrogen.
  $2Na + 2H_2O \rightarrow 2NaOH + H_2$
- During the reaction: $Na_{(atom)} \rightarrow Na^{+}_{(ion)} + e^{-}$
- Electrons are lost so this is oxidation.
- Going **down** the group, they get **more** reactive.
- They also get softer, less dense and easier to melt.
- In bigger atoms, the outer electron is further from the pull of the positive nucleus, and is lost more easily.

TOP TIP The alkali metals are dangerously reactive but their compounds are vital components of living things, like sodium chloride.

Now try this

b Are the following statements **true (T)** or **false (F)**?

Group 1 metals fizz in water ______

Na displaces **H** from water ______

Li is more reactive than **Na** ______

K is strong and shiny ______

KOH is an alkali ______

Li has a lilac flame ______

Na has one electron in its outer shell ______

Na is oxidised when it reacts ______

Li loses electrons more easily than **Na** ______

Li forms 1+ ions, **Na** forms 2+ ions ______

Homework

4. Prepare a presentation about the reactions of alkali metals.
5. What trends do their melting points and densities show?
6. Based on what you know about Na and K, predict the properties of caesium.

THE GROUP 7 ELEMENTS 1

- The halogens in group 7 are reactive non-metals.
- They have similar properties because they have seven electrons in their outer shell, for example, $Cl_{(2.8.7)}$.
- Going down the group, they get less reactive, their colours darken and boiling points increase: Cl_2 (green gas), Br_2 (brown liquid), I_2 (grey solid).
- They react with metals to make salts: sodium + chlorine → sodium chloride. $2Na_{(s)} + Cl_{2(g)} \rightarrow 2NaCl_{(s)}$
- The reaction is very vigorous.
- NaCl is used for flavouring food, as a preservative and as a raw material for chlorine manufacture.
- Chlorine is used to sterilise water and make pesticides and plastics; iodine to sterilise wounds.

Now try this

c Match each property to the correct halogen.

	sterilises water
Chlorine	grey solid
	green gas
	makes white salts
	sterilises wounds
Bromine	brown liquid
	used in some polymers
	only displaces iodine
Iodine	has seven electrons in its outer shell
	most reactive

TOP TIP Halogens lose their colour when they form ionic compounds.

Homework

7 What would you see when sodium reacts with each halogen?

8 What patterns are there in the colours, states and melting points of group 7?

9 Use what you know about Cl_2, Br_2 and I_2 to predict the properties of F_2 and At_2.

THE GROUP 7 ELEMENTS 2

- Halogens react with metals by gaining one electron, to form 1– ions with stable electronic structures, for example, $Cl_2 + 2e^- \rightarrow 2Cl^-$.
- This is reduction because electrons are gained.
- Smaller atoms gain electrons more easily, as their outer shell is closer to the nucleus.
- The order of reactivity is F, Cl, Br, I, At
- More reactive halogens displace less reactive ones. bromine + sodium iodide → sodium bromide + iodine $Br_2 + 2NaI \rightarrow 2NaBr + I_2$.

TOP TIP I_2 molecules are purple but form brown solutions.

Now try this

d Finish the following equations.

chlorine + lithium bromide → lithium chloride + ____________

Cl_2 + 2LiBr → 2LiCl + ____________

bromine + potassium iodide → ____________ + ____________

Br_2 + 2KI → ____________ + ____________

chlorine + sodium iodide → ____________ + ____________

Cl_2 + 2KI → ____________ + ____________

Homework

10 Draw chlorine and sodium bromide solutions before and after they react.

11 What would you see when Cl_2 reacts with KBr and KI? Give reasons.

12 Find out how bromine is extracted from sea water.

The periodic table 3

ELECTROLYSIS 1

- Electrolysis decomposes solutions by turning charged ions into atoms. Any gases formed escape from solution.
- The ions are melted or dissolved so that they are free to move.
- Metal cations (+) and H^+ ions are attracted to the cathode (–).
- Non-metal anions (–) move to the anode (+).
- Sulfuric acid releases H_2 and O_2.
  At the negative cathode: $2H^+(aq) + 2e^- \rightarrow H_{2(g)}$
  At the positive anode: $4OH^-_{(aq)} - 4e^- \rightarrow 2H_2O_{(l)} + O_{2(g)}$
- Hydrogen 'pops' with a lit splint.
- Oxygen relights a glowing splint.

TOP TIP When dilute sulfuric acid is electrolysed, hydrogen and oxygen are released.

Now try this

a Fill in the missing words.

During electrolysis the H^+ __________ in sulfuric acid solution are attracted to the __________ __________ where they gain electrons and form __________ of H_2. Opposites attract so the OH^- ions in the solution move to the __________ __________ where they lose __________. This produces __________ and oxygen.

Homework

1 What is different about the anode and cathode?
2 Find out which products form when a solution of NaCl is electrolysed.
3 Prepare a presentation to explain electrolysis of sulfuric acid to a Year 9 class.

ELECTROLYSIS 2

- Aluminium is expensive because it takes a lot of electricity to extract it from the aluminium oxide in bauxite.
- Aluminium oxide → aluminium + oxygen
- The aluminium oxide is dissolved in molten cryolite to lower its melting point.
- The electrodes are made from graphite (carbon).
- At the anode (+) oxygen forms. $2O^{2-} \rightarrow O_2 + 4e^-$
- This oxidises the electrode to CO_2.
- At the cathode (–) aluminium forms. $Al^{3+} + 3e^- \rightarrow Al$

TOP TIP It takes a lot of energy to extract aluminium so it is worth recycling it even though it is not in short supply.

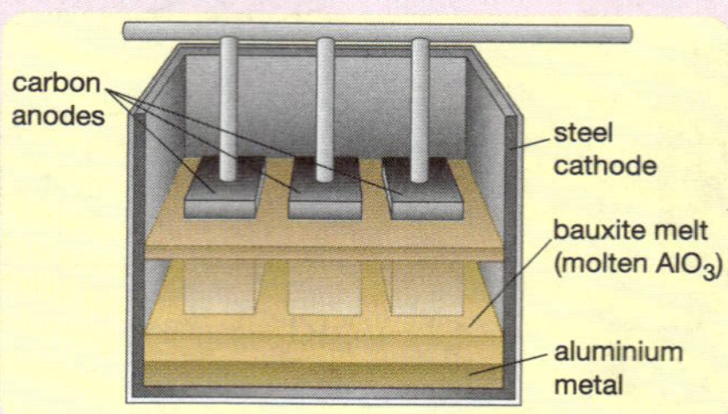

Now try this

b Decide if these things happen at the anode (A) or cathode (C).

Aluminium deposited __________
Ions collect electrons __________
Al^{3+} ions attracted __________
Negative ions attracted __________
Electrode regularly replaced __________
Reduction __________
Non-metal discharged __________
Ions donate electrons __________
Oxidation __________
Electrode oxidised to CO_2 __________

Homework

4 Prepare a presentation to explain aluminium extraction.
5 Titanium is the second most common metal – how is it extracted?
6 Explain what oxidation and reduction have to do with electrolysis.

See pages 116–127 of Collins GCSE Additional Science

TRANSITION ELEMENTS

- Iron and copper are transition metals.
- Their compounds are coloured: copper$_{(blue)}$, iron(II)$_{(light\ green)}$, iron(III)$_{(orange)}$.
- Both metals and compounds can be catalysts, for example, iron in the Haber Process, nickel in margarine manufacture.
- Precipitates form if their ions mix with alkali. $Cu^{2+}_{(blue)}$, $Fe(II)^{2+}_{(grey/green)}$, $Fe(III)^{2+}_{(brown)}$
  For example, $Cu^{2+}_{(aq)} + 2OH^{-}_{(aq)} \rightarrow Cu(OH)_{2(s)}$
- Thermal decomposition splits their carbonates up, changes their colour and releases CO_2.
  For example, $CuCO_3 \rightarrow CuO + CO_2$
- The carbon dioxide turns limewater cloudy.

TOP TIP Transition metals have similar properties and their own block in the periodic table.

Now try this

c Link each substance to its properties.

Fe	orange
	green
$Fe(II)(OH)_2$	conductor
	grey
$Fe(III)(OH)_3$	catalyst in Haber process
	decomposes on heating
	precipitated by alkali
$Fe(II)CO_3$	releases CO_2 on heating

Sc	Ti	V	Cr	Mn	Fe	Co	Ni	Cu	Zn
Y	Zr	Nb	Mo	Tc	Ru	Rh	Pd	Ag	Cd
La	Hf	Ta	W	Re	Os	Ir	Pt	Au	Hg
Ac									

The transition metals.

Homework

7 Prepare a presentation on copper and its compounds.
8 Write equations for: iron hydroxide forming; iron carbonate decomposing.
9 How could you find the transition metal with the most stable carbonate?

METAL STRUCTURE AND PROPERTIES

- Metals are hard, strong, lustrous and dense.
- They form alloys like brass$_{(copper)}$ and steel$_{(iron)}$.
- They have high melting/boiling points.
- They conduct heat and electricity well.
- Each atom contributes delocalised electrons to a regular crystal structure.
- *Metallic bonding is the electrostatic attraction between the sea of delocalised electrons and the close-packed positive metal ions.*
- Superconductors have little or no resistance.
- They allow loss-free power transmission, super-fast circuits and powerful electromagnets, but they only work at very low temperatures.
- *We need to develop superconductors that work at 20 °C.*

TOP TIP When a voltage is applied, delocalised electrons move and form an electric current.

Now try this

d Link each metallic property to a use.

Lustrous	wiring
Electrical conductor	bridges
Tensile strength	weights
High melting point	nails
Strong	mirror
Hard	lift cables
Dense	saucepan
Thermal conductor	light bulb filament

Homework

10 Find **two** images of metal atoms and say which best explains their properties.
11 Suggest reasons to account for some metals conducting better than others.
12 Conduct some research to compare the conductivities of copper and a superconductor.

Chemical economics 1

ACIDS AND BASES 1

- *Acids contain H^+ ions.*
- They have pH values below 7.
- Sulfuric acid is used as car battery acid and to prepare metal surfaces and make fertilisers.
- Acids are neutralised by bases and carbonates.
- Bases are oxides and hydroxides.
- Alkalis are soluble bases.
- *They contain OH^- ions.*
- They have pH values greater than 7.
- *Acids and alkalis neutralise each other.*
  $H^+_{(aq)} + OH^-_{(aq)} \rightarrow H_2O_{(l)}$

TOP TIP Replacing the hydrogen in an acid with a metal gives a neutral salt.

Now try this

a Circle the correct answers. There may be more than one.

An acid	HCl	NaCl	NaOH
An alkali	KOH	HNO_3	KCl
A salt	NaOH	H_2SO_4	$NaNO_3$
An oxide	CuO	NaOH	$CuSO_4$
A carbonate	$CaCO_3$	CaO	H_2SO_4
Bases	CuO	$CuCO_3$	NaOH
Weak alkali	pH 5	pH 13	pH 8
Strong acid	pH 1	pH 6	pH 3

Homework

1 Draw particle pictures to show an acid reacting with an alkali.
2 Describe what happens to the pH when H^+ ions are added to OH^- ions.
3 Find out why acid/base indicators change colour. Is it always at pH 7?

ACIDS AND BASES 2

- Acids are neutralised by carbonates, bases and alkalis.
- *CARBONATE + ACID → SALT + WATER + CO_2*
  for example, $CaCO_{3(s)} + 2HCl_{(aq)} \rightarrow CaCl_{2(aq)} + H_2O_{(l)} + CO_{2(g)}$
- *OXIDE + ACID → SALT + WATER*
  for example, $CuO_{(s)} + 2HCl_{(aq)} \rightarrow CuCl_{2(aq)} + H_2O_{(l)}$
- *HYDROXIDE + ACID → SALT + WATER*
  for example, $NaOH_{(aq)} + HCl_{(aq)} \rightarrow NaCl_{(aq)} + H_2O_{(l)}$
- *Ammonia makes ammonium salts:*
  for example, $NH_{3(aq)} + HCl_{(aq)} \rightarrow NH_4Cl_{(aq)}$

TOP TIP An indicator is needed to show when an acid has been completely neutralised by an alkali.

Now try this

b Which pairs from the right react to make the chemicals on the left?

H_2O	magnesium
CO_2	OH^- ion solution
	H^+ ion solution
H_2	carbonate
A salt	copper oxide

Homework

4 Write step-by-step instructions for making copper sulfate and sodium chloride.
5 Write equations for reacting: HCl + KOH; H_2SO_4 + CuO; HNO_3 + Na_2CO_3.
6 Design a test to show which students understand how salts are made.

REACTING MASSES 1

- The relative formula mass is the sum of the relative atomic masses (M_r) of the atoms.
  $SO_2 = 32 + 16 + 16 = 64$
  $CaCO_3 = 40 + 12 + 16 + 16 + 16 = 100$
  $Ca(OH)_2 = 40 + 16 + 16 + 1 + 1 = 74$
- *Formulae cannot change and equations must be balanced. Atoms cannot be gained or lost.*
- The total reactant mass equals the total product mass.
- *Equations can be used to calculate how much product will form:*
  $CaCO_3 \rightarrow CaO + CO_2$
  100 g $CaCO_3$ make 44 g CO_2
  1 g $CaCO_3$ makes 0.44 g CO_2 etc.

Now try this

c Balance each equation and calculate the mass of magnesium needed to make the amount of product shown.

_____ $Mg + O_2 \rightarrow$ _____ MgO (80 g) _______g

$Mg + Cl_2 \rightarrow MgCl_2$ (190 g) _______g

$Mg +$ _____ $HCl \rightarrow MgCl_2 + H_2$ (1 g) _______g

$Mg +$ _____ $HNO_3 \rightarrow Mg(NO_3)_2 + H_2$ (4 g) _______g

$Mg + H_2SO_4 \rightarrow MgSO_4$ (60 g) $+ H_2$ _______g

TOP TIP Multiply everything in brackets by the number outside.

Homework

7 Put these gases in order of mass: CH_4, CO_2, Cl_2, H_2, N_2, SO_2, NH_3, NO_2.
8 Calculate the masses of **10** different oxides that contain 32 g of oxygen.
9 Calculate the grams of CO_2 made by heating 800 g $CaCO_3$ and burning 800 g CH_4.

REACTING MASSES 2

- The percentage yield compares the mass of product made with the expected mass.
- $\% \text{ yield} = \dfrac{\text{actual yield (g)}}{\text{predicted yield (g)}} \times 100\%$
- 100% yield means no product is lost.
- 0% yield means no product is made.
- Percentage yields below 100% are due to:
  - losses in filtration
  - losses in evaporation
  - losses in transferring liquids.

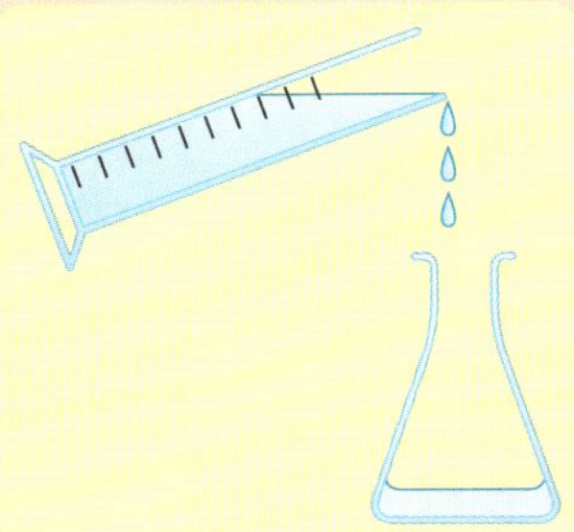

Now try this

d Calculate the theoretical yield and the percentage yield for each reaction.

12 g of C makes 22 g of CO_2 ____________

48 g of Mg makes 16 g of MgO ____________

16 g of S makes 32 g of SO_2 ____________

16 g of Cu makes 15 g of CuO ____________

12 g of C makes 14 g of CO ____________

TOP TIP Reactions with higher percentage yields are more profitable.

Homework

10 Explain why it is useful for chemists to know the percentage yield of a reaction.
11 Explain where losses are likely to occur when ammonium sulfate is made.
12 Why can percentage yields appear higher than 100% when CuO is made by heating $CuCO_3$?

Chemical economics 2

FERTILISERS AND CROP YIELD

- Fertilisers increase yields by adding essential elements like nitrogen as soluble compounds.
- Ammonia is neutralised with acid to make fertilisers like ammonium nitrate: NH_4NO_3.
- The more nitrogen is incorporated into plant protein, the faster and bigger crops grow.
- *Eutrophication occurs when fertiliser run-off adds nitrate or phosphate to river water.*
- *This kills living organisms because algal blooms block light, other plants die and decomposers reduce oxygen levels.*

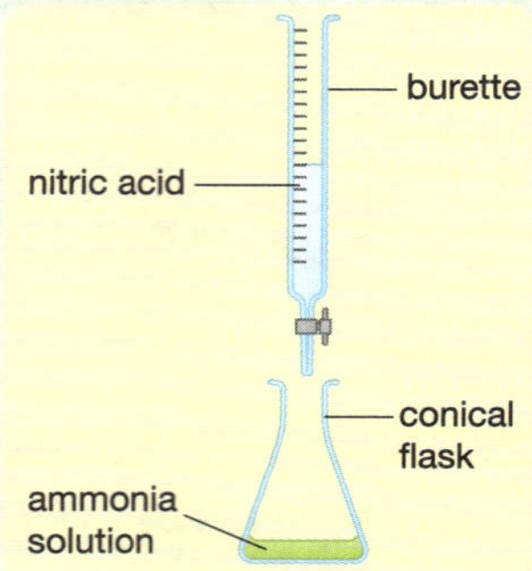

Now try this

a Calculate the percentage of nitrogen in each of these fertilisers.

Ammonia – NH_3 ______

Urea – $CO(NH_2)_2$ ______

Ammonium nitrate – NH_4NO_3 ______

Ammonium sulfate – $(NH_4)_2SO_4$ ______

Ammonium phosphate – $(NH_4)_3PO_4$ ______

TOP TIP $\% \text{ nitrogen} = \frac{\text{number of atoms} \times 14}{\text{relative formula mass}}$

Homework

1 Explain why ammonium phosphate is a better fertiliser than ammonia.

2 Write a step-by-step method for making ammonium nitrate in a laboratory.

3 Find out what causes ‘blue baby’ syndrome.

HABER PROCESS AND COSTS 1

- Ammonia is used to make nitric acid and cleaning fluids, and is essential for world food production.
- It is made using a reversible reaction. $N_{2(g)} + 3H_{2(g)} \rightleftharpoons 2NH_{3(g)}$
- The N_2 is from air and H_2 from cracking oil.
- The conditions used are: 450 °C, 200 atmospheres of pressure and an iron catalyst.
- Unreacted N_2 and H_2 are continually recycled.
- Higher pressures give a higher percentage yield.
- Higher temperatures reduce the percentage yield but make the reaction faster and therefore more economic.
- Catalysts increase the reaction rate and cut costs.

TOP TIP The cost of making NH_3 depends on energy, wages, equipment, catalyst and raw material costs, and how fast it can be made.

Now try this

$N_{2(g)} + 3H_{2(g)} \rightleftharpoons 2NH_{3(g)}$

b Would the following cause an increase (I) or decrease (D) in the percentage yield of ammonia?

Raising the pressure ______

Raising the temperature ______

Adding more N_2 ______

Adding more H_2 ______

Adding a catalyst ______

Homework

4 Explain why ammonia is much more valuable than nitrogen and hydrogen.

5 Find out who invented the Haber process and what the consequences were.

6 Find out what Le Chatelier said about equilibrium reactions.

See pages 142–149 and 152–155 of Collins GCSE Additional Science

HABER PROCESS AND COSTS 2

- The conditions used in the Haber process are a compromise between those that give high rates and those that give high percentage yields.
- *They give the lowest cost rather than the fastest reaction or highest percentage yield.*
- *Higher pressures would increase the percentage yield but would increase plant costs.*
- *Higher temperatures reduce percentage yields and boost energy costs, but increase the rate.*
- Catalysts increase the reaction rate and cut costs.

TOP TIP Automation reduces the wages bill.

Now try this

c **Decide whether each of these modifications to the Haber process would increase the percentage yield (PY), the profitability (P), both (B) or neither (N).**

Increasing automation	______
Using pressures > 200 atmospheres	______
Transferring heat from NH_3 to N_2	______
Lowering the temperature to 100 °C	______
Oil and gas prices rise	______
A cheaper catalyst is found	______

Homework

7 Find the location of a Haber process plant and list the advantages it offers.
8 Explain why the conditions used in the Haber process are a compromise.
9 Find an estimate for the amount of fertiliser used each year.

DETERGENT

- Many detergents are soluble salts made by neutralisation of acids with alkalis.
- Washing-up liquids have detergents, water to ease pouring, colour and fragrance, water softeners and rinse agents to help water run off.
- Washing powders have detergents, bleaches to remove coloured stains, water softeners, enzymes for food stains and optical brighteners to give a whiter than white glow.
- *Detergent molecules have ionic heads (hydrophilic), which attract water molecules, and hydrocarbon tails (hydrophobic) which attract grease.*
- Dry cleaning uses organic solvents to remove stains that are insoluble in water.
- *The intermolecular forces between solvent and stain molecules are stronger.*

Now try this

d **Match each word to the correct description(s).**

Solvent	removes coloured stains
Hydrophobic	soluble salt
Bleach	will not dissolve
Enzymes	what things dissolve in
Hydrophilic	the material that dissolves
Detergent	digest food stains
Brightener	makes water drain off
Rinse agent	attracts water molecules
Solute	makes whites look whiter
Insoluble	made by neutralising an acid
	repels water molecules

Homework

10 Prepare a presentation to show how detergents work.
11 Research the best wash conditions for a variety of fabrics.
12 Find out how water can be softened to make detergents work better.

Chemical economics 3

BATCH OR CONTINUOUS

- Ammonia is made in a continuous process.
- Speciality chemicals like medicines are made on a much smaller scale by a batch process.
- The cost includes research and testing, labour, energy, raw materials, development time and marketing.
- The raw materials can be synthetic or from plants.
- Extraction of chemicals from plants involves crushing them, dissolving the chemicals in a suitable solvent and chromatography.
- Years are needed for testing and human trials to comply with legislative demands.
- Raw materials can be rare or involve expensive extraction from plants.

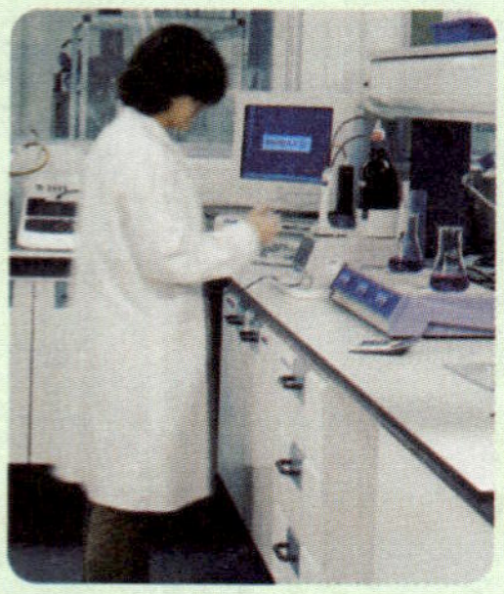

Now try this

a Decide whether each factor applies to **batch (B)** or **continuous (C)** processes.

Best for chemicals produced in bulk ______
Best for making chemicals to order ______
Plant needs a higher initial investment ______
Produces small quantities ______
Difficult to automate ______
Low labour costs ______

TOP TIP Drugs are only developed if the anticipated demand gives a reasonable pay-back time on the investment costs.

Homework

1. Many existing drugs come from plants. Find some examples.
2. Explain the differences between batch and continuous processes.
3. Research typical times taken for each stage in drug development.

NANOCHEMISTRY 1

- *Diamond, graphite and fullerenes are allotropes of carbon.*
- *They have melting points because so many strong covalent bonds would need breaking to melt them.*
- In diamond, each carbon forms four bonds to make a hard 3D network suitable for cutting tools.
- It is used for jewellery because it is lustrous and colourless.
- In graphite, each atom bonds to three others in a layer, and has one delocalised electron – so it conducts and is used to make electrodes for electrolysis.
- The layers are only loosely attracted to each other.
- Graphite is black, lustrous, opaque and slippery.
- It is used as a lubricant and for pencil leads.

Now try this

b Decide if each description matches **diamond (D)** or **graphite (G)**.

Soft ______
Transparent ______
Used in pencils ______
Has delocalised electrons ______
Used in drill bits ______
A lubricant ______
Insulator ______
Hard ______
Abrasive ______

Homework

4. Explain why graphite is a good conductor and lubricant but diamond is not.
5. Which form of carbon is used in brake linings and why?
6. Find out how fake diamonds are made.

NANOCHEMISTRY 2

- Buckminsterfullerene (C_{60}) is a black solid made from hollow balls. It makes a deep red solution in petrol.
- *It can 'cage' molecules, for example, for drug delivery.*
- *In nanotubes, graphite sheets roll into tubes, which provide a large surface area for catalysts and have high tensile strength.*
- They are used as semiconductors in circuits, as industrial catalysts, and to reinforce tennis rackets.
- These nanoparticles give materials unique properties.

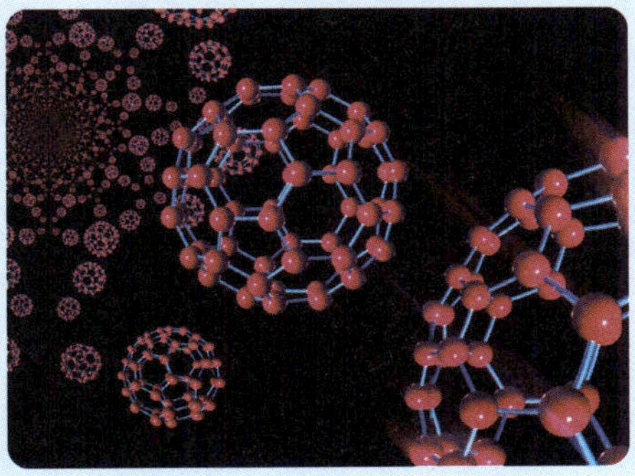

- *Molecular manufacturing uses positional chemistry to build molecule-by-molecule or removes matter from structures to leave nanoscale features.*

Now try this

c Are the following characteristics of a **fullerene (F)**, **nanotubule (N)** or **both (B)**?

Resembles a football	______
Used to hold catalysts	______
High tensile strength	______
Conductor	______
C_{60}	______
Black	______
Can act as a cage	______
Used for drug delivery	______

TOP TIP Chemistry works with materials on a large scale, but nanotechnologies work with clusters of atoms.

Homework

7 Find out why titanium dioxide nanoparticles are useful in sunscreens.
8 Conductors stronger than steel! Find out what nanotubes could be used for.
9 Research the role chance played in the discovery of fullerenes.

HOW PURE IS OUR WATER?

- Water is stored in lakes, rivers, aquifers and reservoirs.
- It is a cheap raw material, a coolant and a solvent.
- It may contain nitrates from fertiliser, lead from pipes, or pesticides. Purification may not remove these solutes.
- Pure water is needed for drinking and cooking.
- Its collection and purification takes time.
- Distillation of sea water takes a lot of energy.
- Sewage treatment involves filtration, sedimentation of organic waste, microbial action and chlorination.
- This should remove enough salts, minerals, microbes, pollutants and insoluble materials to make water safe to drink.
- Cl^-, Br^- and I^- precipitate with $AgNO_3$ by making AgI(yellow), AgBr(cream), AgCl(white).
- Sulfate ions (SO_4^{2-}) make white precipitates with barium chloride solution.

Now try this

d Match the pollutants to their sources.

Lead	households
Pesticide	rocks
Minerals	fertiliser
Organic waste	pipes
Sulfates	farm sprays
Nitrates	acid rain

TOP TIP Chlorination kills microbes in water.

Homework

10 Prepare a presentation on pollutants found in water.
11 Research water supply problems in a developing country.
12 Produce a flowchart to show how domestic water is purified.

Understanding motion

SPEED

- The speed of an object is defined as 'the rate of change of distance travelled'.
- *For an object travelling at a constant speed, the speed is given by the equation:*

  $$\textit{speed} = \frac{\textit{distance}}{\textit{time}}$$

- *Other helpful equations are: distance = speed × time*

  $$\textit{time} = \frac{\textit{distance}}{\textit{speed}}$$

- For an object not travelling at constant speed, the average speed is given by the equation:

  $$\text{average speed} = \frac{\text{distance travelled}}{\text{time taken}}$$

- Velocity may be defined as speed in a certain direction.

Now try this

a Circle the correct answers.

What is the correct unit for speed?

km m/s

An object has speed 5 km/h. What distance does it travel in two hours?

2.5 km 10 km

Does doubling the speed double the distance travelled in a given time?

Yes No

Homework

1. Describe how you would determine your average speed.
2. Use the Internet to find the typical speed of **three** objects (for example, aeroplanes). Use this to determine the distance travelled by each object in a time of 10 s.
3. List similarities and differences between speed and velocity.

ACCELERATION

- An object 'speeding up' has acceleration.
- An object 'slowing down' has a negative acceleration or 'deceleration'.
- *Acceleration is equal to the rate of change of velocity* (or *speed).*
- $\textit{acceleration} = \dfrac{\textit{change in speed}}{\textit{time taken}}$
- $\textit{acceleration} = \dfrac{\textit{(final speed – initial speed)}}{\textit{time taken}}$
- Acceleration is measured in m/s^2.
- Uniform acceleration means an object with a constant acceleration.
- The speed of an object with an acceleration of 10 m/s^2 increases by 10 m/s every second.
- An object moving in a circle has acceleration because its direction changes.
- Example: A car changes its speed from 10 m/s to 15 m/s in a time of 4.0 s. What is its acceleration?

  $$\text{acceleration} = \frac{\text{change in speed}}{\text{time}} = \frac{15 - 10}{2.0} = 2.5\ m/s^2$$

Now try this

b Are the following statements **true** (T) or **false** (F)?

Acceleration is the same as speed. ______

A planet moving round the Sun has acceleration because its direction changes. ______

A car starting from rest and speeding up has acceleration. ______

A car has deceleration when its speed decreases with time. ______

TOP TIP An object has acceleration when it changes **direction** or **speed.**

See pages 174–181 of Collins GCSE Additional Science

Homework

4 In your own words, define acceleration and deceleration.

5 Make a list of **five** objects that show acceleration.

MOTION REPRESENTED BY GRAPHS

- The gradient of a distance–time graph is equal to the speed of the object.

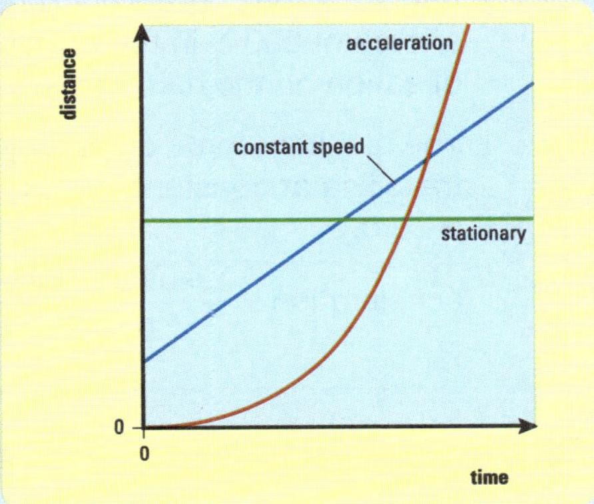

- The gradient of a speed–time graph is equal to the acceleration of the object.

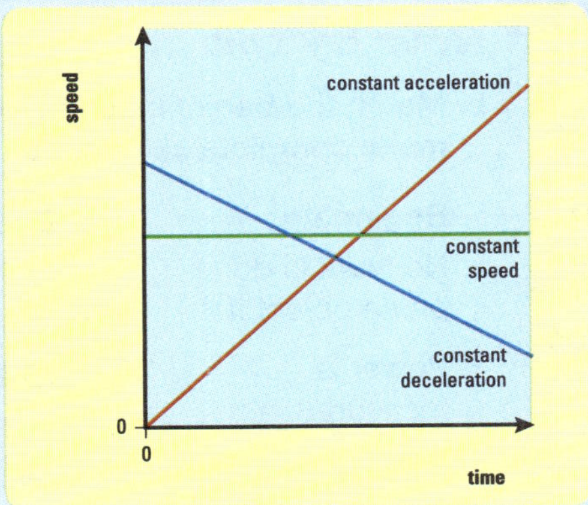

- The area under a speed–time graph is equal to the distance travelled by the object.

TOP TIP Remember: gradient = $\frac{\text{vertical change}}{\text{horizontal change}}$

Now try this

c Find the following key words in this word search:

speed time velocity gradient distance

T	A	Y	D	E	E	P	S
T	N	E	I	D	A	R	G
G	T	P	A	P	A	P	T
G	I	G	A	B	I	W	E
D	M	S	I	T	Y	A	E
V	E	L	O	C	I	T	Y
D	I	S	T	A	N	C	E
M	A	M	A	G	T	G	N

Homework

6 Write a short paragraph on distance–time graphs.

7 Write a short paragraph on velocity–time graphs.

Force, work, energy and power

FORCE AND MOTION

- An object remains at rest or travels at constant velocity when acted upon by a resultant force of zero.
- An object has acceleration when the resultant force is not zero.
- For an object of a given mass, doubling the force will double the acceleration.
- For a given force, doubling the mass of an object will halve its acceleration.
- *resultant force = mass × acceleration* ($F = ma$)
- Force is measured in newtons (N).
- A force of 1 N acting on an object of mass 1 kg causes an acceleration of 1 m/s^2.
- When two bodies interact, each exerts an equal but opposite force on the other – 'action' = 'reaction'.

Now try this

a Are the following statements true (T) or false (F)?

Force is measured in kilograms. ______

A hammer hits a nail with a force of 200 N. The nail exerts a force of 200 N in the opposite direction on the hammer. ______

The resultant force on an object travelling at constant velocity is zero. ______

$\text{acceleration} = \frac{\text{resultant force}}{\text{mass}}$ ______

Homework

1 Write **five** examples of 'action' = 'reaction'.

2 Use '$F = ma$' to explain why massive cars tend to have smaller acceleration.

WORK AND POWER

- Work done is measured in joules (J).
- Work is done on an object when it moves in the direction of the applied force.
- *work done = force × distance moved in the direction of the force*
- 1 joule is the work done on an object when a force of 1 N moves the object a distance of 1 m in the direction of the force.
- Power is measured in watts (W). *Power is equal to the rate of work done.*
- $\text{power} = \frac{\text{work done}}{\text{time}}$ *or* $\text{power} = \frac{\text{energy transfer}}{\text{time}}$
- 1 W is equal to 1 J per second.
- A power of 60 W means 60 J of work done per second.
- A moving object has kinetic energy.
- *kinetic energy* $= \frac{1}{2} \times \text{mass} \times \text{speed}^2$ ($KE = \frac{1}{2}mv^2$)

Now try this

b Match the beginnings and endings to make complete sentences.

Beginning	Ending
No work is done on an object if it	joules.
Power is measured in	kinetic energy.
Work is measured in	remains stationary.
A car travelling faster has greater	watts.

TOP TIP: Energy and work are both measured in joules (J).

Homework

3 Write a short paragraph on work, power and kinetic energy.

4 List all the quantities and their associated units.

5 According to a student the 'kinetic energy of a car is proportional to its speed'. Discuss whether this statement is true or false.

CAR SAFETY

- Thinking distance is the distance travelled by a car before the brakes are applied. (It is the distance travelled in a time equal to the reaction time of the driver.)
- Thinking distance is increased if the driver is tired, under the influence of drugs or alcohol or the car is travelling at a greater speed.
- thinking distance = speed of car × reaction time of driver
- Braking distance is the distance travelled by a car as the brakes are applied and the car comes to a halt.
- Braking distance is increased when the road is wet or icy, the brakes are worn, the tyres are bald or the speed of the car is greater.
- stopping distance = thinking distance + braking distance
- The safety features in cars are seatbelts, airbags and crumple zones. They change shape, reduce injuries and absorb energy.
- When a car slows down:
  loss in kinetic energy = work done by car brakes
- Seatbelts prevent collisions with the dashboard and windscreen.
- *Seatbelts, airbags and crumple zones increase a person's time for stopping and therefore decrease the person's deceleration and the force acting on the person.*
- Airbags inflate rapidly during a collision. They prevent collisions with the dashboard and steering wheel.
- CO_2 emissions are higher from cars with high fuel consumption.

Now try this

c Fill in the missing words.

The reaction time of a driver is 0.6 s. The thinking distance when the car is travelling at a speed of 10 m/s is _______ m. Wet conditions will increase the ___________ distance and tiredness increases the ___________ distance. Driving in wet conditions and being tired will increase the overall ___________ distance of the car.

Homework

6 List the safety features in a car and describe how they reduce injuries.

7 Describe the factors that affect the thinking and braking distances of a car.

8 Look at your parents' or a friend's car and list its safety features.

Falling and theme park rides

FALLING DOWN

- A falling object is pulled towards the centre of the Earth due to gravity.
- All objects falling in a vacuum on the Earth have the same acceleration of 10 m/s^2 and experience no air resistance.
- Friction between moving parts of a machine can be reduced by lubricating (oiling) it.
- Air resistance or drag can slow down falling objects.
- Air resistance opposes the motion of an object.
- Air resistance acting on an object can be reduced by streamlining its shape.
- Air resistance increases when the cross-sectional area of the falling object is increased.
- A falling object in air has two forces acting on it – its weight (downwards) and air resistance or drag (upwards).
- Weight and drag are both forces and hence measured in newtons (N).
- *weight = mass × gravitational field strength* ($W = mg$)
- When an object is dropped, the only force acting on it is its weight and hence it accelerates at 10 m/s^2.
- *As the speed of the falling object increases, the resistance due to air also increases. This decreases the acceleration of the object.*
- *After some time, the drag is equal to the weight of the object. The resultant force is zero. The acceleration is also zero and the object has a constant velocity known as terminal velocity.*
- $\text{acceleration} = \dfrac{(\text{weight} - \text{drag})}{\text{mass}}$

TOP TIP A falling object will accelerate as long as the weight and drag are **unbalanced**.

Now try this

a Are the following statements **true (T)** or **false (F)**?

An object falling through air has an upward force called drag. ______

Drag decreases as the velocity of the object increases. ______

A stone of weight 1.2 N reaches terminal velocity. The drag is 1.2 N. ______

When an object is dropped, the only force acting on it is its weight. ______

Homework

1. Discuss all the factors that affect the air resistance acting on an object like a car.
2. A skydiver jumps off a helicopter. In your own words, describe how the size of the forces acting on the skydiver change with time.
3. Use the Internet to find the typical terminal velocity of a skydiver.

• See pages 200–207 of Collins GCSE Additional Science

THEME PARK RIDES

- An object has gravitational potential energy (PE) because of its mass and its position in the Earth's gravitational field.
- Greater mass implies greater PE.
- Greater height also implies greater PE.
- The gravitational potential energy of an object increases as it gains vertical height.
- *potential energy transfer = mass × gravitational field strength × change in height*

  PE = mgh (g = 10 N/kg on the Earth's surface)
- A moving object has kinetic energy (KE).
- *kinetic energy* = $\frac{1}{2}$ × *mass* × *speed*^{2}

  KE = $\frac{1}{2}mv^2$
- *Doubling the mass of an object doubles its KE.*
- *Doubling the speed of an object quadruples its KE.*
- Energy is always conserved, that is: total initial energy = total final energy
- For a roller coaster:

As it is gains height:	The KE decreases and the PE increases. loss in KE = gain in PE + energy lost as heat and sound
At the top of the ride:	The PE is at a maximum.
As it falls:	The PE decreases and the KE increases. loss in PE = gain in KE + energy lost as heat and sound
When it comes to a stop:	The KE is transferred into heat in the brakes.

TOP TIP Potential energy and kinetic energy are both measured in joules.

Now try this

b Circle the correct answer for each statement.

KE and PE are both measured in:

kg N J.

The PE of a falling object:

decreases increases stays the same.

Kinetic energy can be doubled by doubling the:

mass height of the object.

A ball does not bounce back to its starting height because some energy is lost as:

chemical heat to the ground.

Homework

4 Write a short paragraph on gravitational potential energy (PE), kinetic energy (KE) and conservation of energy.

5 Design your own theme park ride. Describe the energy changes taking place as you go on this ride.

Sparks and electrostatics

CHARGING INSULATORS

- Rubbing can charge insulators like wool, plastic and rubber.
- There are two types of charges: positive and negative.
- Charged insulators (for example, TV screens) can attract dust, fibres and small pieces of paper.
- The transfer of electrons charges an insulator.
- *An insulator losing electrons will have a positive charge.*
- *An insulator gaining electrons will have a negative charge.*
- Like charges repel; opposite charges attract.
- A polythene rod rubbed with a duster acquires a negative charge and the duster acquires an equal but opposite positive charge.

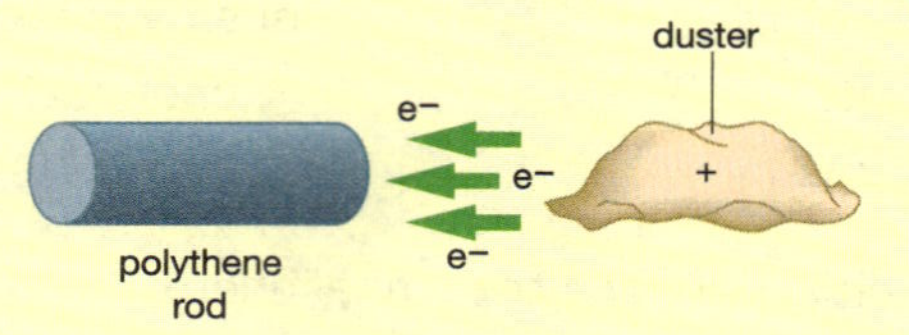

Now try this

a Tick the statements that are correct.

All insulators can be charged by friction. ☐

An insulator becomes positive because it gains protons. ☐

Two positively charged balloons attract each other. ☐

A duster is used to shine a mirror. The duster becomes negatively charged because it has gained electrons. ☐

Homework

1 In your own words explain the terms 'insulators' and 'charge'.

2 Rub a plastic ruler with a duster or jumper. Use it to attract tiny pieces of paper. Use your knowledge of physics to describe why the ruler attracts the pieces of paper.

ELECTRIC SPARKS

- You will get an electrostatic shock when:
  - you touch something that is charged
  - you become charged by walking on a carpet/vinyl floor and then become earthed by touching a water pipe or metal door handle.
- Static charges are a nuisance as they cause synthetic clothes to 'cling'.
- The transfer of charges between two objects creates an electric spark.
- Electric sparks generate high temperatures and therefore are dangerous near inflammable gases and vapours (for example, refuelling aircraft).
- *The chance of receiving an electric shock can be reduced by correct earthing, using insulating mats or wearing shoes with insulating soles.*

TOP TIP The risk of electric sparks can be reduced by securing a metal strap between the object and the ground.

Now try this

b Fill in the missing words.

An electric ____________ is created through the ____________ when charges are transferred between objects. Electric sparks are very ____________ because they increase the ____________ of the air and can cause explosions near petrol fumes and other inflammable vapours.

Homework

3 List situations where an electric spark would be extremely dangerous.

4 List situations in the home where electrostatic attraction is a nuisance.

USES OF ELECTROSTATICS

- Some uses of static electricity include: defibrillators (restarting the heart when it has stopped), photocopiers/laser printers, removing dust/soot from smoke chimneys and paint spraying.
- A defibrillator has two charged paddles. These are used to pass a charge through the patient to make the heart contract. The operator has to be careful not to be shocked!
- Good electrical contact is necessary between the patient and the paddles.
- Electrostatic dust precipitators are used in the chimneys of coal-burning power stations. They have metal plates/grids connected to high voltage. Dust particles are attracted to the plates/grid.
- When the dust particles are large enough they fall down the chimneys.
- In spray painting the gun is charged. The paint particles are repelled to produce fine spray. The object to be painted is charged opposite to the paint. Attraction between the object and the paint ensures an even coat of paint.
- There is less waste in spray painting.

Now try this

c Find the following key words in this word search:

static laser paddle spray paint charge attract

S	P	R	A	Y	Y	A	T
S	T	T	S	I	P	L	N
P	L	A	S	E	R	A	I
A	A	S	T	Y	T	V	A
D	C	S	P	I	P	A	P
D	N	E	E	T	C	K	U
L	C	H	A	R	G	E	A
E	A	T	T	R	A	C	T

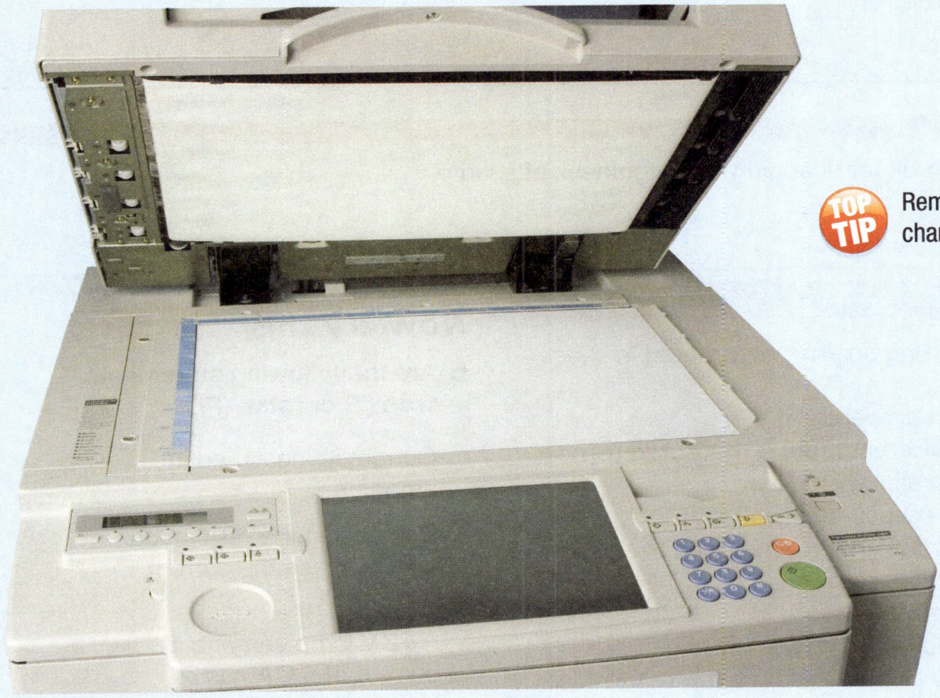

TOP TIP Remember that opposite charges attract.

Homework

5 Construct a mind map of the uses of electrostatics.
6 Draw labelled diagrams to illustrate how spray painting works.
7 Use the Internet to research how a laser printer uses electrostatics.

Safe electricals

CIRCUITS

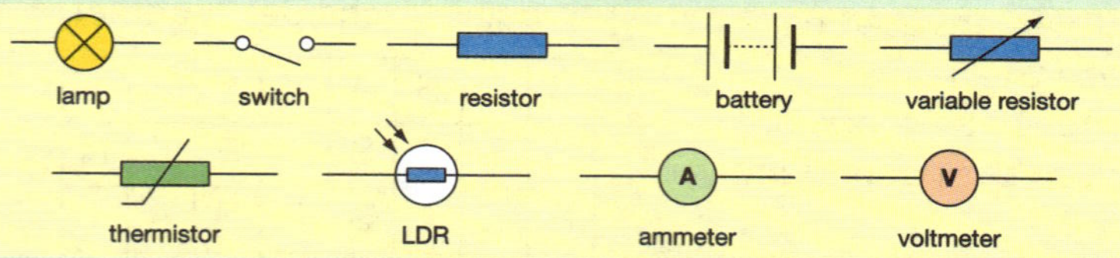

- A complete loop is required for an electrical circuit to work.
- A resistor can be used in a circuit to change the current.
- Electric current is the rate of flow of charge.
- In a circuit, electric current is due to the movement of electrons.
- The size of the current for a given circuit depends on the resistance. Less resistance in a circuit means greater current; greater resistance means smaller current.
- A variable resistor can be used to change the resistance in a circuit and hence the current.

TOP TIP A circuit will not work if there is a break in the circuit.

Now try this

a Complete the sentences.

A battery is connected to a lamp. The lamp is brightly lit because the circuit is ___________. The lamp is replaced by another lamp of greater resistance. The current in the circuit now is ___________ and the lamp will be ___________.

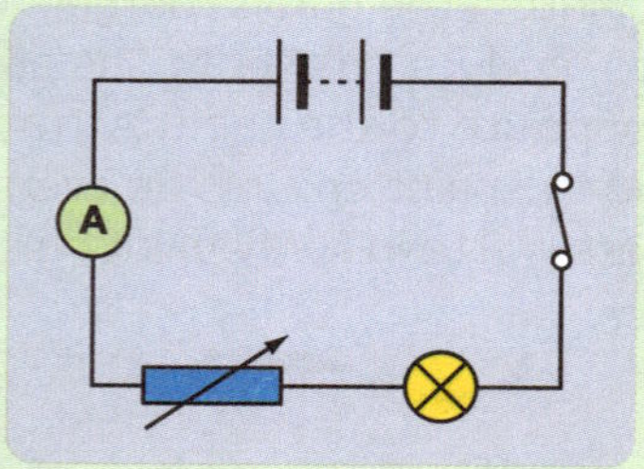

Homework

1 Design a simple circuit for changing the brightness of a lamp.
2 Draw a mind map for 'Circuits'.

RESISTANCE

- Current is measured using an ammeter placed in series with a component.
- Current is measured in amperes (A).
- Voltage or potential difference (pd) is measured using a voltmeter placed in parallel with a component.
- Potential difference is measured in volts (V).
- The resistance of a component is found using the equation:

$$resistance = \frac{potential\ difference}{current} \quad \text{or} \quad R = \frac{V}{I}$$

- Resistance is measured in ohms (Ω).
- For a given pd, current decreases as resistance increases and vice versa.
- For a given resistor, current is increased as pd increases and vice versa.

Now try this

b Are the following statements true (T) or false (F)?

Current is measured in amperes. _______

Decreasing the resistance will decrease the current in a circuit. _______

A 12 V lamp carrying a current of 6.0 A has a resistance of 2.0 Ω. _______

Voltage = current × resistance _______

Homework

3 Write about current, potential difference and resistance.
4 Make a list of electrical quantities and their associated units.

See pages 222–227 of Collins GCSE Additional Science

SAFETY

- A mains cable has three coloured wires: brown, blue and green/yellow.
- The brown wire is wired to the live terminal, the blue wire to the neutral terminal and the green/yellow wire to the earth terminal.
- Charges can safely flow to the ground if a conductor is earthed.
- Metal appliances are earthed in order to protect you from accidental shocks.
- An earthed conductor cannot become live.
- Double-insulated appliances have plastic casing and do not need to be earthed.
- The fuse is attached to the live terminal.
- The fuse is a safety device. A large current will melt the fuse and cut off the supply.
- A fuse prevents large currents from starting a fire.
- *Circuit breakers are safety devices and can be described as 're-settable fuses'.*

Now try this

c **The diagram shows a mains three-pin plug. Label the earth, live and neutral terminals and the fuse.**

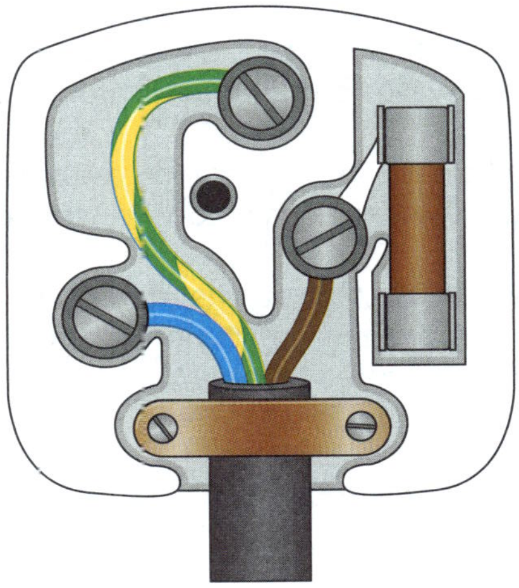

TOP TIP A fuse has to be replaced after a fault whereas circuit breakers just have to be reset.

Homework

5 Describe how a fuse prevents electrical fires.

6 Make a list of double-insulated items in your home or in your friend's home.

7 List all the electrical safety devices in your home or in your friend's home.

Ultrasound and radiation

X-RAYS AND GAMMA RAYS

- Ultrasound is a longitudinal wave.
- *For a longitudinal wave, the particles vibrate in the same direction as the wave.*
- *For a transverse wave, the particles vibrate at right angles to the direction of the wave.*
- Longitudinal waves cannot travel through a vacuum.
- Ultrasound creates regions of high pressure called compressions and regions of low pressure called rarefactions.
- The amplitude of a wave is the maximum distance of a particle from its normal (or equilibrium) position.
- The wavelength of a wave is the distance occupied by one complete wave.
- The frequency of a wave is the number of complete waves in one second.
- Frequency is measured in hertz (Hz).
- Ultrasound is used for 'seeing' inside our bodies without surgery.
- Ultrasound scans are used to check the condition of the foetus, breaking down kidney and other stones and measuring the speed of blood flow in the body.
- Ultrasound is reflected by different layers of tissues.
- Unlike X-ray scans, ultrasound scans can be used to produce images of soft tissues and they do not damage living cells.

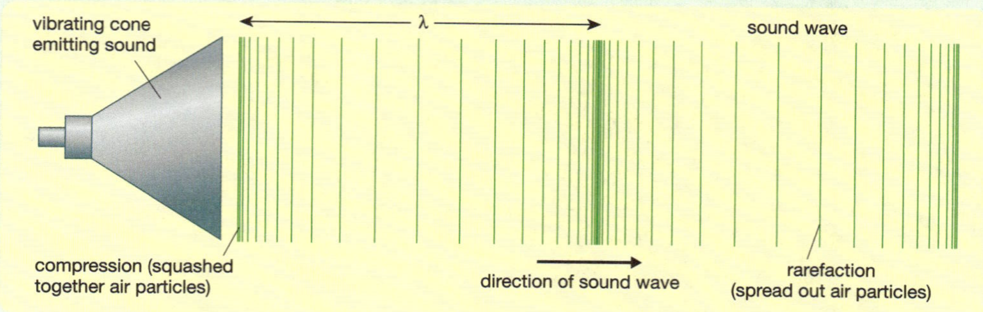

Now try this

a Match the questions with the correct answers.

What is the unit of frequency?	kidney
Ultrasound can be used to find the speed of what in the body?	longitudinal
What type of wave is ultrasound?	blood
What type of stones can ultrasound break down?	hertz

TOP TIP We cannot hear ultrasound.

Homework

1. In your own words, describe the amplitude, frequency and wavelength of an ultrasound.
2. List some of the applications of ultrasound.
3. Use a search engine like Google to search for some images of ultrasound scans.

TREATMENT

- Some radioactive nuclei of atoms emit nuclear radiation (alpha particles, beta particles and gamma rays).
- Gamma rays and X-rays are both used in medicine for treatment (therapy) and for finding out what is wrong (diagnosis).
- X-rays and gamma rays are electromagnetic waves. They have similar wavelengths.
- *X-rays are produced when high-speed electrons hit a target metal.*
- *Gamma rays are short wavelength electromagnetic waves emitted from some unstable nuclei (for example, cobalt-60).*
- X-rays and nuclear radiation cause ionisation and can damage living cells.
- Gamma rays are used to sterilise bandages, syringes and other hospital instruments.
- Gamma rays are used for the treatment of cancer.
- *In radiotherapy, several gamma ray sources producing wide beams are directed towards cancerous tissues to destroy the cancer cells.*
- A radioactive tracer is a radioactive substance that is drunk or injected into the body.
- *Only beta particles and gamma rays can pass through skin. Hence a tracer is either a beta or gamma emitter. (Alpha particles are easily stopped by skin.)*
- The function of some vital organs can be diagnosed using a radioactive tracer.
- The gamma rays or beta particles from the tracer are detected using a radiation detector (for example, gamma camera).

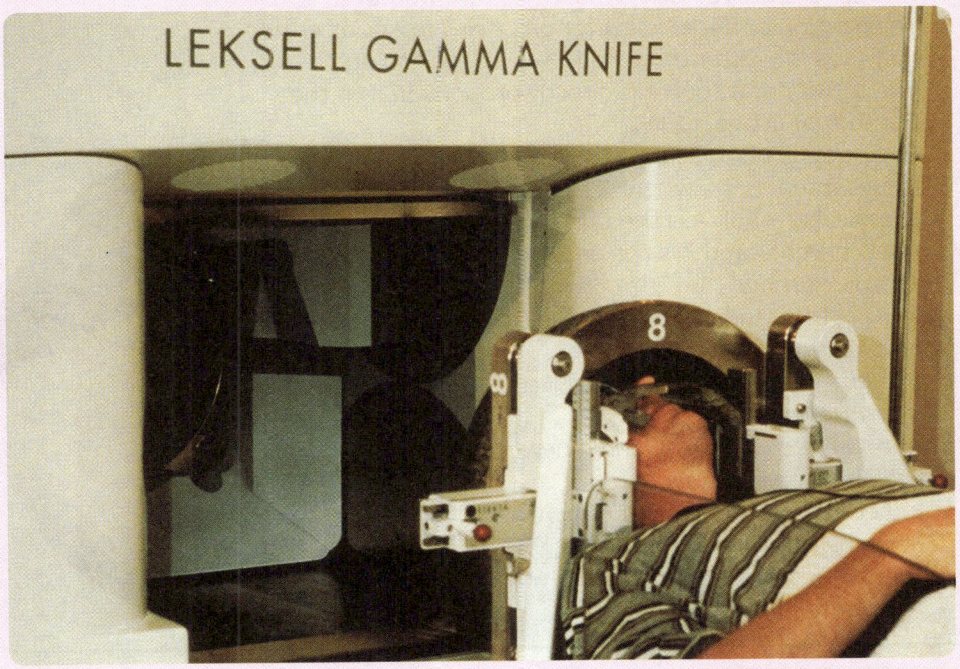

Now try this

b Find the following six key words in this word search:

X-ray gamma ionise
sterile tracer cell

A	Q	L	K	I	T	S	F
G	D	G	R	O	U	S	G
O	B	A	C	N	C	T	Q
M	D	M	E	I	V	E	T
G	X	M	G	S	C	R	Y
T	R	A	C	E	R	I	O
S	A	J	L	H	X	L	P
M	Y	L	J	D	D	E	E

TOP TIP Hospital syringes come in sealed sterile plastic bags. Exposure to gamma rays sterilises both the bag and the syringe.

Homework

4 Outline some of the similarities and differences between X-rays and gamma rays.
5 Describe the uses of gamma sources in the hospitals.
6 Write a few sentences on the **three** different types of nuclear radiation.

Nuclear physics

RADIOACTIVITY

- Radioactivity is to do with unstable nuclei.
- The nucleus of a radioactive atom emits either an alpha (α) particle or a beta (β) particle and/or gamma (γ) rays.
- An alpha particle is a slow-moving helium nucleus ($^{4}_{2}He$). It has a positive charge.
- A beta particle is a fast-moving electron. It has a negative charge.
- Gamma rays are short-wavelength electromagnetic waves. These have no charge and travel at the speed of light.
- The activity of a source is the average number of nuclei decaying per second.
- Activity is measured in becquerels (Bq).
- The activity of a radioactive substance decreases with time.
- Radioactivity is a random process because it is impossible to predict which nucleus will decay at a particular time.
- The half-life of a radioisotope is the average time taken for half the active nuclei to decay or disintegrate.
- *The fraction of nuclei left after one half-life is $\frac{1}{2}$, after two half-lives is $\frac{1}{4}$, after three half-lives is $\frac{1}{8}$ and so on.*
- The activity of a source is directly proportional to the number of active nuclei.
- The nucleus of an atom may be represented as $^{A}_{Z}X$, where X is the chemical symbol, A is the nucleon or mass number and Z is the proton or atomic number.
- The protons and neutrons are also known as the nucleons.
- *In alpha decay, the mass number decreases by 4, the proton number decreases by 2 and a new radioisotope is formed.*
- *In beta decay, the mass number remains the same, the proton number increases by 1 and a new radioisotope is formed.*

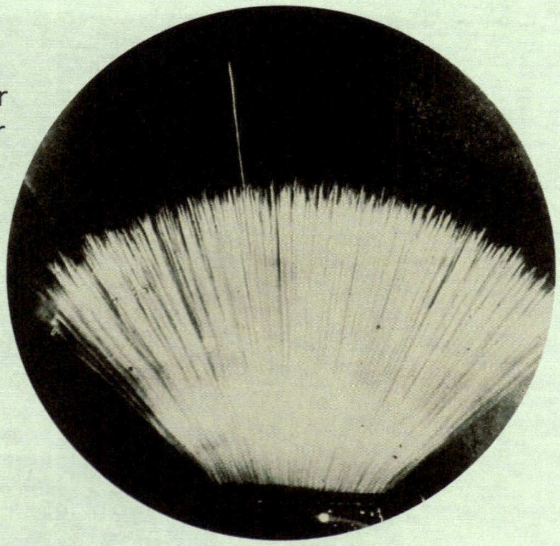

Now try this

a Tick the statements which are correct.

Alpha radiation are particles. ☐

Three-quarters of the nuclei decay after two half-lives. ☐

Activity is measured in Bq. ☐

A neutron is a nucleon. ☐

TOP TIP Radioactivity is to do with unstable nuclei.

Homework

1 Write a paragraph on radioactive nuclei.

2 Use the Internet to find some radioactive isotopes and their half-lives.

3 Explain why a source will have a high activity if there are lots of nuclei and the half-life is very short.

USES OF RADIOISOTOPES

- Background radiation is always present and is due to radioactive substances in rocks, soil, air and cosmic rays.
- Some background radiation comes from man-made sources, for example, nuclear and hospital waste.
- Radioisotopes are used as tracers in industry and hospitals.
- Gamma-emitting tracers are used to find leaks or blockages in underground pipes.
- Smoke detectors contain an alpha emitter.
- Carbon dating is used to date bone, cloth, wood and paper. *It relies on the radioactive isotope of carbon-14.*

Now try this

b Fill in the missing words.

Leaks in pipes can be detected using a ______________. A radioactive substance emitting gamma rays is put into the pipe. A gamma-emitting source is used because gamma rays can ______________ through the pipe and soil. An ______________ in the activity above the ground locates the leaks.

TOP TIP Cosmic rays come from outer space and the Sun.

Homework

4 Tracers are used in industry and in hospitals. List all their applications.

5 Research smoke detectors on the Internet and write a short paragaph to explain how they work.

FISSION

- Nuclear power stations use uranium as a fuel. Most of the waste is radioactive for thousands of years.
- Reactions produce the heat to produce steam to turn the turbines, which turn the generators to produce electricity.
- *In a fission reaction, a neutron is captured by a uranium-235 nucleus and splits into two smaller (daughter) nuclei and either two or three neutrons.*
- Energy is released when a uranium nucleus splits.
- Materials become radioactive when they capture neutrons in a nuclear reactor.
- *In a chain reaction, the neutrons can cause further fission reactions.*
- One destructive use of fission is the atomic bomb. One peaceful use is electricity production.

Now try this

c Are the following statements true (T) or false (F)?

Fission reactions release chemical energy. ______

Fission means splitting of a nucleus. ______

Fission is used in atomic bombs and nuclear power stations. ______

A metal placed in a nuclear reactor becomes radioactive. ______

Homework

6 Draw a labelled diagram to show how a nuclear power station produces electricity.

7 With the help of a labelled diagram, describe a chain reaction.

Bones, joints and circulation

BONES

- Some animals (for example, worms) do not have a skeleton.
- Some animals (for example, insects) have an exoskeleton (outside skeleton) made from chitin.
- Some animals (for example, humans) have an internal skeleton made from cartilage or bone which is living tissues.
- An internal skeleton gives a framework to which to attach muscles.
- A long bone has a head covered with cartilage and a shaft with bone marrow and blood vessels.
- Long bones are hollow.
- *In humans the cartilage skeleton is slowly replaced by bone (ossification).*
- *Calcium and phosphorus are deposited in bone formation.*

Now try this

a Complete these sentences.

An exoskeleton is made from ____________. It is on the ____________ of an animal. An internal skeleton is made from ____________ or ____________. It is ____________ the animal. Bones can repair themselves because they are made from ____________ cells. The insides of long bones contain ____________ and ____________ ____________. Ossification is the replacement of __________ by ____________. Bone contains the elements ____________ and ____________.

Homework

1 Make a table to show differences between external and internal skeletons.
2 Draw a labelled diagram to show the structure of a long bone.
3 Draw labelled diagrams to show ossification.

JOINTS AND MOVEMENT

- Bones can be fractured (broken).
- Simple, compound and greenstick are types of fracture.
- Some old people have osteoporosis (soft bones).
- A joint is where two bones meet.
- Tendons join muscles to bones. Ligaments join bones together.
- Hinge joints (elbow) and ball and socket joints (shoulder) are synovial joints.
- The forearm is raised by the biceps and triceps muscles acting as antagonistic muscles.
- *The movement of the forearm is an example of a lever.*
- *Synovial fluid cushions and lubricates a joint.*

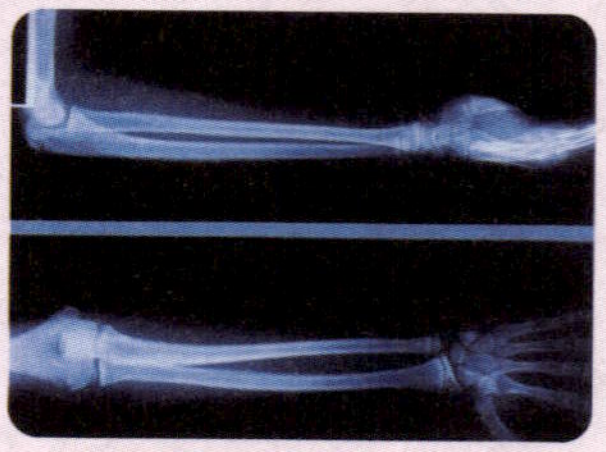

Now try this

b Fill in the missing words.

Osteoporosis is ____________ ____________. Ligaments join ____________. Tendons join ____________ to ____________. ____________ and ____________ are examples of hinge joints. ____________ and ____________ are examples of ball and socket joints. To raise the forearm, the biceps ____________ and the triceps ____________. The biceps and triceps are called ____________ muscles.

Homework

4 Describe the **three** types of fractures.
5 Draw and label the bones and muscles in the arm.
6 Explain how the arm movement operates as a lever.

BLOOD CIRCULATION

- Some animals (for example, amoeba) do not have a blood system.
- Some animals (for example, insects) have an open circulation system.
- Some animals (for example, humans) have a closed circulation system.
- In a closed system, blood flows in blood vessels called arteries, veins and capillaries.
- Some animals (for example, fish) have a single circulatory system; there is only one circuit from the heart.
- Some animals (for example, humans) have a double circulatory system; there are two circuits from the heart.
- More blood will flow to those body organs using most energy.
- *A single circulatory system has a two-chambered heart.*
- *A double circulatory system has a four-chambered heart.*
- *Harvey and Galen contributed to our understanding of blood circulation.*

Now try this

c Look at the diagram and complete the following sentences.

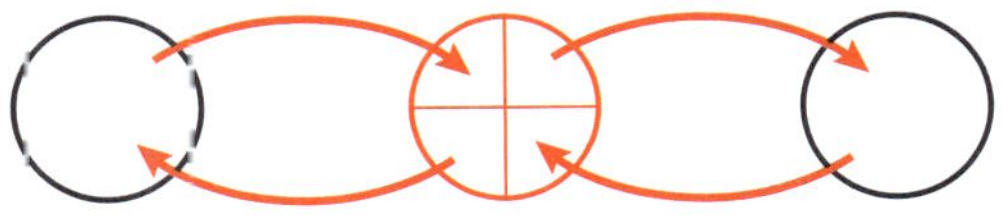

This is a ___________ circulatory system. There are ___________ heart chambers. The heart chambers are called ___________ and ___________. The three types of blood vessels are ___________, ___________ and ___________.

Name an animal with a single circulatory system. ___________

Name an animal without blood.___________

Homework

7 Draw and label a diagram of a single circulatory system.
8 Use a text book to explain why amoeba do not 'need' a blood system.
9 Use a search engine to find out about the work of Harvey and Galen.

THE HEART

- The heart is made from muscle.
- The heart has its own blood supply (coronary artery).
- Heart muscle contraction puts the blood under pressure.
- The pulse is a measure of heart beat.
- The pulse can be measured at the wrist, temple and ear.
- Pacemaker cells control heart muscle contraction.
- Pacemaker cells produce a small electric current.
- An ECG and echocardiograms investigate heart action.
- *SAN and AVN are pacemaker cells.*
- Heart rate is linked to activity and *adrenalin levels.*
- *The heart cycle shows the working of atria and ventricles.*

d Complete these sentences.

The ___________ artery supplies the heart. The heart beat can be measured as a ___________. The pulse can be measured at the ___________, ___________ and ___________. Pacemaker cells control heart ___________ ___________. Pacemaker cells produce an ___________ ___________. Exercise causes the heart rate to ___________. Hormones such as ___________ affect heart rate.

Homework

10 Why does the pulse rate increase during exercise?
11 Use a search engine to find out about artificial pacemakers.
12 Draw labelled diagrams to explain the heart cycle.

The heart and respiration

HEART PROBLEMS

- Damaged or weak heart valves cause poor circulation. They can be repaired or replaced.
- A hole in the wall between atria and ventricles is called a hole in the heart.
- A hole in the heart causes oxygenated and deoxygenated blood to mix. It can be fixed by surgery.
- A blocked coronary artery can be bypassed by a transplanted blood vessel.
- The circulatory system can be affected by a poor lifestyle, such as excessive alcohol, smoking, drugs, stress and a poor diet.

TOP TIP Remember to give a full explanation to a question, for example, explain that a poor diet can cause plaque to build up in the coronary artery, leading to poor circulation.

Now try this

a Complete these sentences.

Heart valves make blood flow in ________ direction. A hole in the heart is a hole between the ____________ and ____________ sides of the heart. This causes the blood to carry less ____________.

Bypass surgery is used when the ____________ artery is partly blocked.

Homework

1 Draw a labelled diagram of the heart to show the valves.
2 Use a search engine to find out about bypass surgery.
3 Use a table to show the advantages and disadvantages of heart transplants.

BLOOD GROUPS AND CLOTTING

- Blood is made from plasma containing red blood cells, white blood cells and platelets.
- Red blood cells contain haemoglobin to carry oxygen.
- White blood cells destroy microorganisms.
- Platelets help blood clotting to seal wounds.
- Anticoagulants (warfarin, heparin, aspirin) reduce clotting.
- Vitamin K, alcohol, green vegetables and cranberries aid clotting.
- Haemophilia is an inherited condition.
- There are four blood groups (A, B, AB and O).
- These are subdivided into rhesus positive or negative.
- Blood can be donated and transfused into others.
- *Agglutinins in red blood cells and serum determine blood groups and blood donation.*
- *Blood clotting involves many steps: a cascade process.*

TOP TIP Red blood cells carry oxygen for respiration.

Now try this

b Complete the following.

Name the liquid part of the blood.

____

Which chemical in red blood cells combines with oxygen? ________

Aspirin ________ clotting while vitamin K ________ clotting.

The four main blood groups are ______, ______, ______ and ______.

People with blood group O can donate to ______ ______.

People with blood group O can receive only group ______ blood.

Homework

4 Draw and label the components of blood.
5 Find out your blood group and find out which blood groups you can receive and donate to.
6 Draw a diagram of the main steps in blood clotting.

RESPIRATION

- All living things respire to get oxygen to release energy from food.
- The exchange of gases is breathing.
- Simple animals exchange gases through their moist skin.
- Complex animals use gills or lungs.
- The intercostal muscles and diaphragm alter the volume and pressure of the air in the lungs.
- Our respiratory system has many parts.
- Vital lung capacity varies in individuals.
- *Our respiratory system is efficient due to large surface area of alveoli, a good blood supply, a thin lining and a moist surface.*

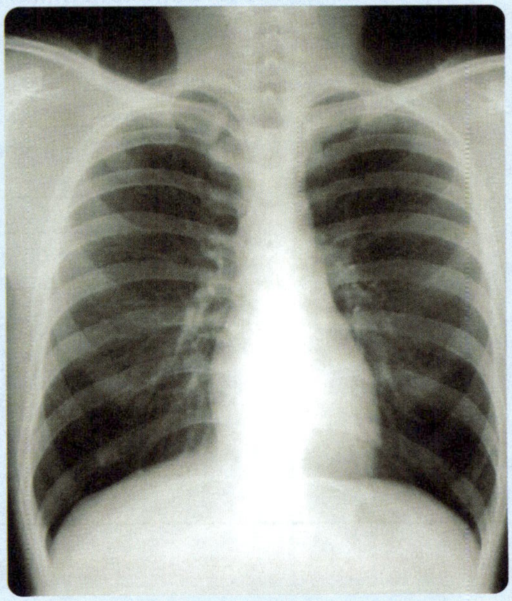

Now try this

c Complete these sentences.

The exchange of gases is called ______________. The oxidation of food is called ______________. Big animals do not breathe through their skin because they would not get enough ______________ for respiration. When we breathe in, the intercostal muscles ______________, moving the ribs ______________ and ______________. The diaphragm also ______________ and moves ______________. These actions ______________ the volume and ______________ the pressure inside the chest.

Homework

7 Explain the difference between respiration and breathing.
8 Draw a labelled diagram of the structure of the lungs.
9 Explain how the thin lining of air sacs helps respiration.

RESPIRATORY CONDITIONS

- Ciliated cells and mucus protect the respiration system from dust and disease.
- Lung diseases are asbestosis (industrial disease), cystic fibrosis (inherited) and lung cancer (by smoking).
- Asthma is an allergic reaction.
- Asbestosis is caused by inhaling asbestos fibres.
- Cystic fibrosis is inherited through a recessive allele.
- Lung cancer is when cells divide out of control.
- Bronchitis and pneumonia are other respiratory diseases caused by microorganisms.

Now try this

d Match each disease to its cause.

Asbestosis	smoking
Cystic fibrosis	microorganisms
Lung cancer	inherited
Bronchitis	allergy
Asthma	industrial

TOP TIP Asthma is an allergic reaction.

Homework

10 Use a search engine to find information on asthma.
11 Write a short explanation of lung cancer.
12 Use a search engine to find out which respiratory diseases are increasing.

Organs and growth

KIDNEYS

- Excretion is getting rid of waste produced by the body.
- Getting rid of solid waste through the anus is defecation.
- The main excretory organs are lungs, kidneys, liver and skin.
- The liver produces urea from excess amino acids.
- The kidney excretes urea, water and salt as urine.
- The kidneys filter the blood at high pressure; the waste is excreted; water and useful substances (glucose) are reabsorbed.
- The amount of urine produced is affected by water intake, heat and exercise.
- *A kidney has a filter unit (glomerulus and capsule), a region for selective reabsorption and a region for water regulation.*
- *A dialysis machine works as a kidney.*
- *The concentration of urea is controlled by the anti-diuretic hormone (ADH) using negative feedback.*

Now try this

a Complete these sentences.

Waste produced by the body is got rid of by __________. Urea is produced by the __________. The blood is __________ in the kidney. The kidney excretes __________ which contains __________, __________ and __________. On a hot day, __________ urine is excreted. The kidney 'chooses' to reabsorb some chemicals but not others. This is called __________ __________. If the kidney is not working correctly a __________ machine is used.

Homework

1 Explain the difference between excretion and defecation.
2 Draw and label a diagram of the structure of a kidney.
3 Use a search engine to find out about dialysis.

SKIN AND LUNGS

- The skin excretes sweat containing water and salt.
- The sweat evaporates from the skin and then diffuses into the air.
- Evaporation uses energy from the skin which is cooled down.
- The skin has two main layers: the outer epidermis and inner dermis.
- The skin contains hair follicles and sweat glands.
- The lungs excrete carbon dioxide and some water.
- High levels of carbon dioxide in the body are dangerous.
- *High levels of carbon dioxide in the blood are detected by the brain and trigger an increased breathing rate.*

TOP TIP The skin, lungs and kidneys all excrete water.

Now try this

b Label this diagram of the skin.

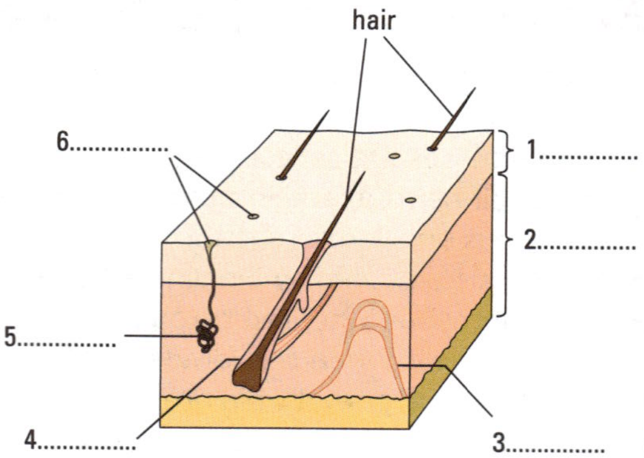

Homework

4 Draw and label the main parts of the skin.
5 Use a search engine to find out how mouth-to-mouth resuscitation works.
6 Write a short description of how high levels of carbon dioxide are detected.

FERTILISATION AND GROWTH

- Fertilisation is the fusion of a male gamete (sperm) and a female gamete (egg).
- Testes produce sperm; sperm ducts carry sperm.
- Ovaries produce eggs; oviducts carry them to the uterus.
- The menstruation cycle synchronises ovulation and preparation of the uterus.
- *Hormones such as oestrogen, progesterone, FSH and LH control the menstruation cycle.*
- Infertility can be treated by IVF, surrogacy, egg donation or artificial insemination.
- Growth is the production of new cells by mitosis.
- Growth can be an increase in height or mass.
- Extremes in height are caused by genes or hormone imbalance.
- A baby's length, mass and head size are monitored to ensure any growth problems are recognised at an early stage.
- *The human growth hormone is produced by the pituitary gland.*

Now try this

c Are the following statements **true (T)** or **false (F)**?

Testes produce eggs. ______

Oviducts carry eggs. ______

The menstruation cycle is controlled by hormones. ______

One of these hormones is insulin. ______

The thickness of the uterus wall varies during the menstruation cycle. ______

The average menstruation cycle lasts seven days. ______

In growth, new cells are produced by meiosis. ______

Homework

7 Write a short description of the menstruation cycle.

8 Use a search engine to find information on IVF.

9 Make a table showing hormones that control the menstruation cycle and their function.

REPLACEMENT OF BODY PARTS

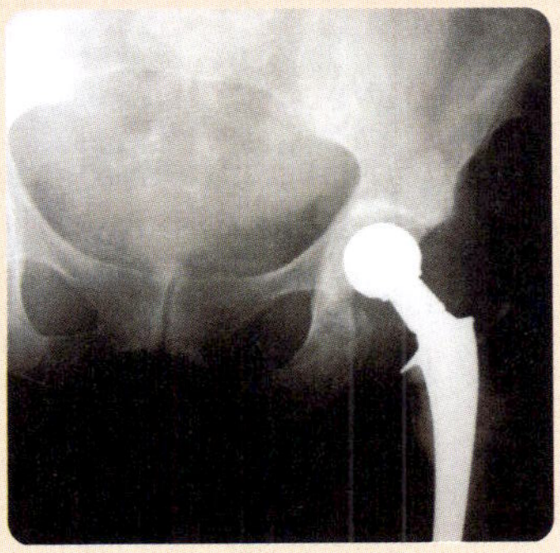

- Body parts can have mechanical replacements (for example, kidney, joints, heart, eye lens).
- The use of mechanical replacements is limited by their size, need for power supply and material suitable.
- Body parts can have living replacements (for example, blood, cornea, heart, lungs, kidney, bone marrow). They can be donated by living or dead donors.
- Living replacements must be matched for blood and tissue type (to avoid rejection) as well as size.
- There is a donor shortage.

Now try this

d Complete the following.

Name one body organ that can have a mechanical or biological replacement.

____

Living replacements must be matched to avoid ___________.

People who agree for their body organs to be used carry ___________ cards.

While still living, and without harming yourself, you can donate ___________ and ___________.

Mechanical replacements may need a ___________ supply to keep them working.

Homework

10 Draw an outline of a human body and show which body parts can be replaced.

11 Use a search engine to find out about bone marrow transplants.

12 Write down reasons for and against carrying a donor card.

Microorganisms and fermentation

BACTERIA

- Bacteria are different from plant and animals cells because they lack mitochondria, chloroplasts, vacuole and a 'true nucleus'.
- Bacteria can be classified by their shape (spherical, rod, spiral, curved rods).
- A bacterium like E.coli has a flagellum (movement), cell wall (shape) and DNA (genetic information).
- Bacteria reproduce rapidly by binary fission (asexual reproduction).
- Some bacteria are used in making yoghurt, cheese, vinegar, silage and compost.
- *Bacteria can survive on different energy sources and in a wide range of habitats.*

TOP TIP Bacterium is singular, bacteria is plural (many bacteria).

Now try this

a Are the following statements **true** (T) or **false** (F)?

Bacteria are plants. _______

Bacteria do not have a proper nucleus but they contain DNA. _______

E.coli is a bacterium. _______

Bacteria are classified by their colour. _______

Bacteria are classified by their shape. _______

Bacteria are used to make alcohol. _______

Bacteria are used to make yoghurt. _______

Bacteria reproduce by a type of asexual reproduction. _______

All bacteria get their energy from photosynthesis. _______

Homework

1 Describe the process of making yoghurt.
2 Draw a diagram to show the structure of E.coli.
3 Use a search engine to find which energy sources are used by bacteria.

HARMFUL MICROORGANISMS

- Microorganisms can enter the body through the nose, mouth, skin and reproductive organs.
- Microorganisms that cause disease are pathogens. They cause infectious diseases.
- Bacteria cause TB and food poisoning.
- Viruses cause flu, chicken pox and smallpox.
- A fungus causes athletes foot.
- Protozoans cause malaria and dysentery.
- Antibiotics can control bacteria inside the body. Antiseptics kill bacteria outside the body.
- Natural disasters cause the rapid spread of infectious diseases such as dysentery, cholera and food poisoning.
- Pasteur, Lister and Fleming were all involved in research into microorganisms and disease.

Now try this

b **Match up the two columns then answer the questions below.**

Bacteria	malaria
Fungi	tuberculosis
Virus	athletes foot
Protozoan	influenza

What is a pathogen? __________

What are diseases that can be transmitted to other people called? __________

TOP TIP Antibiotics kill bacteria but not viruses.

Homework

4 Use your textbook to write a short description of how malaria is transmitted.
5 Use a search engine to find out about the work of Pasteur, Lister and Fleming.
6 Write a brief guide explaining how to avoid catching infectious diseases in a disaster zone.

See pages 54–69 of Collins GCSE Biology

FERMENTATION

- Yeast is a fungus and can be stored in a dry condition.
- Yeast uses anaerobic respiration to break down sugars to produce alcohol. It also produces wine from grapes, beer from barley and cider from apples.
- Yeast reproduces very quickly by budding (asexual reproduction). Its growth is affected by temperature, food availability, pH and removal of alcohol produced.
- Some fermentation products can be distilled to increase their alcohol content (for example, whisky from barley).
- High alcohol levels kill yeast.
- *The yeast growth rate doubles for every 10 °C rise.*
- *Pasteurisation is used when bottling beers.*
- *The balanced chemical equation for anaerobic respiration is:*

$$C_6H_{12}O_6 \longrightarrow 2C_2H_5OH + 2CO_2$$

glucose → ethanol + carbon dioxide.

TOP TIP In animals, anaerobic respiration produces lactic acid, not alcohol.

Now try this

c Complete these sentences.

Yeast uses ______________ respiration to make alcohol. This type of respiration does not use ______________. Budding is a type of ______________ reproduction. Yeast grows best at a ______________ temperature. If the yeast's waste products are not removed it will ______________. Anaerobic respiration produces ______________ energy than aerobic respiration because the ______________ is not completely broken down.

Homework

7 Use your textbook to help you describe the main stages in brewing beer.
8 Write a short description of fermentation.
9 Use a table to compare and contrast aerobic and anaerobic respiration.

BIOFUELS

- Bacteria rot organic material producing biogas which contains methane.
- Biogas is produced in marshes and septic tanks, or commercially using a digester.
- Biogas can be used as a fuel in buses, to provide electricity or to power central heating systems.
- Alcohol from yeast can also be used as a fuel in cars.
- Biofuels produce less carbon dioxide than fossil fuels and produce no particulates.
- *A low amount of methane in biogas is explosive.*
- *Although biogas is a cleaner fuel than diesel it produces less energy.*

TOP TIP Biogas is made by **bacteria**.

Now try this

d Complete the following.

Biogas contains the gas ______________. A digester produces ______________. The process of ______________ transfers energy from fuels. Biofuels are better than fossil fuels because they produce less ______________ ______________ and no ______________. Diesel is better than biofuels because it produces ______________ ______________.

Homework

10 Write a short comparison of fossil fuels and biofuels.
11 Use a search engine to help you draw and label a digester.
12 Explain why vent pipes are fitted to landfill sites.

Soil and life in water

SOIL STRUCTURE

- Soil contains rock particles, humus, living organisms, air and water.
- Humus is dead material such as leaves.
- Earthworms, insects, snails, nematode worms and bacteria live in the soil and depend on air and water.
- Soil anchors and provides plants with minerals.
- *Soil should have a good drainage and aeration system otherwise it becomes waterlogged and lacking in oxygen.*
- *Most crop plants prefer a neutral soil. An acid soil can be neutralised by adding lime.*

Now try this

a Add the following labels to the diagram below.

soil particles   living organism
air and water   humus

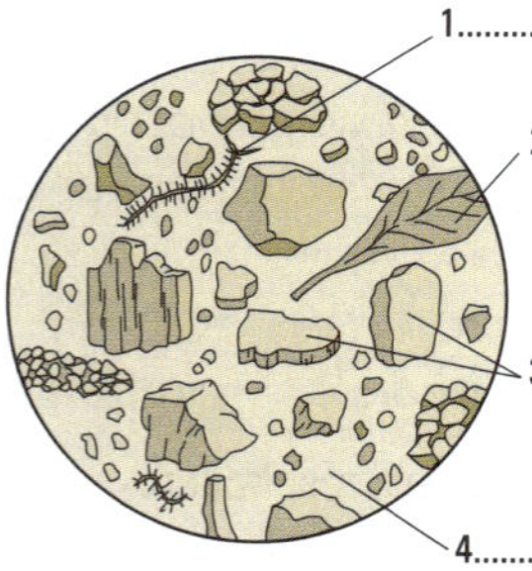

Homework

1 Use a search engine to find drawings of organisms found in the soil.
2 Use your text book to help you find out how some plants are grown without soil.
3 Use a search engine to find the pH of **five** common crops.

FOOD WEBS AND EARTHWORMS

- A typical soil food web contains herbivores (for example, slugs), detritivores (for example, earthworms) and carnivores (for example, spiders).
- Earthworms help soil structure by aerating and mixing up soil layers. They improve soil fertility by burying organic material such as leaves and neutralising acid soils.
- Elements such as nitrogen, carbon, sulfur and phosphorus are recycled.
- This recycling depends on different types of bacteria.
- *Saprophytic soil bacteria start decomposition of organic material.*
- *Nitrifying and nitrogen-fixing bacteria help to recycle nitrogen.*

Now try this

b Are the following statements true (T) or false (F)?

Carbon and nitrogen are recycled naturally. ______
Viruses help the nitrogen cycle. ______
Earthworms bury leaves. ______
Earthworms neutralise an alkaline soil. ______
Earthworms mix up soil layers. ______
An animal that gets its food from dead organic matter is a detritivore. ______
A plant that gets its food from dead organic matter is a saprophyte. ______

Homework

4 Why is the recycling of minerals important?
5 Explain why burying plant leaves helps soil fertility.
6 Use a search engine to find out about Charles Darwin's work on earthworms.

ADVANTAGES OF LIFE IN WATER

- There is a wide variety of life in water.
- There are no problems of water shortage or dehydration.
- Water temperatures show less variation.
- Organisms are supported in water.
- Waste products are easily disposed of.
- Some animals (for example, frogs) spend part of their life cycle in water (as tadpoles) and part on land.
- Plankton are microscopic organisms in water.
- Plankton contains phytoplankton (plants) and zooplankton (animals).
- Phytoplankton are producers; they use photosynthesis to produce food.
- Seasonal changes in light, temperature and minerals such as nitrates and phosphates cause seasonal variations in plankton.

Now try this

c Complete these sentences.

Aquatic organisms live in ____________. Plankton contains plants which form ____________ and animals which form ____________. The plant plankton uses ____________ to produce ____________ so they are called ____________. Phytoplankton will grow and reproduce faster when there is more ____________, more ____________ and a ____________ temperature. When there are more phytoplankton there will be more ____________. During the season of ____________ there will be more plankton.

Homework

7 Plankton can contain krill. Use a search engine to find out the importance of krill.

8 Write **one** food chain from a lake and **one** from the sea.

9 Use a search engine to find out about the migration of salmon.

DISADVANTAGES OF LIFE IN WATER

- Aquatic organisms have been affected by pollution and acid rain.
- Aquatic organisms have problems with regulating their water content.
- *Water enters aquatic organisms by osmosis.*
- *Animals such as amoeba have contractile vacuoles to get rid of this excess water.*
- Water pollution can be by sewage, oil, PCBs, fertilisers, pesticides and detergents.
- Sewage and fertiliser run off can cause eutrophication.
- Eutrophication causes a lack of oxygen so animals such as fish die.
- Some organisms are sensitive to oxygen levels or pH. These are indicator species.

TOP TIP A process like eutrophication has many steps. A short answer will gain few, if any, marks.

Now try this

d Complete the following.

The stages in eutrophication are mixed up. Put them in the correct order.

	oxygen used up
1	sewage and fertiliser run off
	rapid growth of algae and plankton
	animals die
	algae and plankton die

Water enters fresh water animals because their insides have a ______ concentration of solutes. Water leaves marine animals because their insides have a ______ concentration of solutes.

Homework

10 Use a search engine to find out how acid rain affects aquatic organisms.

11 Use your textbook to help explain why pollutants can build up in food chains.

12 Write a short description of osmosis.

Enzymes and genetic engineering

ENZYMES

- Enzymes are specific; they each work on a different substrate.
- Biological washing powders contain amylases to digest carbohydrates, lipases to digest fats and proteases to digest proteins.
- *Carbohydrates are broken down into sugars, fats into fatty acids and proteins into amino acids.*
- *The chemicals are digested into soluble substances so they dissolve in the water and leave the clothing.*
- Most biological washing powders work best in a neutral pH and a low temperature.
- *In the food industry, invertase is used to break down sucrose into fructose and glucose which tastes much sweeter.*

TOP TIP Sugars end in -ose (for example, glucose). Enzymes end in -ase (for example, protease).

Now try this

a Complete these sentences.

Enzymes only work on specific ______________. Biological washing powders contain ______________ such as ______________, ______________ and ______________. Enzymes speed up chemical ______________. They break down chemicals into simpler chemicals that ______________ in water. This breakdown is called ______________. An example of an enzyme is ______________ and an example of a sugar is ______________.

Homework

1 Using bullet points, list what you know about enzymes.
2 Use a search engine to find out about sweeteners.
3 Explain how biological washing powders work.

IMMOBILISED ENZYMES

- An immobilised enzyme is when an enzyme is attached to another chemical to prevent it being lost.
- Enzymes can be immobilised using alginate.
- Immobilised enzymes are used in reagent sticks such as those used to measure glucose levels in blood or urine.
- Immobilised enzymes prevent contamination.
- Immobilised enzymes in alginate beads can be used in continuous flow systems.
- *The immobilised enzyme lactase is used to produce lactose-free milk by converting lactose into glucose and galactose.*

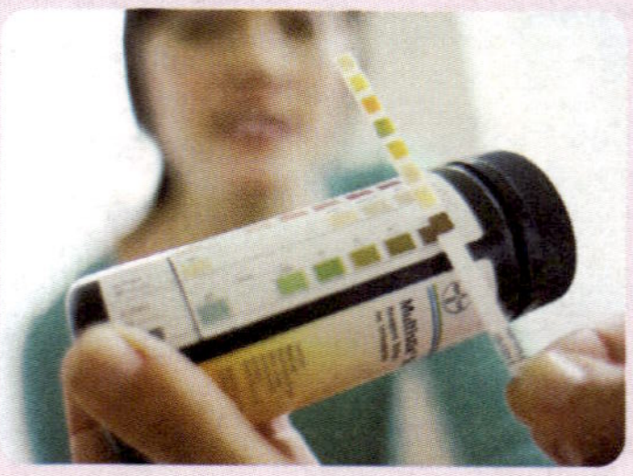

Now try this

b Are the following statements true (T) or false (F)?

An immobilised enzyme doesn't work. ______

An immobilised enzyme is attached to another chemical. ______

Immobilised enzymes are used in reagent sticks. ______

Alginate beads can contain immobilised enzymes. ______

Lactose is an enzyme. ______

Lactase acts on lactose to produce lactose-free milk. ______

Homework

4 Write a short description of an immobilised enzyme.
5 Explain why it is important to have an accurate blood glucose reading.
6 Use a search engine to find out about lactose intolerance.

See pages 80–87 of Collins GCSE Biology

WHAT IS GENETIC ENGINEERING

- DNA carries genetic information in the form of a genetic code.
- Genetic engineering (also called genetic modification) alters the genetic code.
- In genetic engineering a gene is removed from one organism and put into a different organism.
- Genes from one organism work in a different organism.
- By inserting a gene, the organism becomes transgenic.
- There are a number of stages in the procedure.
- *Restriction enzymes are used to cut open DNA and ligase enzymes are used to rejoin the DNA strands.*

Now try this

c Complete the following.

Put the following stages in genetic engineering in the correct order.

☐	Transgenic organism cloned
☐	New gene inserted into the DNA
☐	Gene removed from DNA
1	Wanted gene identified
☐	DNA in another organism cut open
☐	Gene works in transgenic organism

Which enzyme cuts open DNA? ___________

Which enzyme rejoins DNA strands?

____

Homework

7 Explain what is meant by the genetic code.

8 Use your text book to help you draw the sequence of events in genetic engineering.

9 Use a search engine to find out when genetic engineering was first used.

USES OF GENETIC ENGINEERING

- Genetic engineering can be used to produce human insulin. The gene for human insulin production is inserted into bacteria which then multiply, producing insulin.
- Genetic engineering is used to improve many crops such as beans, maize and cotton.
- Genetic engineering can increase the yield, make them resistant to weed killers, make plants produce other useful chemicals such as vitamins and make plants more resistant to cold or drought.
- *Some scientists are concerned about the interference to gene pools and unknown consequences.*

TOP TIP Remember: some people do not agree with the use of genetic engineering.

Now try this

d Complete these sentences.

A gene for human insulin can be put into the _______________ of bacteria. Bacteria are used because they reproduce _______________ and will make a lot of _______________.

Genetic engineering is used to produce weed _______________ crops. This means that the crops are not _______________ by weed killers. They get more _______________, _______________ and _______________ and grow _______________.

Homework

10 Complete a table to show the advantages and disadvantages of genetic engineering.

11 Use a search engine to find out which countries grow genetically engineered crops.

12 Explain why the method of producing insulin described is so useful.

How much? Part 1

MOLES AND EMPIRICAL FORMULAE 1

- Amounts of chemicals are measured in moles.
- A molar mass is the relative formula mass in grams.
- So: $\text{moles} = \frac{\text{grams}}{\text{molar mass}}$ $\quad$ $\text{grams} = \text{moles} \times \text{molar mass}$
- The number in front of each formula shows the number of moles that react together.
  For example, $\underset{\text{2 moles}}{2H_2} + \underset{\text{1 mole}}{O_2} \longrightarrow \underset{\text{2 moles}}{2H_2O}$
- Moles can be used to calculate the product formed.
  For example, CO_2 from 200 g of limestone:
  $CaCO_3 \rightarrow CaO + CO_2$
  1 mole $CaCO_3$ makes 1 mole CO_2
  200g $CaCO_3$ is $\frac{200}{100} = 2$ moles
  2 moles $CaCO_3$ makes 2 moles CO_2
  2 moles $CO_2 = 2 \times 44$ g $CO_2 = 88$ g CO_2

Now try this

a Convert the grams to moles and the moles to grams.

80 g Ca ________

4 g H_2 ________

36 g H_2O ________

68 g NH_3 ________

11 g CO_2 ________

0.5 moles Ca ________

10 moles H_2 ________

0.5 moles H_2O ________

2 moles NH_3 ________

Homework

1 Calculate the masses of **10** different chlorides that contain 71 g of chlorine.

2 Calculate the grams of CO_2 made by heating 800 g $CaCO_3$ and burning 800 g CH_4.

3 Calculate the mass of CO_2 that a plant would need to make a 1000 g bag of glucose ($C_6H_{12}O_6$).

MOLES AND EMPIRICAL FORMULAE 2

- An empirical formula shows the simplest whole number ratio of each type of atom.
- It can be found from reacting masses.
  Example: S has a mass of 32, O a mass of 16. If 32 g of S reacts with 32 g of O, 1 mole of S reacts with 2 of O.
  Formula = SO_2.
- Example: A compound is 80% C and 20% H.
  Divide by relative atomic mass to get moles.
  $C = \frac{80}{12} = 6.67 \qquad H = \frac{20}{1} = 20$
  Divide by the smaller number to get a ratio.
  $C = \frac{6.67}{6.67} = 1 \qquad H = \frac{20}{6.67} = 3$
  So empirical formula = CH_3.

Now try this

b Calculate each formula.

48 g of Mg with 32 g of O ________

20 g of Ca with 8 g of O ________

24 g of C with 64 g of O ________

24 g of C with 8 g of H ________

8 g of S with 8 g of O ________

28 g of N with 6 g of H ________

24 g of C with 6 g of H ________

8 g of H with 64 g of O ________

TOP TIP If the percentage composition is given, assume you have 100 g altogether.

Homework

4 Which compound has an empirical formula of CH_2, and a molar mass of 28?

5 Find the formula of an acid which is 2.44% H, 39.02% S and 58.54% O.

6 What compound has mass 180 and is 40% C, 6.67% H and 53.33% O.

ELECTROLYSIS 1

- Electrolysis decomposes molten electrolytes like $PbBr_2$ if inert carbon electrodes are used.
- A battery or dc supply pushes electrons to the negative electrode where they cause reduction, for example: Pb^{2+} + 2 electrons → Pb.
- Oxidation releases electrons at the positive electrode, for example: $2Br^-$ – 2 electrons → Br_2. These travel through wires to the negative electrode.
- Ions in the electrolyte move to the electrodes to complete the circuit.
- *Solutions like $KNO_{3(aq)}$ may discharge ions from the water rather than the solute.*
- At the negative cathode: $2H^+_{(aq)} + 2e^- \rightarrow H_{2(g)}$.
- At the positive anode: $4OH^-_{(aq)} - 4e^- \rightarrow 2H_2O_{(l)} + O_{2(g)}$.

Now try this

c Finish the half equations to show what happens at the anode and cathode.

$Al_2O_{3(l)}$	Anode:	$2O^{2-} \rightarrow$ ____ + ____
	Cathode:	Al^{3+} + ____ → ____
$PbI_{2(l)}$	Anode:	$2I^- \rightarrow$ ____ + ____
	Cathode:	Pb^{2+} + ____ → ____
$KCl_{(l)}$	Anode:	$Cl^- \rightarrow$ ____ + ____
	Cathode:	K^+ + ____ → ____
$K_2SO_{4(aq)}$	Anode:	$4OH^- \rightarrow$ ____ + ____ + ____
	Cathode:	$2H^+$ + ____ → ____

TOP TIP Electrolysis only works when ions are melted or dissolved so that they are free to move.

Homework

7 Explain why electrolysis only breaks aluminium oxide down when it is molten.
8 Why is it no use electrolysing a potassium salt solution if you want the metal?
9 Titanium is the second most common metal – how is it extracted?

ELECTROLYSIS 2

- When copper is purified, the copper at the positive electrode dissolves – so it loses mass. $Cu_{(s)} \rightarrow Cu^{2+}_{(aq)} + 2e^-$
- The Cu^{2+} are attracted to the negative electrode.
- Uncharged impurities fall to the bottom.
- Reduction makes copper plate onto the negative. $Cu^{2+}_{(aq)} + 2e^- \rightarrow Cu_{(s)}$
- The gain at the negative equals the loss at the positive.
- The amount transferred depends on the total charge transferred, which increases with current and time: charge = $current_{(amps)} \times time_{(seconds)}$ (Q = It)

TOP TIP The current in wires is carried by electrons. In electrolytes it is carried by ions.

Now try this

d Decide if the following happen at the positive (P) or negative (N) electrode.

Metals deposited	____
Wire collects electrons	____
Cu^{2+} ions attracted	____
Non-metals discharged	____
Reduction	____
Negative ions attracted	____
Electrolyte collects electrons	____
Oxidation	____

Homework

10 Prepare a presentation to explain copper purification.
11 Find out how electroplating works and what it is used for.
12 How much copper would be transferred in two hours by a current of 2 A?

How much? Part 2

QUANTITATIVE ANALYSIS

- Solubility is measured in grams dm^{-3} or mol dm^{-3}.
- 1 dm^3 of water = 1000 cm^3 = 1000 g.
- 1 M solutions contain 1 mole of solute per dm^3.
- *mol dm^{-3}(molarity) = $\frac{moles}{dm^3} = \frac{grams\ dm^{-3}}{M_r}$.*
- *grams dm^{-3} = mol $dm^{-3} \times M_r$*
- If a 1 mol dm^{-3} solution is mixed with nine volumes of water, the concentration becomes 0.1 mol dm^{-3}.
- Dilution of medicines and baby milk must be accurate.
- Food packages usually give recommended daily allowances (RDA) per 100 g. For sodium chloride this is 4 g/day.
- *Na(23) has less than half the mass of NaCl(58.5). Multiply the sodium content by 2.54 to give the mass of sodium chloride present.*
- Sodium ions may come from several sources, so this conversion may be inaccurate.

Now try this

a Convert the grams dm^{-3} to mol dm^{-3} and vice versa.

80 grams dm^{-3} NaOH ______
63 grams dm^{-3} HNO_3 ______
146 grams dm^{-3} HCl ______
7 grams dm^{-3} NH_4OH ______
49 grams dm^{-3} H_2SO_4 ______
0.5 mol dm^{-3} NaOH ______
2 mol dm^{-3} HNO_3 ______
0.2 mol dm^{-3} HCl ______
2 mol dm^{-3} NH_4OH ______
2 mol dm^{-3} H_2SO_4 ______

Homework

1 Collect **two** food labels and calculate the mass of NaCl per 100 g of food.
2 How would you make 0.1, 0.2, 0.5 and 0.8 mol dm^{-3} acids from 1 mol dm^{-3} acid?
3 4 g of NaOH dissolves in 0.5 dm^3 of water. What is the concentration in mol dm^{-3}?

TITRATIONS

- Solutions with known molarities are titrated to find the concentrations of other solutions.
- A fixed volume of alkali is transferred to a flask. Indicator is added.
- A known concentration of acid is added until the indicator changes colour.
- *Single indicators give a sharp end-point.*
- *The volume of a known concentration shows the number of moles used.*

  moles = concentration × volume in dm^3

  $= mol\ dm^{-3} \times dm^3 \left(\frac{cm^3}{1000}\right)$
- *If: acid + alkali → salt + water, the moles of alkali equal the moles of acid*

  So: alkali concentration = $\frac{moles\ of\ acid}{volume\ in\ dm^3}$

Now try this

b What concentration is HCl if 20 cm^3 is neutralised by:

20 cm^3 0.5 M NaOH ______
10 cm^3 2 M NaOH ______
40 cm^3 0.5 M NaOH ______
20 cm^3 1 M NH_4OH ______
5 cm^3 1 M NH_4OH ______
40 cm^3 0.2 M KOH ______
20 cm^3 0.5 M NH_4OH ______
10 cm^3 0.010 M KOH ______

Homework

4 Write step-by-step instructions for carrying out an acid/base titration.
5 List the sources of error in a titration and say how they can be minimised.
6 Find the colour and pH changes for **five** different indicators.

GAS VOLUMES

- Gas volumes are usually measured in cm^3 or dm^3.
- The limiting reactant is the one that runs out first.
- Doubling it doubles the volume of gas produced.
- Gas can be collected in upturned measuring cylinders, burettes or gas syringes.
- The mass of gas lost can be read from a balance.
- A mole of gas occupies 24 000 cm^3 or 24 dm^3.
- moles = $\frac{\text{volume } (dm^3)}{24}$ volume (dm^3) = moles × 24
- Reacting volumes are easily calculated. For example, $N_2 + 3H_2 \longrightarrow 2NH_3$ (1 mole, 3 moles, 2 moles)

  1 mole N_2 makes 2 moles NH_3
  24 dm^3 N_2 makes 48 dm^3 NH_3
  1 dm^3 N_2 makes 2 dm^3 NH_3

TOP TIP A mole of any gas occupies the same volume – 24 dm^3.

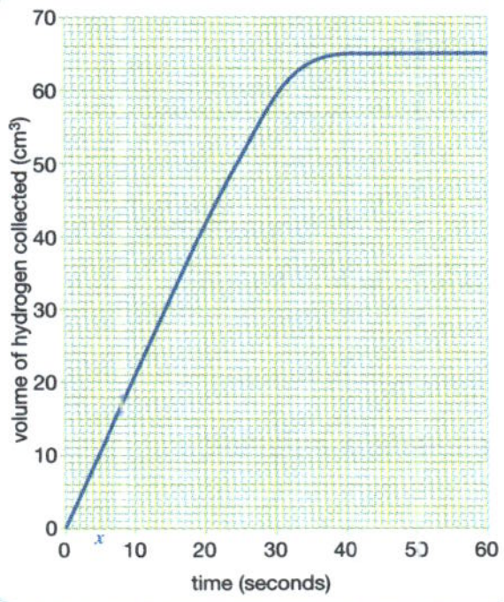

Now try this

c Convert the volumes to moles and the moles to dm³.

48 dm^3 He ________
12 000 cm^3 H_2 ________
6 dm^3 O_2 ________
24 dm^3 NH_3 ________
48 dm^3 CO_2 ________
48 dm^3 CO ________
0.5 moles He ________
0.25 moles H_2 ________
0.05 moles O_2 ________
2 moles NH_3 ________
1 mole CO_2 ________

Homework

7 Find the volume of hot gas made when moles of CH_4, H_2, C_2H_4 or C_2H_5OH burn.
8 What mass of air fills a 24 000 dm^3 room? (Assume 80% N_2 and 20% O_2.)
9 How much glucose could you burn, or use for respiration, with this much air?

EQUILIBRIA

- The Contact Process, used to make sulfuric acid, has one reversible step.
- Molten sulfur is sprayed into a furnace. $S + O_2 \rightarrow SO_2$
- *SO_2 is oxidised to SO_3 at 450 °C and 1 atmosphere in the presence of a catalyst (vanadium oxide).* $2SO_{2(g)} + O_{2(g)} \rightleftharpoons 2SO_{3(g)}$
- *SO_3 is dissolved to form H_2SO_4.*
- Reversible reactions reach equilibrium in closed systems.
- The forward and reverse reactions go at the same rate.
- The conditions are a compromise. Yields are higher at lower temperatures and higher pressures but these are not economical.
- *Removing products, or adding reactants, moves the position of equilibrium to the right, or vice versa.*

TOP TIP Catalysts don't affect the position of equilibrium (yield) because they have the same effect on the forward and backward reactions.

Now try this

d Fill in the missing words.

Sulfur is burned to make ________ ________. This is mixed with more ________ and passed over a catalyst called ________ ________ at ________ °C and ________ atmosphere. The ________ ________ formed is dissolved in ________ sulfuric acid and then diluted to give ________ sulfuric acid.

Homework

10 Produce a poster to show some uses of sulfuric acid.
11 Find out why sulfur trioxide is dissolved in sulfuric acid instead of water.
12 Research what Le Chatelier said about equilibrium reactions.

How much? Part 3

STRONG AND WEAK ACIDS

- Concentration is measured in moles per dm^3 (M).
- *Strength is determined by the degree of ionisation.*
- *Hydrochloric, nitric and sulfuric acids are strong.*
  $HCl \rightarrow H^+ + Cl^-$ (fully ionised)
- *Ethanoic acid is weak. It has a higher pH, and lower conductivity, than the same concentration of HCl.*
  $CH_3COOH \rightleftharpoons CH_3COO^- + H^+$ (partially ionised equilibrium mixture)
- It makes a safer descaling agent.
- The same amounts of hydrochloric and ethanoic acid make the same volume of H_2 with magnesium and CO_2 with calcium carbonate.
- HCl reacts faster because the higher H+ ion concentration makes the collision frequency higher during reactions.

Now try this

a Decide if each acid is **weak (W)**, **strong (S)** or could be **either (E)**.

1 M sulfuric acid ______

0.001 M hydrochloric acid ______

Gives off CO_2 with carbonates ______

A partially ionised acid ______

2 M acid with pH = 4 ______

Gives off H_2 with magnesium ______

0.1 M acid with high conductivity ______

Gives off H_2 during electrolysis ______

Homework

1. If 1 M HCl gives 100 cm^3 of H_2 in 20 s, what might 1 M CH_3COOH give and why?
2. Find titration curves for HCl and ethanoic acid and explain their differences.
3. Draw particle pictures of solutions of HCl and CH_3COOH.

IONIC EQUATIONS

- Ions are in fixed positions in solids, but they can move around when melted or dissolved.
- When their solutions are mixed, the ions of insoluble compounds collide and precipitate.
- The other ions in the mixture stay in solution – they are spectator ions.
- Precipitates can be filtered out, washed and dried to give the pure salt.
- Cl^-, Br^- and I^- ions precipitate with silver nitrate.
  $Ag^+_{(aq)} + I^-_{(aq)} \rightarrow AgI_{(s)}$
- AgI (yellow), AgBr (cream), AgCl (white)
- Sulfate ions make white precipitates with barium ions.
- barium chloride + sodium sulfate → barium sulfate + sodium chloride
- $Ba^{2+}_{(aq)} + SO_4^{2-}{}_{(aq)} \rightarrow BaSO_{4(s)}$

Now try this

b Complete these equations.

silver nitrate$_{(aq)}$ + sodium **iodide**$_{(aq)}$ →

____

$\mathbf{Ag^+_{(aq)} + I^-_{(aq)}} \rightarrow$ ______

barium nitrate$_{(aq)}$ + sodium **sulfate**$_{(aq)}$ →

____

$\mathbf{Ba^{2+}_{(aq)} + SO_4^{2-}{}_{(aq)}} \rightarrow$ ______

lead nitrate$_{(aq)}$ + sodium **iodide**$_{(aq)}$ →

____

$\mathbf{Pb^{2+}_{(aq)}}$ + ______ $\mathbf{I^-_{(aq)}} \rightarrow$ ______

Homework

4. Lead sulfate is insoluble. Explain how it could be made.
5. Write a step-by-step method for the preparation of lead iodide.
6. Use particle pictures to explain how precipitates of barium sulfate form.

ENERGY TRANSFERS – FUEL CELLS

- Hydrogen (H_2) pops with a lit splint.
- Oxygen (O_2) relights a glowing splint.
- The car industry is developing fuel cells.
- They are very efficient and pollution-free.
- They provide electrical power in spacecraft.
- The overall reaction in a fuel cell is:
  $2H_2 + O_2 \rightarrow 2H_2O$ (exothermic)
- Fuel and oxygen react and the energy released creates a potential difference.
- *Hydrogen is oxidised at the anode:*
  $H_2 \rightarrow 2H^+ + 2e^-$.
- *Oxygen is reduced at the cathode:*
  $O_2 + 4e^- + 4H^+ \rightarrow 2H_2O$.

TOP TIP Hydrogen-oxygen fuel cells are pollution-free because their only product is pure water.

Now try this

c In cars, hydrogen can be burned or used in a fuel cell. Decide if the following apply to **burning hydrogen (BH)**, a **fuel cell (FC)**, **both (B)** or **neither (N)**.

Heat energy released	______
H_2 reacts with O_2	______
A redox reaction	______
Needs a catalyst	______
Pollution-free	______
Potential difference generated	______
Very efficient	______
Used in spacecraft	______

Homework

7 Explain why vehicles that run on fuel cells are useful in cities.
8 Write a step-by-step method for making a simple fuel cell.
9 Find out what fuel cells look like and where they are used.

REDOX REACTIONS

- Rust is hydrated iron(III) oxide.
- Rusting needs oxygen and water:
  iron + oxygen + water → hydrated iron(III) oxide.
- *This is oxidation (loss of electrons).*
- *Reduction is gain of electrons.*
- *Oxidising agents take electrons.*
- *Reducing agents donate them.*
- Rusting is stopped by oil and grease, paint, tin, galvanising, sacrificial protection and alloying.
- Oil, grease, paint, tin and galvanising stop oxygen and water reaching the iron.
- *If the surface of the tin coating is scratched, the iron rusts faster.*
- *Zinc provides sacrificial protection. It donates electrons more easily than iron so rusting is prevented even if the layer is scratched.*

Now try this

d Label the reactions **oxidation (O)** or **reduction (R)**.

$Fe^{2+} \rightarrow Fe^{3+} + 1e^-$	______
$O_2 + 4H^+ + 4e^- \rightarrow 2H_2O$	______
$Fe \rightarrow Fe^{2+} + 2e^-$	______
$Pb^{2+} + 2e^- \rightarrow Pb$	______
$Cl_2 + 2e^- \rightarrow 2Cl^-$	______
$Mg \rightarrow Mg^{2+} + 2e^-$	______
$Zn + 2OH^- \rightarrow ZnO + H_2O + 2e^-$	______
$2H_2 \rightarrow 4H^+ + 4e^-$	______

TOP TIP These metals are in decreasing order of reactivity: magnesium, zinc, iron and tin.

Homework

10 Cars are made from steel. How could you stop yours rusting?
11 Find out why rusting is more serious than the corrosion of aluminium.
12 Explain why the displacement of copper by zinc is a redox reaction.

Chemistry out there 1

ALCOHOLS

- Alcohols are like water molecules with one hydrogen replaced by a hydrocarbon chain.
- They are solvents and renewable fuels.
- Their general formula is $C_nH_{(2n+1)}OH$.
- Example: C_2H_5OH – ethanol – which also makes alcoholic beverages.
- It is made by fermenting glucose, using yeast enzymes, in the absence of oxygen:
  sugar → ethanol + carbon dioxide.
  $C_6H_{12}O_6 \rightarrow 2CO_2 + 2C_2H_5OH$ (H)
- *Ethanol also forms when ethene and steam pass over a heated phosphoric acid catalyst: ethene + water → ethanol.* $C_2H_4 + H_2O \rightarrow C_2H_5OH_{(hydration)}$
- Ethanol is dehydrated to ethene by passing its vapour over heated aluminium oxide.

Now try this

a Match the compounds with their descriptions.

Methanol	dehydrated ethanol
Butanol	found in wine
Ethene	CH_3OH
Ethanol	C_3H_7OH
Propanol	hydrated ethene
	C_4H_9OH

TOP TIP If fermentation is not carried out in the absence of air, ethanol is oxidised to ethanoic acid.

Homework

1. Draw the displayed formulas of methanol and butanol.
2. Compare and contrast the **two** methods of making ethanol.
3. Find out how alcohol is concentrated to make fuels or spirits.

SODIUM CHLORIDE

- Salt is mined as rock salt, or by pumping water down to dissolve it (solution mining).
- Mining can cause subsidence.
- Electrolysis of sodium chloride solution (brine) gives sodium hydroxide to make soap, chlorine for sterilising water and making PVC, and hydrogen for margarine.
- Ions in solution Na^+, $Cl^-_{(from\ salt)}$ H^+, $OH^-_{(from\ water)}$.
- *At the cathode* $2H^+ + 2e^- \rightarrow H_2$.
- *At the anode* $2Cl^- - 2e^- \rightarrow Cl_2$.
- The ions not discharged make sodium hydroxide.
- Dilute sodium chloride solution produces oxygen.
- *Molten sodium chloride gives Na and* Cl_2.
- Sodium hydroxide and Cl_2 react to make bleach.

TOP TIP Chlorine bleaches damp indicator paper.

Now try this

b Tick the statements that are true.

- Sodium chloride is a mixture. ☐
- Electrolysis decomposes salty water. ☐
- Sodium is made by electrolysis of brine. ☐
- H_2, Cl_2 and NaOH are made from salt. ☐
- Cl_2 and NaOH react with each other ☐
- Cl_2 is produced at the anode (+). ☐
- O_2 is released by electrolysis of dilute salt solutions. ☐
- Electrolysis of $NaCl_{(l)}$ and $NaCl_{(aq)}$ gives the same products. ☐

Homework

4. Find out how bleach is made.
5. Prepare a presentation about products made from salt.
6. Explain how a solution of NaCl is converted to NaOH during electrolysis.

DEPLETION OF THE OZONE LAYER 1

- Ozone is a form of oxygen with the formula O_3, which absorbs harmful ultraviolet (UV) radiation.
- Increased UV can lead to sunburn, ageing skin, cataracts and skin cancer.
- Chlorofluorocarbons (CFCs) are organic molecules containing chlorine, fluorine and carbon atoms.
- *Scientists were initially enthusiastic about CFCs.*
- They were used as refrigerants and aerosol propellants.
- They are inert, insoluble and have low boiling points.
- *Since their role in ozone depletion was discovered*, most countries agreed they should be banned.
- Hydrocarbons or HFCs are a safer alternative.

TOP TIP As ozone levels fall, more UV light reaches Earth.

Now try this

c Fill in the missing words.

CFCs are small molecules containing ____________, ____________ and ____________ atoms. They were originally thought to be completely ____________. Later it was realised that they ____________ down in the stratosphere to release ____________ free radicals. These remain in the atmosphere for a ____________ time and are responsible for ____________ depletion.

Homework

7 Find out what CFCs were used for before their link with ozone was discovered.

8 Replacing CFCs can be expensive. Should countries be forced to ban them?

9 Which parts of the world are most affected by ozone depletion?

DEPLETION OF THE OZONE LAYER 2

- *Covalent bonds can break unevenly to form ions or evenly to form highly reactive free radicals.*
  For example, $CF_2Cl_2 \rightarrow CF_2Cl^+ + Cl^-$ *(ions)*
  $CF_2Cl_2 \rightarrow CF_2Cl^\cdot + Cl^\cdot$ *(free radicals)*
- Free radicals are produced when UV light hits CFCs in the stratosphere. They persist for a long time and deplete ozone, so more UV light reaches the Earth.
- *The chlorine catalyses a chain reaction.*
  $Cl + O_3 \rightarrow ClO + O_2$
  sunlight + $O_3 \rightarrow O + O_2$
  $O + ClO \rightarrow Cl + O_2$
  Overall $2O_3 \rightarrow 3O_2$

Now try this

d Match each formula to its name.

O_3	hydrocarbon
CF_2Cl_2	HFC
Cl^-	ozone
Cl	chloride ion
O	chlorine free radical
C_4H_{10}	CFC
CF_2H_2	oxygen free radical

TOP TIP CFCs deplete ozone long after their use has been banned because they persist in the atmosphere.

Homework

10 Research safe alternatives to CFCs.

11 Find out how ozone concentrations are monitored.

12 Explain why a single free radical can break down thousands of O_3 molecules.

Chemistry out there 2

HARDNESS OF WATER 1

- Calcium and magnesium ions make water hard.
- Permanent hardness is caused by calcium sulfate, temporary hardness by calcium hydrogen carbonate.
- Carbon dioxide makes water slightly acidic.
- Calcium carbonate (from chalk, limestone and marble) is insoluble, but it reacts with carbon dioxide solution to form soluble calcium hydrogen carbonate.
- *calcium carbonate + water + carbon dioxide → calcium hydrogen carbonate*
- Soft water makes lather with soap. Hard water does not.
- Both lather well with soapless detergents.

Now try this

a Match the chemicals with the correct descriptions.

Calcium carbonate	causes temporary hardness
Carbon dioxide	makes scum with hard water
Detergent	found in many rocks
Calcium sulfate	makes water acidic
Soap	causes permanent hardness
Calcium hydrogen carbonate	lathers with any water

TOP TIP Hard water helps produce strong teeth and bones, and prevent heart disease.

Homework

1. Plan an experiment to compare the hardness of **two** different sources of water.
2. Explain why some regions of the UK have harder water than others.
3. Find out how water softeners work.

HARDNESS OF WATER 2

- Hard water deposits limescale (calcium carbonate) in kettles etc, but it is removed by acids, for example, $CaCO_3 + 2HCl \rightarrow CaCl_2 + H_2O + CO_2$
- Weak acids are safer to use as descalers.
- Boiling removes temporary hardness.
- *calcium hydrogen carbonate → calcium carbonate + water + carbon dioxide*
- *Washing soda (sodium carbonate) softens hard water by precipitating the calcium ions.*
- *Ion-exchange resins swap calcium ions for sodium, which does not form insoluble compounds.*

TOP TIP Boiling removes temporary hardness.

Now try this

b Tick the statements that are true.

- Ion-exchange purifies water. ☐
- Carbonate ions precipitate calcium. ☐
- Acid breaks down limescale. ☐
- Boiling removes calcium ions. ☐
- Permanent hardness cannot be removed. ☐
- Washing soda removes any hardness. ☐
- Sulfate ions are removed by ion-exchange. ☐
- Boiling decomposes hydrogen carbonates. ☐

Homework

4. Research the ingredients used in domestic limescale removers.
5. Make a presentation to show how an ion-exchange resin works.
6. Use equations to show how sodium carbonate softens hard water.

See pages 153–167 of Collins GCSE Chemistry

NATURAL FATS AND OILS

- Oils and fats are esters of long chain fatty acids.
- Those with one C=C are 'monounsaturated'.
- Those with several C=Cs are 'polyunsaturated'.
- Unsaturated fats decolourise bromine water.
- Immiscible liquids (oil and water) make emulsions.
- Milk has oil drops dispersed in water.
- Butter has water drops dispersed in oil.
- Extra C=Cs make oils more runny, less viscous.
- Vegetable oils are reacted with H_2 to reduce the number of C=Cs and make fats for margarine.
- Sodium hydroxide makes fats undergo hydrolysis. fat + sodium hydroxide → soap + glycerol
- The process is called saponification.

Now try this

c Match each word to a description.

Sodium hydroxide	alkali
Soap	decolourises bromine
Unsaturated fat	hydrolysis of fats
Saponification	mixture of fats and oils
Hydrogen	contains C=C bonds
Margarine	used to saturate oils
	made from fats

TOP TIP Unsaturated fats are less likely to cause heart disease. There are more in plant oils than animal fats.

Homework

7 Draw a table to show the types of fat in **four** brands of margarine.

8 Prepare a presentation to show how oils react with hydrogen.

9 Research the health problems blamed on saturated fats.

ANALGESICS

- Drugs modify reactions in the body.
- Analgesics like aspirin, paracetamol and ibuprofen reduce pain, lower body temperature and thin the blood to reduce the risk of clots.
- Aspirin is manufactured from pure chemicals, but was originally extracted from willow bark.
- *Salicylic acid is heated with acid anhydride and phosphoric acid to make aspirin, which is an ester.*
- *Aspirin can cause stomach ulcers.*
- *The sodium or calcium salt of aspirin is more soluble because it has charged ions.*
- It is easier to swallow and is absorbed faster.
- It converts to aspirin in the stomach.

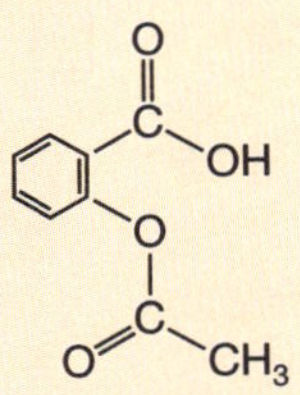

aspirin

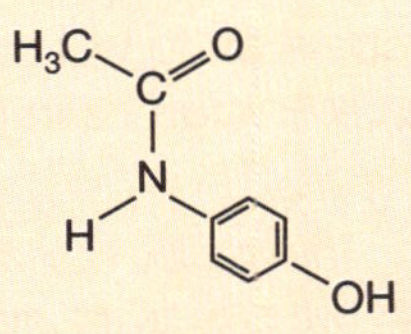

paracetamol

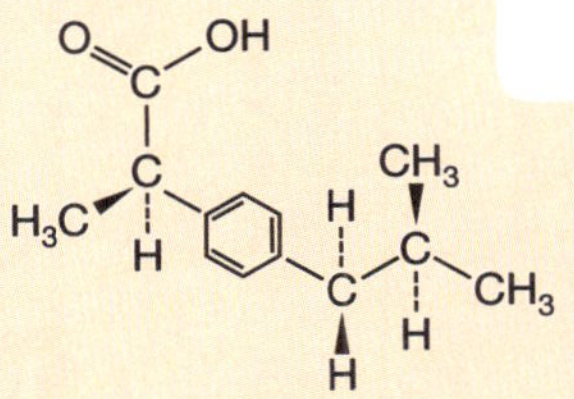

ibuprofen

Now try this

d Match the analgesic(s) to each description. Write A for aspirin, I for ibuprofen and P for paracetemol.

Found in willow bark ______

Contains an acid (O=C–O–H) group ______

Contains an amide (O=C–N–H) group ______

Is an ester of salicylic acid ______

Contains three methyl (–CH_3) groups ______

Contains a hydroxyl (–O–H) group that is not part of an acid ______

TOP TIP Pharmacists supervise medicine sales. Analgesics are sold in limited quantities to reduce the risk of a fatal overdose.

Homework

10 Work out the molecular formulae of aspirin, paracetamol and ibruprofen.

11 Plan an experiment to compare the solubility of aspirin and soluble aspirin.

12 Write an illustrated description of the preparation of aspirin from salicylic acid.

Space for reflection 1

GRAVITY AND CIRCULAR MOTION

- Gravitational force keeps a satellite (natural or artificial) or a planet in orbit.
- The planets orbit the Sun and satellites orbit planets.
- Gravitational force is an attractive force and it decreases with increased separation.
- A geostationary satellite orbits the Earth once every 24 hours.
- The gravitational force on a satellite provides the centripetal force for its circular orbit.
- The orbital period of an artificial satellite increases with increasing height from the Earth's surface.
- Gravitational force decreases when the distance or separation is increased:

  (gravitational force $\propto \frac{1}{distance^2}$*).*
- *A planet closer to the Sun has a shorter orbital period because the gravitational force of the Sun is stronger.*

Now try this

a Circle the correct word in each sentence.

Planets move round the Sun because of:

gravitational   magnetic force.

The gravitational force between objects is always:

repulsive   attractive.

A satellite orbits the:

Sun   planet.

Homework

1 Describe the motion and uses of artificial satellites.

2 Draw a mind map for this section.

VECTORS AND EQUATIONS OF MOTION

- A scalar quantity only has size (magnitude) – for example, speed and mass.
- A vector quantity has both size (magnitude) and direction – for example, velocity and force.
- Average speed does not depend on the direction of travel.
- *Two vectors can be added by drawing a vector diagram.*
- For an accelerating object, the equations of motion are:

$v = u + at \quad s = (\frac{v + u}{2})t \quad v^2 = u^2 + 2as \quad s = ut + \frac{1}{2}at^2$

Now try this

b Tick the correct statements.

Force and speed are both vectors. ☐

Two cars are travelling at 10 m/s in the same direction. Their relative speed is 20 m/s. ☐

The final speed of a car accelerating will be greater than its initial speed. ☐

TOP TIP The relative speed is higher if two objects are moving in opposite directions.

Homework

3 Make a list of some vector and some scalar quantities.

4 An object is acted upon by forces of 10 N and 30 N. Using diagrams, explain the maximum and minimum values of the total force.

PROJECTILES AND MOMENTUM

- A projectile is an object thrown or fired at an angle to the Earth's gravitational field.
- The trajectory or path of an object projected horizontally on the earth is curved or parabolic.
- For an object projected horizontally, the horizontal velocity remains the same but there is acceleration in the vertical direction.
- You can use the equations of motion for the vertical motion of a projectile.
- When two objects interact, each object exerts an equal but opposite force on the other object. 'Action' = 'Reaction'.
- momentum = mass × velocity (Unit: kg m/s)
- *force* = $\frac{\textit{change in momentum}}{\textit{time}}$
- *In all collisions and explosions, momentum is always conserved.*

Now try this

c **Are the following statements true (T) or false (F)?**

A football is an example of a projectile. ______

Momentum is a vector quantity. ______

A car hits a wall with a force of 2000 N. The force on the car due to the wall is also 2000 N. ______

Two cars collide. The total momentum remains the same. ______

Homework

5 Make a list of projectiles.

6 Use the ideas of momentum and force to explain how a seat belt works.

SATELLITE COMMUNICATIONS

- Radio waves below 30 MHz are reflected by the Earth's upper atmosphere called the ionosphere.
- Radio waves are 'spread' around or diffracted by large objects.
- *Diffraction of a wave is more noticeable when the size of the gap is comparable to the wavelength.*
- Radio waves above 30 GHz are absorbed and scattered by rain and dust.
- An aerial is needed for reception of radio waves and a 'dish' is needed for satellite TV signals.
- Longwave radio waves carry signals by amplitude modulation (AM) and have a very long range.

Now try this

d **Match the questions with the correct answers.**

What is the spreading of a wave called?	ionosphere
What causes low frequency radio waves to be reflected?	rain
What absorbs high frequency radio waves?	diffraction

Homework

7 Use a labelled diagram to show how the ionosphere reflects radio waves.

8 In your own words explain why longwave radio waves have a long range compared with microwaves.

Space for reflection 2

NATURE OF WAVES

- Interference takes place when two waves overlap.
- Interference of two sound waves produces louder and quieter regions of sound.
- Interference of two light waves produces bright and dark regions of light.
- Reinforcement of waves is known as constructive interference. Cancellation of waves is known as destructive interference.
- *The path difference for constructive interference is* $0, \lambda, 2\lambda, 3\lambda$, *etc.*
- *The path difference for destructive interference is* $0, \frac{\lambda}{2}, 1\frac{1}{2}\lambda, 2\frac{1}{2}\lambda$, *etc.*
- Only transverse waves (for example, electromagnetic waves) can be plane polarised.
- A plane polarised wave has vibrations in just one plane.

Now try this

a Are the following statements **true (T)** or **false (F)**?

Interference is the same as diffraction. ______

A bright patch of light is produced when light interferes constructively. ______

Interference occurs when waves combine. ______

Sound cannot be polarised because it is not a transverse wave. ______

TOP TIP Light is a wave because it can be diffracted and made to interfere.

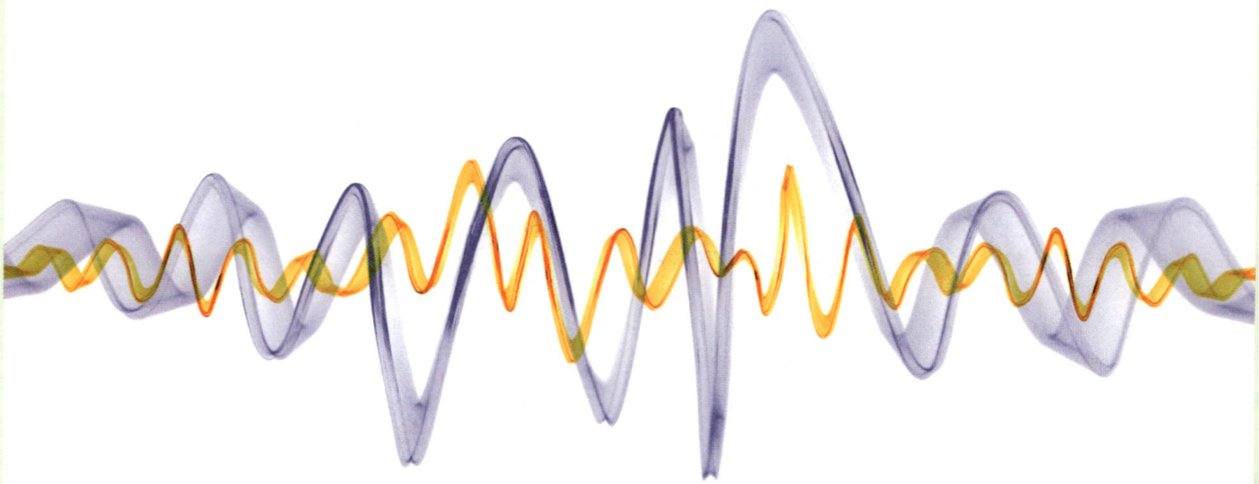

Homework

1 Use diagrams to describe constructive interference and destructive interference.

2 Write a few sentences on diffraction, interference and path difference.

REFRACTION OF WAVES

- Refraction is the bending of a wave as it travels between mediums.
- Refraction at the boundary between two mediums occurs because of change in the speed of light.
- A ray of light bends more if the change of speed is greater or the refractive index is larger.
- *refractive index* = $\dfrac{\textit{speed of light in vacuum}}{\textit{speed of light in medium}}$
- *Snell's law: refractive index* = $\dfrac{\textit{sin (angle of incidence)}}{\textit{sin (angle of refraction)}}$

$$n = \frac{\sin i}{\sin r}$$

- Dispersion is the splitting of light into its different colours by a prism. This is due to refraction.
- Blue light is deviated more than red light through a prism.
- *A material (for example, glass) has different refractive indices for different colours.*

Now try this

b Match each key word with the correct definition.

The bending of light	dispersion
The spreading of light	refraction
The splitting of light into different colours	refractive index
Different materials have different values of …	diffraction

Homework

3 Using a labelled diagram, describe the conditions necessary for total internal reflection.

4 You are given a block of plastic. Describe an experiment to find the refractive index of the plastic.

OPTICS

- A convex lens is a converging lens. It is thicker at its centre.
- Parallel rays of light passing through a convex lens pass through the focal point (focus).
- The focal length of a lens is the distance between the lens and the focus.
- 'Fatter' convex lenses have shorter focal lengths.
- Projectors and cameras produce real images – these can be formed on a screen.
- *Real images formed by a convex lens are always inverted.*
- A convex lens can be used as a magnifying glass when the object is between the lens and the focus.
- A ray diagram can be drawn to find the location of an image.
- *magnification* = $\dfrac{\textit{image size}}{\textit{object size}}$.

Now try this

c Circle the correct word in each sentence.

A convex lens bends parallel rays:
away towards the axis.

A thinner convex lens has a:
shorter longer focal length.

A camera lens produces a:
real virtual image of an object.

A real image is always:
upright inverted.

Homework

5 Draw a ray diagram to show the focal point (focus) and focal length of a convex lens.

6 Draw a ray diagram for an object placed at a distance of 1.5 times the focal length from the centre of the lens. Describe the properties of the image.

Electricity for gadgets 1

RESISTING

- The resistance of wire kept at constant temperature remains the same but increases as its temperature increases.
- Ohm's law states: The current in the conductor is directly proportional to the voltage across its ends as long as its temperature remains constant.
- A graph of current against voltage for an ohmic conductor is a straight line through the origin.
- A filament lamp is a non-ohmic component. Its resistance increases as the current (or pd) is increased.
- *resistance* = $\frac{voltage}{current}$
- A variable resistor can be used to control the size of the current in a circuit.

Now try this

a Circle the correct word in each sentence.

An ohmic conductor has a resistance of 10 Ω at 2.0 A. The resistance is:

doubled the same at 4.0 A.

A resistance of a metal wire:

increases decreases when it is cooler.

Current is voltage:

divided multiplied by resistance.

Homework

1 Sketch the current against voltage graphs for a wire kept at constant temperature and a filament lamp. In each case, describe how the current affects the resistance.

2 Find out how and why the resistance of a wire changes with temperature.

SHARING

- A potential divider has two or more components connected in series to a supply. The voltage is measured across one of the components using a voltmeter.
- The resistance of an LDR decreases as the intensity of light is increased.
- The resistance of a thermistor (ntc type) decreases as its temperature is increased.
- *The output voltage V_{out} across the resistor of resistance R2 for a potential divider is given by:*

$$V_{out} = V_{in} \left(\frac{R_2}{R_1 + R_2}\right)$$

where V_{in} is the input voltage and R_1 is the resistance of the remaining resistor.

Now try this

b Tick the correct statements.

The output from a potential divider is measured using a voltmeter. ☐

Altering the temperature of an LDR will change its resistance. ☐

A thermistor can be used to monitor the temperature of a greenhouse. ☐

Homework

3 Draw a potential divider circuit and write a short paragraph on what it does.

4 Design a potential divider for monitoring the temperature of a greenhouse.

MOTORS AND GENERATING

- A current-carrying wire is surrounded by a circular magnetic field.
- A current-carrying wire placed at right angles to a magnetic field experiences a force.
- *Fleming's left hand-rule:*
  thuMb → **M**otion, **F**irst *finger* → **F**ield *and seCond finger* → **C**urrent.
- An electric motor has a (rectangular) coil that turns in a magnetic field.
- Increasing the current, having more turns on the coil and using a stronger magnetic field will increase the speed of the motor.
- A voltage is induced across the ends of a wire when it 'cuts' the magnetic field.
- The size of the induced voltage across the ends of a wire is bigger when it moves faster through a stronger magnetic field.
- A simple generator consists of a coil rotating in a magnetic field.
- In the UK, the mains voltage is alternating voltage of frequency 50 Hz.

Now try this

c Match the beginnings and endings to make complete sentences.

Beginning	Ending
A generator produces an	50 Hz.
To induce a current in a wire you have to move it in a	frequency and voltage.
The mains frequency is	magnetic field.
Rotating the coil of a generator faster increases the	alternating voltage.

Homework

5 Draw the magnetic field patterns for a straight current-carrying wire and a solenoid. Describe the field pattern in each case.

6 Describe the factors affecting the size of the induced voltage in a coil rotating in a magnetic field.

TRANSFORMERS

- A transformer changes the size of alternating current or voltage.
- A step-down transformer reduces voltage and a step-up transformer increases voltage.
- Step-down transformers are used in phone chargers, radios and laptops.
- Power stations use step-up transformers for transmission cables of the National Grid.
- *Changing the magnetic field in the primary coil induces an output voltage at the secondary coil.*
- The turn-ratio equation for a transformer: $\frac{V_p}{V_s} = \frac{N_p}{N_s}$
- *For a 100% efficient transformer:* $V_pI_p = V_sI_s$

Now try this

d Match each question with the correct answer.

Where might you find a step-down transformer?	AC
What is the name for the output coil of a transformer?	a laptop
What type of current is needed for a transformer to work?	secondary

Homework

7 List the devices in your home that may have transformers.

8 Draw a labelled diagram for a transformer. Explain how the number of turns on the secondary and primary coils affects the output voltage.

Electricity for gadgets 2

CHARGING

- A diode allows current to flow in one direction.
- A silicon diode conducts when the voltage across it is greater than about 0.6 V.
- The conduction in a silicon diode is due to both electrons and holes.
- The resistance of the silicon diode is infinite for negative voltages and voltages less than 0.6 V. The resistance decreases as the voltage increases beyond 0.6 V.
- A single diode and a resistor can be used to produce half-wave rectification.
- A combination of four resistors (bridge circuit) and a resistor can be used to produce full-wave rectification.
- A capacitor stores charge which can be discharged later.
- The voltage across a charging capacitor increases and the voltage decreases when the capacitor discharges.
- A capacitor connected across the resistor of a rectifier can produce a smooth or constant voltage.

Now try this

a Tick the correct statements.

A capacitor stores current. ☐

A half-wave rectifier has one diode and one resistor. ☐

The resistance of a diode depends on the voltage across it. ☐

Homework

1 Draw a diagram of a half-wave rectifier. Show how the circuit can be modified to give a smooth output voltage.

2 Draw a diagram of a full-wave rectifier. Show how the circuit can be modified to give a smooth output voltage.

IT'S LOGICAL

- The input and output for a logic gate can either be a 'high' voltage (logic 1) or 'low' voltage (logic 0).
- NOT gate

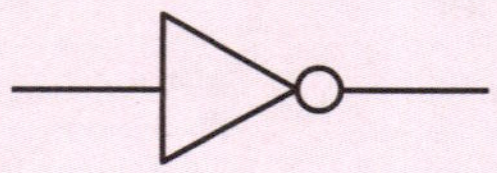

Truth table

input	output
low	high
high	low

- *Other logic gates and their truth tables:*

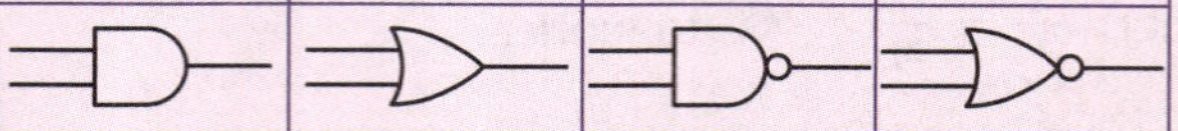

Inputs		AND	OR	NAND	NOR
A	B				
low	low	low	low	high	high
low	high	low	high	high	low
high	low	low	high	high	low
high	high	high	high	low	low

← outputs →

Now try this

b Are the following statements **true (T)** or **false (F)**?

A NOT gate 'inverts' the input signal. ______

A NAND gate is really an AND gate followed by a NOT gate. ______

A NOR gate is really an OR gate followed by a NOT gate. ______

TOP TIP A combination of logic gates can be used as burglar alarms.

See pages 236–247 of Collins GCSE Physics

Homework

3 Draw a mind map for this section with all the logic gates and their truth tables.

4 Make a list of situations where you can use logic gates.

EVEN MORE LOGIC

- A potential divider can provide input signals of 'highs' and 'lows' with a resistor in series with an LDR or thermistor or a switch.

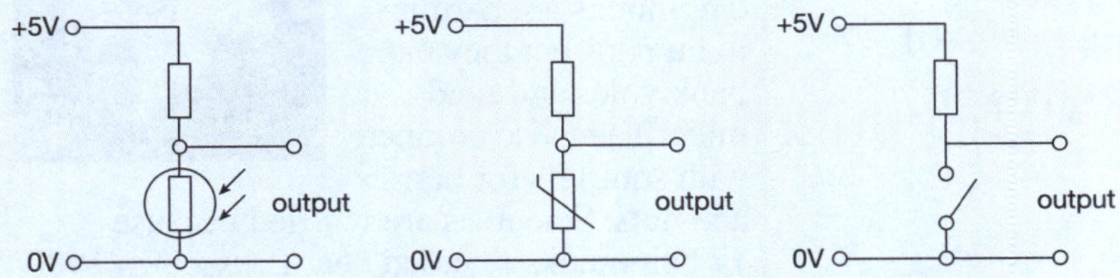

- An LED can be used to show the state of a logic gate.
- The LED always has a safety resistor in series.
- A latch in a car or burglar alarm stays on once triggered.
- *A bistable latch can be constructed from two NAND gates or two NOR gates.*

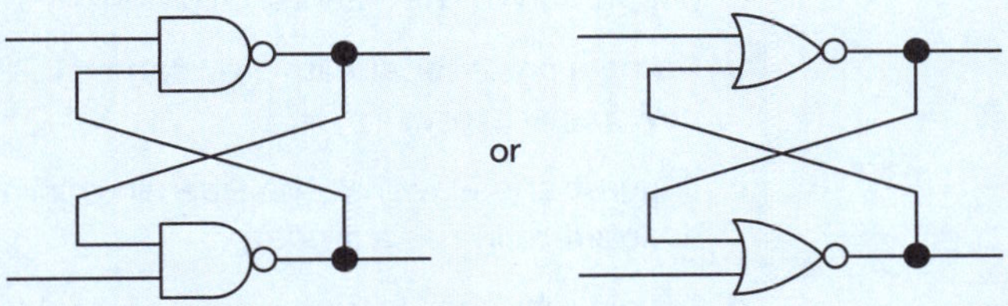

- A relay consists of a coil and a switch.

- A small current in the relay coil can be used to switch on a circuit requiring much larger current (for example, mains circuit).

Now try this

c Tick the correct statements.

An LED is lit when the output is 'high' from a logic gate. ☐

The output from a latch remains either high or low once it is triggered. ☐

A relay has a coil and a separate switch. ☐

A relay can be used to activate a mains circuit. ☐

Homework

5 List possible circuits that use a latch in your home.

6 Draw a circuit for a bistable latch. Explain how your circuit works.

Exam-style questions

Biology Units B1 and B2

1 Rosa is training for the Olympics.

a Her blood pressure is recorded as 140/80 mmHg.

i What do the figures 140/80 show? Circle the correct answer.

arterial and venal   **breathing rate**
diastolic and systolic   **pulse rate** [1]

ii What does mmHg mean? Circle the correct answer.

millimetres of mercury
micromoles of pressure
millilitres of helium [1]

b Rosa sweats when she exercises.

i Why does she sweat? [1]

ii What happens to the sweat on her skin? [2]

c When Rosa is fatigued she has an oxygen debt. Explain what is meant by an oxygen debt.

Include in your answer:

- what happens to glucose
- a word equation for the type of respiration involved
- what happens to the waste product. [3]

d Rosa's body temperature is kept constant.

i What is keeping the body temperature constant called? [1]

ii A negative feedback mechanism is used to control body temperature.
Explain what is meant by a negative feedback mechanism. [1]

[Total marks 10]

2 Read the following newspaper story.

The hunt for invaders

A number of Siberian chipmunks have escaped from an estate in Hampshire. Siberian chipmunks are harmless to humans but they eat bank voles and field mice. They also compete with squirrels for berries and nuts. Scientists are worried because 17 chipmunks released near Brussels in 1980 became 18 000 after 20 years. Local farmers complained that the chipmunks were eating their crops.

a Suggest and explain one way to estimate the population of the Siberian chipmunk. [2]

b Name a predator and its prey named in the newspaper story. [2]

c Suggest one way that the Siberian chipmunk is adapted to live as a predator. [1]

d Explain why the Siberian chipmunk could become successful in England. [2]

e Some scientists think that Natural Selection will limit the numbers of Siberian chipmunks in England. Explain what is meant by Natural Selection. [3]

[Total marks 10]

Chemistry Units C1 and C2

1 Dirty washing-up water looks cloudy because it contains tiny drops of oil.

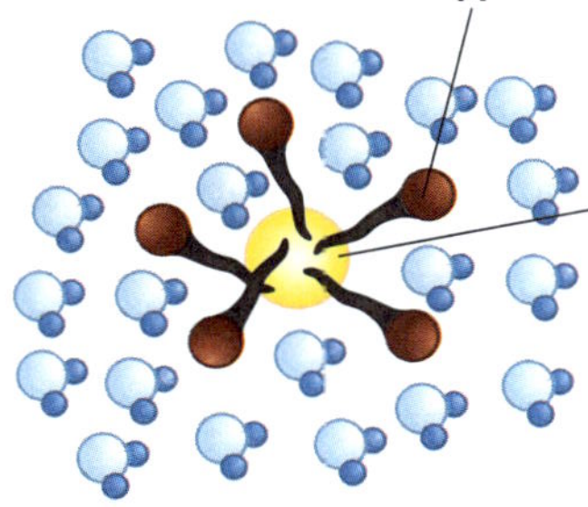

a What type of molecule is X? [1]

b What name is given to mixtures like this? [1]

c What would happen if X was absent? [2]

d Explain why X surrounds each drop of grease. [4]

e Many foods are emulsions. Name one. [1]

[Total marks 9]

2 Eniola is painting with oils.

a Oil paints are colloids. Explain what this means. [2]

b What can be added to make paint more spreadable? [1]

c List the changes that take place as oil paint dries. [3]

d Some paints are thermochromic. What is special about them? [2]

[Total marks 8]

Physics Units P1 and P2

1 For a particular petrol car, 50 MJ of the chemical energy from the fuel is transformed into 24 MJ of kinetic energy.

a Explain why the kinetic energy is not equal to the chemical energy. [1]

b Use the equation below to calculate the efficiency of the car.

$$\text{efficiency} = \frac{\text{output useful energy}}{\text{total input energy}}$$ [3]

[Total marks 4]

2 a Explain what is meant by the wavelength of a wave. [1]

b Light and microwaves are both electromagnetic waves. State two properties of electromagnetic waves. [2]

c Here are some possible statements about microwaves. Place a tick (✓) in the appropriate column. [3]

Statement	False	True
Microwaves can be reflected by metal.		
Microwaves are the same as ultrasound.		
Microwaves can heat or burn body tissues.		

d An insect on the surface of a pond flaps its wings at a frequency of 200 Hz and creates ripples on the surface of the water of wavelength 0.01 m. Use the equation below to find the speed of ripples on the surface of water.

speed = wavelength × frequency [3]

[Total marks 9]

3 A solar panel consists of a number of photocells.

a State the energy transformation for a photocell. [1]

b What type of current does a photocell produce? [1]

c State one advantage and one disadvantage of using a solar panel for a house. [2]

d Describe two ways in which the output power from a solar panel can be increased. [2]

[Total marks 6]

4 **a** Place the following planets in the order of increasing distance from the Sun. [1]

Jupiter **Venus** **Earth** **Uranus**

b Explain why Mercury has a greater orbital speed than Mars. [2]

c Describe two likely problems of manned space travel to a distant planet. [2]

[Total marks 5]

Additional Biology B3 and B4

1 **a** Complete the following sentences about the nucleus using the words below.

chromosomes	**cytoplasm**	**DNA**
FSH	**genes**	**mitochondria**

The nucleus contains strands called

____

They carry coded information in the form of

____

The information is carried in a chemical called

____________________ [3]

b Read these statements about DNA. Tick (✓) the two correct statements.

DNA is an enzyme. ☐

Every person's DNA is the same. ☐

DNA is arranged in a double helix. ☐

DNA controls the synthesis of proteins. ☐

The cross links in DNA are formed by three bases. ☐ [2]

c DNA replicates itself. Explain how this is done. [2]

d DNA fingerprinting can be used to help solve crimes.

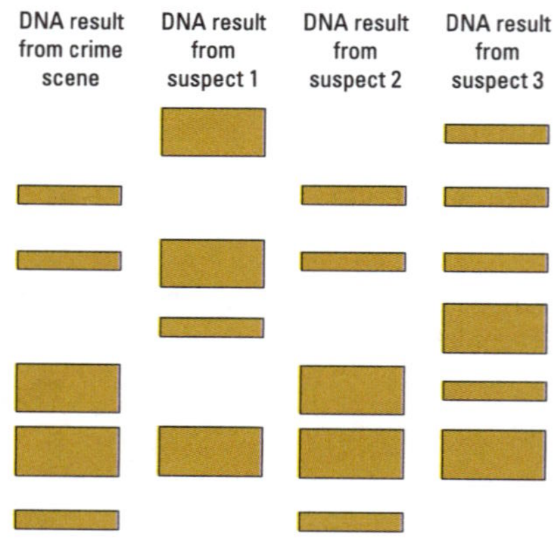

Look at the results of DNA samples taken from three suspects and compare them to the DNA sample taken at the crime scene.

i Which suspect committed the crime? Explain your answer. [1]

ii List the stages in the production of a DNA fingerprint. Write them in the correct order.

1 ____________________

2 ____________________

3 ____________________

4 ____________________ [2]

[Total marks 10]

2 **a** Complete the following sentences about water uptake in plants, using the words below.

leaves **osmosis** **transpiration**
permeable **root hairs** **semi-permeable**

Water is absorbed by ____________

The water is absorbed by the process of

____

This takes place through the ____________ membrane in the cells. [3]

b Plants A, B, and C are each lacking one mineral.

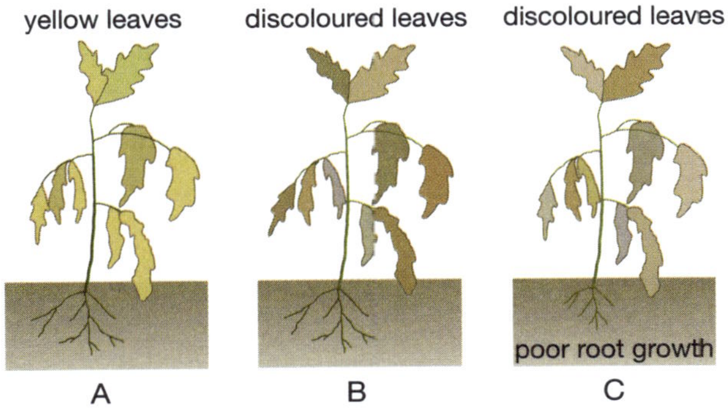

i Which plant is lacking potassium?

ii Which plant is lacking nitrates?

iii Which plant is lacking phosphates? [2]

c Fungi living on plant roots are called mycorrhiza. Look at the graph showing the effect of mycorrhiza on mineral uptake.

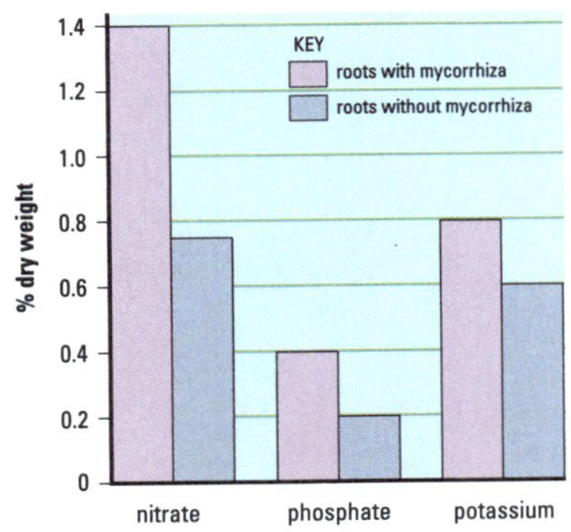

i Describe the general pattern shown by this graph. [1]

ii Write down one advantage and one disadvantage of growing plants in sterile soil. [2]

d Minerals are not absorbed by osmosis or diffusion. Describe how they are absorbed. [2]

[Total marks 10]

Additional Chemistry C3 and C4

1 Magnesium and carbon both burn in air.

Magnesium oxide is a white solid.
Carbon dioxide is a colourless gas.

a Draw the particles in each solid. [4]

b What name is given to the bonding in magnesium oxide? [1]

c Use diagrams to explain why the particles in magnesium oxide are charged. [4]

d Explain why carbon dioxide is:

i very volatile [2]

ii hard to decompose. [2]

e Show how the outer electrons are arranged in a molecule of CO_2. [2]

[Total marks 15]

2 This apparatus can be used to prepare a small sample of fertiliser.

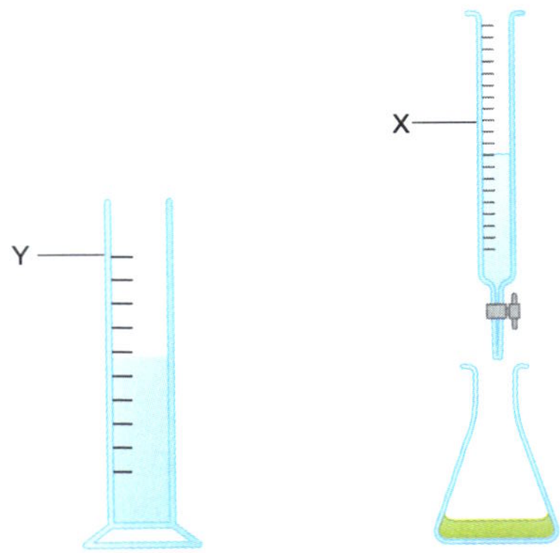

a X is ____________

Y is ____________ [2]

b Name the acid and alkali needed to make ammonium nitrate, NH_4NO_3. [2]

c Calculate the percentage of nitrogen in the compound. [2]

d Explain why the fertiliser should be kept away from river water. [6]

[Total marks 12]

Additional Physics P3 and P4

1 **a** For a particular journey, the distance travelled by a car in a time of 1 hour (3600 s) is 60 km. What is the average speed of the car in m/s? [3]

b A car travelling at 20 m/s has a braking distance of 20 m and a thinking distance of 10 m.

i Explain what is meant by braking distance. [1]

ii Determine the reaction time of the driver. [2]

iii Calculate the stopping distance of the car at this speed. [1]

iv State two factors that would increase the braking distance of the car. [2]

[Total marks 9]

2 **a** Using the axes below, draw a graph for an object:

i travelling at a constant speed [1]

ii travelling with a constant acceleration. [1]

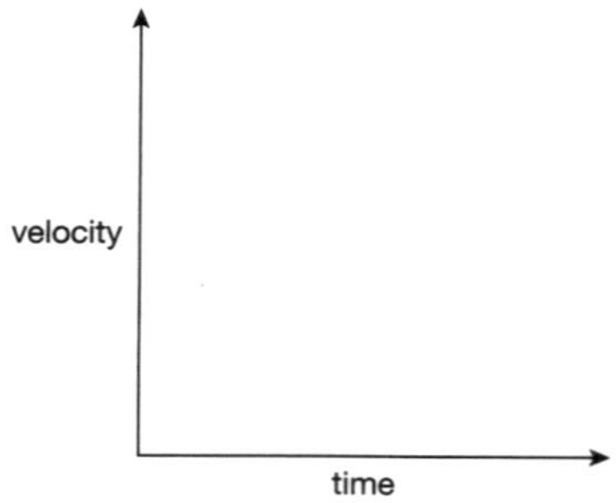

b What is the gradient of a velocity against time graph equal to? [1]

c A racing car travelling at a speed of 40 m/s crashes into a safety barrier and comes to a halt after a time of 2.5 seconds. Calculate the average deceleration of the car. [3]

[Total marks 6]

3 A student connects up the following circuit.

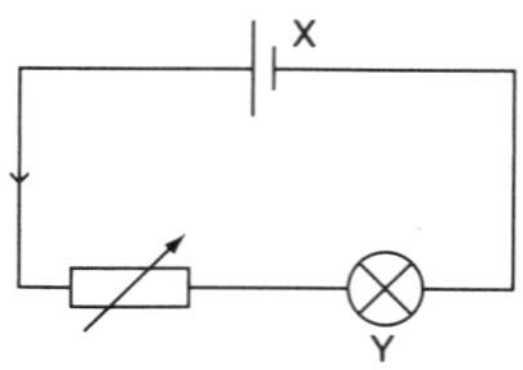

a Name the component X. [1]

b Name the component Y. [1]

c Calculate the resistance of the component Y when the potential difference across it is 6.0 V and the current in the circuit is 0.2 A. [3]

d Explain what happens to the component Y as the resistance of the variable resistor is increased. [2]

[Total marks 7]

4 **a** State one difference and one similarity between gamma rays and X-rays. [2]

b Explain how gamma rays are used in the treatment of cancer. [2]

c What are helium particles? [2]

d A particular nucleus emits an alpha particle. Describe how you can determine the mass and atomic numbers of the nucleus left behind (daughter nucleus). [2]

[Total marks 8]

GCSE Biology B5 and B6

1 **a** What type of blood circulatory system do we have? Tick (✓) the **two** correct descriptions.

open ☐

closed ☐

single ☐

double ☐ [2]

b Look at the diagram of a human heart.

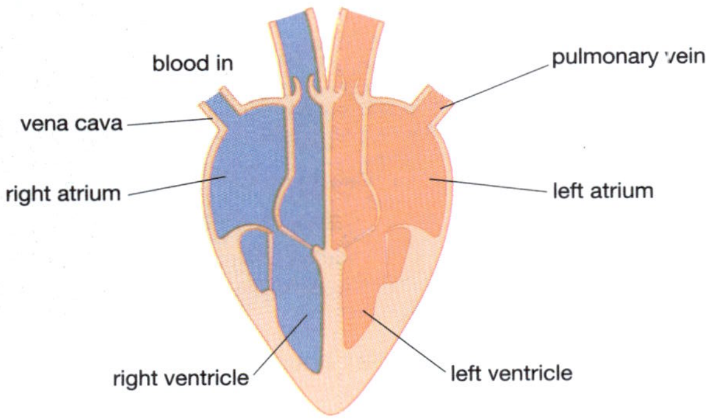

i Draw arrows on a copy of the diagram to show the direction of blood flow through all parts of the heart [1]

ii On your diagram, label a valve. [1]

iii What is the job of a valve? [1]

c Some babies are born with a 'hole in the heart'.

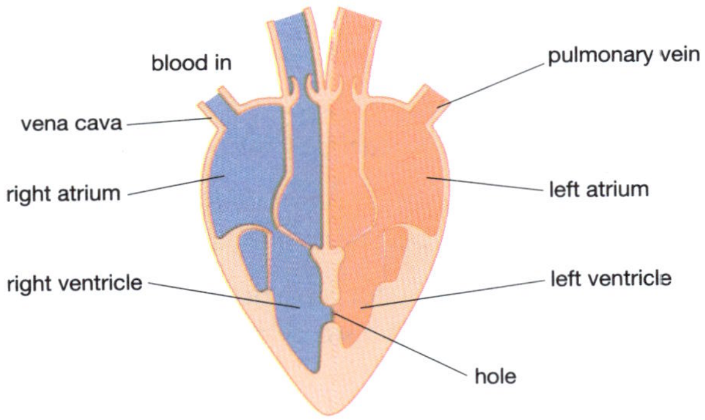

i Explain what problems this will cause to the baby. [3]

ii Serious heart problems can be solved by a heart transplant.
Describe two problems of using a heart transplant. [2]

[Total marks 10]

2 After a party, Mike finds food stains on his shirt. His mum tells him to use a biological washing powder to remove the stains.
The washing powder contains protease and lipase.

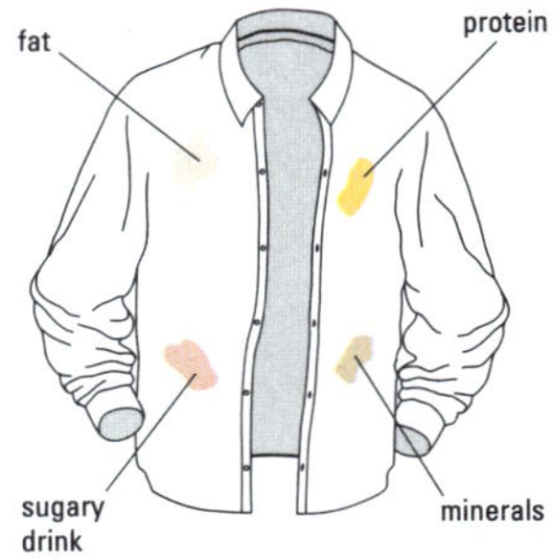

a Which two stains will be removed by this washing powder? [2]

b The instructions on the packet state 'Wash at 40 °C'. Explain what will happen if a higher temperature is used. [2]

c Why will the stains not be removed if the water used in the washing machine has a pH of 4? [1]

d Explain how protease and lipase remove some stains from the shirt. [3]

e Some people are lactose-intolerant.
Explain how immobilised enzymes can be used to produce lactose-free milk. [2]

[Total marks 10]

GCSE Chemistry C5 and C6

1 Sulfur dioxide pollution is decreasing in the UK. Most of the gas produced industrially is converted to sulfuric acid.

a Write a symbol equation for the formation of sulfur dioxide from its elements. [2]

b The reaction that converts sulfur dioxide to sulfur trioxide is reversible.
Write the equation. [2]

c List the conditions used in the Contact Process. [3]

d Why is the temperature used described as a compromise? [3]

[Total marks 10]

2 When the body of a car rusts, it is seriously weakened.

a What is rust? [2]

b Why is rusting classed as a redox reaction? [3]

c How do oil, paint and coatings of tin stop iron rusting? [2]

d Explain why galvanising iron is much more effective in the long term than plating it with tin. [4]

[Total marks 11]

GCSE Physics P5 and P6

1 A satellite is in a geostationary orbit above the equator.

a Name the force that keeps the satellite in an orbit round the Earth. [1]

b What is the period of a satellite in a geostationary orbit? [1]

c The orbit of the satellite is a circle and it has a constant speed. Describe the force acting on the satellite and the acceleration of the satellite. [2]

d What are satellites in a geostationary orbit used for? [1]

[Total marks 5]

2 **a** Explain what is meant by refraction of light. [1]

b Describe two conditions necessary for total internal reflection at an air/glass boundary. [2]

c The critical angle for a particular glass is 42°. Complete the diagram below for the incident ray shown.

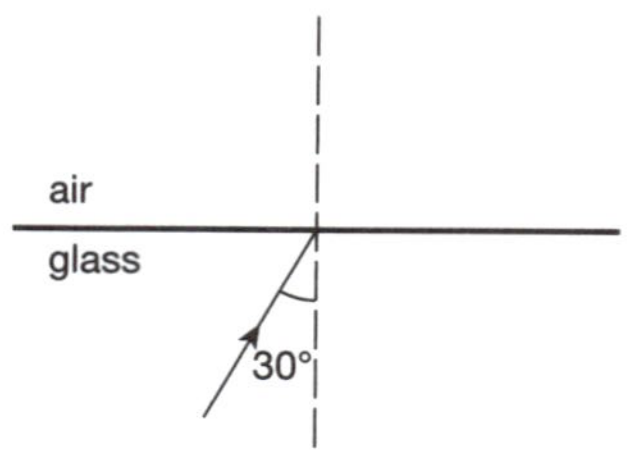

[3]

[Total marks 6]

3 **a** Explain what is meant by an Ohmic component and give one example. [2]

b i Using the axes below, draw a graph to show the characteristic of a filament lamp. [2]

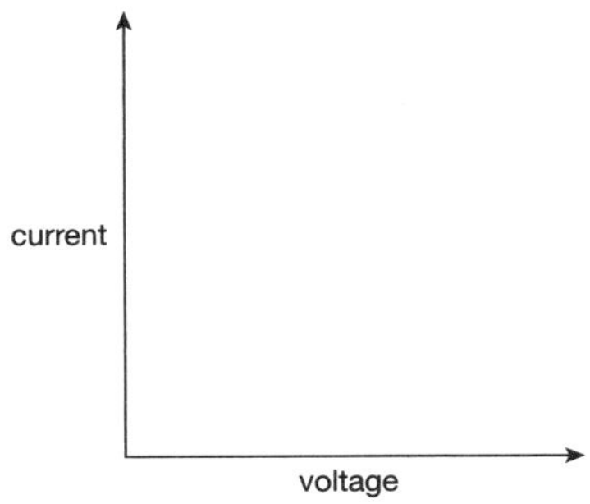

ii Explain how you can determine the resistance of the lamp at a particular voltage. [2]

iii Describe how the resistance of the lamp changes as the current in the lamp increases. [2]

[Total marks 8]

4 All modern digital devices use logic gates to process information.

a Explain what is meant by a digital signal. [1]

b A single OR gate has inputs A and B. Complete the truth table below for this gate. [1]

A	B	Output
0	0	
0	1	
1	0	
1	1	

c A student constructs the logic circuit shown below.

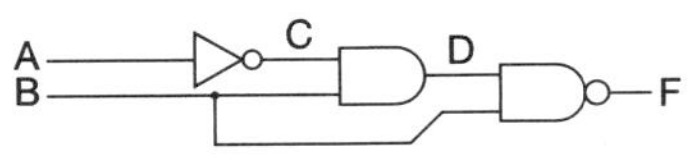

Complete the truth table for this circuit. [3]

A	B	C	D	E
0	0			
0	1			
1	0			
1	1			

[Total marks 5]

Model answers

Biology B1 and B2

1 At school, Josie and Evie do an experiment on exercise.

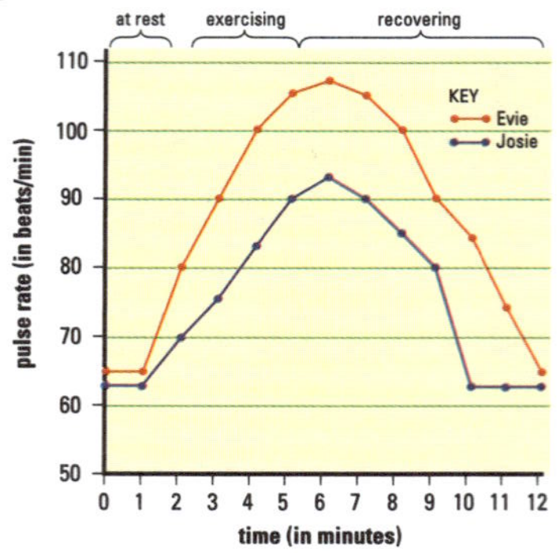

a Which process in their bodies will release energy? [1]

Respiration

b Which gas will be:

i used up? [1]

Oxygen

ii released? [1]

Carbon dioxide

c Josie and Evie measure their pulse rates during the experiment.

i Evie's pulse rate increased by 42 beats per minute.
What is the increase in Josie's pulse rate?
Show your working. [2]

93 – 63 = 30 beats per minute

ii Why do their pulse rates increase during exercise? [3]

To increase the blood supply to their muscles.
To get more food and energy to their muscles.

'To get rid of more carbon dioxide' is also an acceptable answer.

iii After their exercise, their muscles ached.
Explain why. [2]

Lactic acid from anaerobic respiration had collected in their muscles.

2 As part of their experiment on exercise, Josie and Evie measure their pulse rates before, during and after their exercise.

a Look again at their results in the graph in question 1.
How do the results show that Josie is fitter then Evie? [2]

Josie has a faster recovery time than Evie. Her pulse rate shows a smaller increase than Evie's. It increases by only 30, but Evie's pulse rate increases by 42.

b After their hard exercise they breathe heavily.
Explain why. [2]

During hard exercise they will be using anaerobic respiration. This causes an oxygen debt.

'To get more oxygen and get rid of more carbon dioxide' is also an acceptable answer.

c During the exercise they will use both aerobic and anaerobic respiration.

i Write down the word equation for anaerobic respiration in muscles. [2]

glucose → lactic acid + energy

ii Write down the balanced symbol equation for aerobic respiration. [2]

$C_6H_{12}O_6 + 6O_2 \rightarrow 6H_2O + 6CO_2$

'+ energy' is not usually required.

iii Explain why anaerobic respiration releases less energy than aerobic respiration. [2]

The glucose molecules are not broken down completely.

3 Arif has many plants in his garden.

a The plants compete with each other.

i Name two things that plants compete for above ground. [2]

Sunlight and space

ii Name two things that plants compete for below ground. [2]

Water and minerals

b There are ladybirds in Arif's garden. The ladybirds eat greenfly, which feed on Arif's plants. Frogs eat the ladybirds.

i Using only these organisms, name a predator and its prey. [1]

Frogs and ladybirds

'Ladybirds and greenfly' is also an acceptable answer.

ii Animals also compete. Write down two things that animals will compete for. [2]

Food and mates

'Shelter and water' are also acceptable answers.

4 Arif visits a local zoo and sees some camels. Explain three ways in which camels are adapted to life in the desert. [3]

They have bushy eyebrows and hairy nostrils to keep sand out.
They have large feet to spread their weight, so they do not sink into the sand.
They store fat in their hump so they can survive for a long period without food.

5 The plants in Hardeep's garden use photosynthesis to produce glucose.

a What can happen to this glucose? [3]

It can be used as a source of energy for growth.
It can be changed into starch for storage.
It can be changed into other chemicals, such as cellulose to make new cell walls.

b The rate of photosynthesis can be limited by certain conditions.
Name two limiting factors for photosynthesis. [2]

Amount of carbon dioxide and light intensity.

Temperature is also a limiting factor.

c Hardeep grows cacti in her garden. Cacti usually grow in deserts.

i Describe how cacti are adapted to hot, dry conditions. [3]

They have long roots to reach as much water as possible.
They have a thick cuticle to reduce water loss.
Their leaves are reduced to spines to reduce water loss.

'They store water in their fleshy stems' is also an acceptable answer.

ii Explain how and why cacti attract insects and birds. [2]

The cacti flowers have colourful petals and sweet nectar to attract them.
The insects and birds will transfer pollen from one flower to another so that seeds will be produced.

Chemistry C1 and C2

1 **a** What is special about the structures of polymers? [2]

Polymers are large molecules formed by the combination of small molecules.

b How can propene be distinguished from propane? [2]

Propene contains a C=C double bond so it decolourises bromine water.

c Show how the atoms are arranged in polypropene and in a section of polypropene. [2]

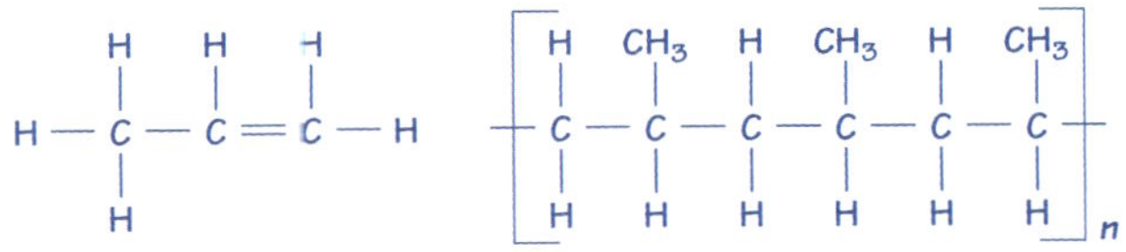

d Boric acid can form temporary cross-links between polyethenol chains. What effect would you expect these to have on the properties of the polymer? [2]

The more boric acid added, the stiffer the polymer would become. Cross-links prevent polymer chains from sliding over each other.

e A number of companies are trying to develop biodegradable polymers. Explain why current plastic disposal methods are unsatisfactory. [2]

Any two from: landfill sites get filled quickly wasting valuable land; burning waste plastics makes toxic gases; it is difficult to separate different polymers for recycling.

2 **a** Name two pollutants with high atmospheric concentrations in city centres. [2]

Carbon monoxide (from incomplete combustion of petrol or diesel in car engine) and oxides of nitrogen (formed in the internal combustion engine).

b What environmental problems do oxides of nitrogen cause? [2]

They are responsible for photochemical smog and acid rain.

c Catalytic converters use one pollutant gas to oxidise the other to a non-toxic gas. Finish this equation to show how they work:

$2CO + 2NO \rightarrow$ [2]

The correct equation is: $2CO + 2NO \rightarrow N_2 + 2CO_2$

d The atmospheric concentration of carbon dioxide cannot be reduced by using catalytic converters. Why is this a problem? [2]

Rising carbon dioxide levels are responsible for the greenhouse effect, which could cause global warming.

e Atmospheric sulfur dioxide levels are falling in the UK. Sulfur is precipitated from power station exhaust gases and used to make sulfuric acid. What problems would sulfur dioxide cause if it did escape? [2]

Sulfur dioxide reacts with water and oxygen to make acid rain. This can kill plants or aquatic life, erode stonework or corrode metals.

Physics P1 and P2

1 **a** The specific heat capacity of water is 4200 J/kg °C. Calculate the energy supplied to 200 g of water to change its temperature from 20 °C to boiling point. [3]

energy = mass × specific heat capacity × temperature change

energy = 0.200 × 4200 × (100 – 20)

energy = 67 200 J

b An ice cube of temperature 0 °C and mass 20 g is left to melt on a table. The specific latent heat of ice is 330 J/g.

i Explain what happens to the temperature of the ice as it melts. [1]

The temperature does not change because there is a change in state from solid to liquid.

ii Where does the ice get the energy for melting? [1]

The ice gets its energy from the surroundings.

iii Calculate its energy absorbed by the ice cube to change state into water. [3]

energy = mass × specific latent heat

energy = 20 × 330

energy = 6600 J

2 An electric kettle has a power rating of 2.2 kW.

a How much energy does the kettle transform in 1 second? [1]

2.2 kJ or 2200 J

b Calculate the energy in joules transformed by the kettle in a time of 3.0 minutes (180 seconds). [3]

energy = power × time

energy = 2200 × 180

energy = 396 000 J

c The kettle is connected to the mains that supplies a potential difference of 230 V. Electrical power is given by the equation:

power = voltage × current.

Calculate the current in the kettle when it is being used to boil some water. [3]

power = current × voltage

2200 = current × 230

$$\text{current} = \frac{2200}{230}$$

current = 9.57 A ≈ 9.6 A

Additional Biology B3 and B4

1 Ross cuts his finger. It bleeds.

a Blood is carried in two types of blood vessel joined by capillaries.
Write down the names of the blood vessels. [2]

Arteries and veins

b Which part of his blood will help to clot the blood and stop his finger from bleeding? [1]

Platelets

c Human blood is red because it contains haemoglobin. What is the job of haemoglobin? [2]

To combine with and carry oxygen around the body.

d The heart pumps blood around the body. It has two types of chamber.
Name the two types of chamber in the heart. [2]

Atria and ventricles.

e Ross' cut finger will heal by making new cells. Describe how new skin cells are made. [3]

New skin cells are made by a type of cell division called mitosis.
Chromosomes in the skin cell nucleus are copied.
So the new cell will be identical to the original one.

2 Ross finds out about his blood circulation.

a He finds out that he has a double circulatory system. What is meant by a double circulatory system? [2]

There are two circuits.
One circuit links the heart and lungs.
Another circuit links the heart and the rest of the body.

b High levels of cholesterol in the blood can be dangerous. Explain why. [3]

Cholesterol can stick to the inside of artery walls.
This can form a plaque and restrict or block blood flow.
If this happens in the coronary artery, the heart's supply of oxygen and food will be reduced and this will result in a heart attack.

3 Chloe finds out about making new cells by meiosis. New cells produced by meiosis have the haploid number of chromosomes. Explain why this is necessary. [4]

Meiosis produces male and female gametes.
These gametes will fuse at fertilisation.
The chromosome number in gametes must be halved (haploid) instead of the original diploid number otherwise the chromosome number in the zygote will be incorrect (doubled).

4 Describe one way in which plant growth is different from animal growth. [1]

Plants mainly grow at their tips, all parts of animals grow.

Alternative answers are:

Animals have a limited time of growth, plants can grow almost indefinitely.
Most plant growth is by cell elongation rather than cell division as in animals.

5 **a** Some scientists are investigating growing food in space.

i Which gas is used by plants to make food? [1]

Carbon dioxide

ii What is this process called? [1]

Photosynthesis

Note: Do not get confused with respiration, which uses oxygen.

b The scientists looked at three different algae. Their cells contain green chloroplasts.

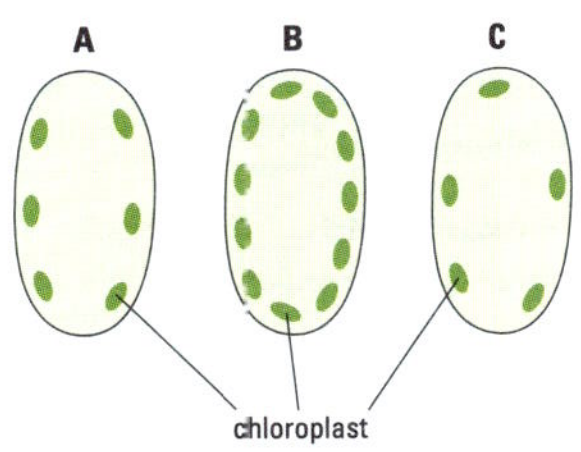

Which algae will produce the most food? Explain your answer. [3]

The algae B has the most chloroplasts and so will make the most food. This is because food is made in the chloroplasts.

c The scientists thought that they could use the excretory wastes of the space travellers to make the algae grow quickly. Explain why the algae would grow quickly. [3]

The excretory wastes contain nitrogen compounds, which act as a fertiliser. The algae use them to make proteins for growth.

d The algae produce a waste gas when they make food. How is this gas useful to animals? [2]

The waste gas is oxygen, which animals use to release energy in respiration.

6 **a** Charlie is a farmer. He uses intensive farming methods to grow crops.

i What do you understand by the term 'intensive farming'? [2]

Growing crops to produce food quickly by using artificial fertilisers and pesticides.

ii Write down one disadvantage of using intensive farming to grow crops. [1]

Insecticides can kill useful as well as harmful insects.

iii Charlie says that using intensive farming is more energy efficient. Explain why it is more energy efficient. [2]

There will be fewer weeds in his fields.
Less water and minerals will be wasted on growing fewer weeds.

b **i** Charlie uses the urea in animal waste to increase the nitrogen content of his soil. Explain what happens to the urea in the soil to improve the nitrogen content and make it available to plants. [3]

Nitrifying bacteria in the soil convert the urea into ammonia. They also convert the ammonia into nitrites and nitrates. The nitrates are soluble in the soil water.

ii Suggest one other way, without using artificial fertilisers, he could improve the nitrogen content of his soil.
Explain how it works. [2]

Grow crops such as peas and beans to improve the nitrogen content. Their root nodules contain nitrogen fixing bacteria.

Additional Chemistry C3 and C4

1 **a** Name a strongly coloured solid element. [1]

This must be iodine. All the coloured elements are halogens and iodine is a solid.

b Name a strongly coloured element that is a liquid. [1]

This must be bromine. All the coloured elements are halogens and bromine is a liquid.

c Name the group both elements belong to. [1]

Halogens.

d The melting points of the elements in this group are shown in the table. Plot a graph of melting point against mass and estimate the melting point of astatine, which has a mass of 210. [5]

Element	Mass	Melting point (°C)
Cl_2	35.5	−100
Br_2	80	−10
I_2	127	110

If the points are plotted correctly, the line of best fit should give a melting point of 300 plus or minus 10 °C.
Check the scales carefully. Small squares often correspond to more than one.

e The table below compares chlorine with air. Suggest two ways of collecting the gas. [2]

Gas	Solubility	Density (g/cm^3)
Cl_2	slight	0.0016
Air	n/a	0.0013

Choose any two from: by downward delivery (because it is denser than air); in a gas syringe (because this is a suitable technique for any gas); over water (because chlorine is not very soluble).

2 **a** List two common sources of water pollution. [2]

Two from: nitrate from fertiliser run off; lead compounds from lead pipes; pesticide from spraying near to water resources.

b A sample of river water gave a cloudy white precipitate with aqueous silver nitrate and barium chloride solutions. What must have been present in the water? [2]

Precipitates form when ions mix that can form insoluble compounds. Silver halides are all insoluble and silver chloride is white, so chloride ions must be present.

c Write an equation for the reaction that produces the precipitate. [2]

$Ag^+{}_{(aq)} + Cl^-{}_{(aq)} \rightarrow AgCl_{(s)}$
It is essential to include the state symbols to make it obvious that the solid precipitated when two solutions were mixed.

d Nitrates cannot be precipitated from solution. Suggest a reason for this. [2]

There are no insoluble compounds that contain nitrate ions.

e When 50 cm^3 of river water was analysed, the silver chloride precipitated gave an average reading of 0.01 grams on a balance sensitive to two decimal places. This gave an estimate of 0.2 $grams/dm^3$. How could a more precise estimate be obtained? [2]

The sensitivity of the balance is limiting the precision of the mass readings. To get a more precise value a bigger volume of water should be tested or a more sensitive balance should be used.

Additional Physics P3 and P4

1 A 15 kg monkey falls 5.0 m. The monkey lands on the ground with a speed of 4.0 m/s.

a Describe the energy changes taking place as the monkey falls towards the ground. [2]

The monkey loses potential energy and gains kinetic energy.

b The equations for gravitational potential energy and kinetic energy are:

potential energy = mgh (g = 10 N/kg)
kinetic energy = $\frac{1}{2}mv^2$

Calculate:

i the initial potential energy of the monkey. [2]

potential energy = mgh
potential energy = $15 \times 10 \times 5.0$
potential energy = 750 J

ii the kinetic energy of the monkey just before it lands on the ground. [2]

kinetic energy = $\frac{1}{2}mv^2$
kinetic energy = $\frac{1}{2} \times 15 \times (4.0)^2$
kinetic energy = 120 J

c Explain why the answers to **b i** and **b ii** are not the same. [2]

The falling monkey experiences friction due to the air.
Some of the energy is also transformed into heat.
(Hence the final kinetic energy is less than the initial potential energy.)

2 **a** Name the two different types of charge. [1]

The two different types of charge are positive and negative.

b A plastic ruler can be charged by rubbing it on a dry cloth. Explain how an insulator acquires a charge. [2]

Friction between the cloth and the ruler removes electrons from one of the insulators and they are transferred to the other.
(The insulator will be positively charged if it loses electrons.)

c State two examples of the practical applications of static electricity. [2]

Photocopiers and removing smoke or dust from chimneys.

GCSE Biology B5 and B6

1 Some animals have an exoskeleton, others have an internal skeleton.

a Write down two differences between an exoskeleton and an internal skeleton. [2]

An exoskeleton is found on the outside of an animal; an internal skeleton is inside the animal.
An exoskeleton is made of chitin; an internal skeleton is made of bone or cartilage.

b **i** What is a joint? [1]

A joint is where two or more bones meet.

ii Complete the table about joints. [4]

Type of joint	Example in the body	Range of movement
hinge joint	*elbow*	*only up and down*
ball and socket joint	*shoulder*	*can rotate in three planes*

c Explain how the biceps and triceps muscles raise the forearm. [3]

The biceps and triceps muscles are antagonistic muscles.
As the biceps muscle contracts, the triceps muscle relaxes.

Details such as 'the muscles use energy from respiration' could also be included.
A common error is to state that the triceps muscle expands. This is wrong.

2 **a** Charlie is 16 years old. He wants to know if he is still growing. Explain how X-rays of his joints can show this. [3]

Cartilage and bone look different in X-rays. If there is still cartilage in his finger joints, he is still growing.

Stating that 'Not all the cartilage has been ossified' is also correct.

b Michael injures his knee playing football. His knee joint swells up.

i What liquid is inside a knee joint? [1]

Synovial fluid

ii What are the functions of this fluid? [2]

Synovial fluid lubricates the joint. It also absorbs shock.

c Many old people develop osteoporosis.

i What is the main cause of osteoporosis? [1]

A lack of calcium in the diet.

(Note: A lack of vitamin D can also cause osteoporosis.)

ii What problems can result from osteoporosis? [2]

Because the bones are soft, they fracture easily.

iii Why can bones repair themselves? [1]

Bones contain living cells.

3 Emma is a farmer.

a **i** Emma knows that soil contains rock particles and living organisms.
Write down two other components of soil. [2]

Two from: humus, water, air

ii Explain how rock particles can be useful to plants. [2]

They help to anchor plant roots so the plants are not blown away.
They also contain useful minerals.

b Emma knows that earthworms help the soil. Describe how they do this. [3]

Earthworms bury leaves, which decay releasing minerals.
As acid soil passes through their bodies, it is neutralised.
Their burrows improve soil drainage.

c Many chemical elements, such as sulfur and phosphorus, are recycled in the soil.

i Name two other elements that are recycled in the soil. [2]

Nitrogen and carbon.

ii Which type of living organisms help in this recycling? [1]

Bacteria

(Note: Fungi also help in recycling.)

4 **a** Emma finds that the house drains are blocked. She buys a drain cleaner. The label on the cleaner is shown below.

This drain cleaner:	This drain cleaner contains:
• digest stains • removes smells • cleans drains	bacteria enzymes minerals sand

i Explain why the drain cleaner does not work in high temperatures. [3]

It contains enzymes, which are denatured at high temperatures.
Bacteria are killed at high temperatures.

ii Explain how the drain cleaner can clear drains that are blocked with waste food. [3]

Bacteria will digest the waste food. Enzymes will also digest the food, breaking it down into smaller molecules which are soluble in water.

b Emma wonders if the enzymes are immobilised.

i What are immobilised enzymes? [2]

An immobilised enzyme is attached to another chemical, such as alginate.

ii Write down two advantages of using immobilised enzymes. [2]

They can be used in continuous flow systems.
They also prevent contamination.

GCSE Chemistry C5 and C6

1 A chemical leak has allowed ammonium hydroxide (NH_4OH) to contaminate a lake. In order to assess the seriousness of the situation the water board plans to measure the lake's hydroxide concentration.

a What technique could they use? [1]

Acid-base titration

b 1 dm^3 of 0.01 mol/dm^3 hydrochloric acid was made by diluting a 1 mol/dm^3 acid solution with water. What volume of 1 mol/dm^3 acid was used? [2]

1 dm^3 of 0.01 mol/dm^3 hydrochloric acid contains 0.01 moles in 1000 cm^3

1 dm^3 of 1 mol/dm^3 acid contains 1 mole in 1000 cm^3

This is 0.01 moles in $1000 \times 0.01 = 10$ cm^3

So, 10 cm^3 of the 1 mol/dm^3 acid solution needs making up to 1 dm^3 with water

c Name the glassware used to measure lake water into a flask. [1]

A pipette should be used to measure the volume accurately.

d Name the glassware used to add acid to the flask a bit at a time. [1]

A burette should be used to measure the volume of acid added.

e Write a symbol equation for the reaction. [1]

$NH_4OH + HCl \rightarrow NH_4Cl + H_2O$

f 40 cm^3 of 0.01 mol dm^{-3} hydrochloric acid reacted with 20 cm^3 of lake water. What is the lake water's hydroxide ion concentration? [2]

The equation shows that 1 mole of acid reacts with 1 mole of alkali

$$\text{Moles of acid} = \text{concentration} \times \text{volume in dm}^3 = 0.01 \times \frac{40}{1000} = 0.0004$$

$$\text{Moles of alkali} = \text{concentration} \times \frac{20}{1000} = 0.01 \times \frac{40}{1000}$$

So the concentration of NH_4OH is 0.02 mol/dm^3

(A simpler method is to say: If the acid and alkali had equal concentrations their volumes would be equal. There is half as much alkali, so it must be twice as concentrated.)

g How would the results be affected if the analyst took too long to realise that the indicator had changed colour? [2]

If the colour change was not noticed immediately, too much acid would be added. This would make the alkali seem more concentrated than it really was.

2 **a** List two uses of ethanol. [2]

Any two from: used in alcoholic beverages; as a solvent; as a fuel for cars.

b Ethanol can be made by hydration of ethene. Write a balanced symbol equation for this reaction. [2]

The equation is: $C_2H_4 + H_2O \rightarrow C_2H_5OH$

c Ethanol for human consumption is made by fermentation of sugar. Write a balanced symbol equation for this reaction. [2]

The equation is: $C_6H_{12}O_6 \rightarrow 2CO_2 + 2C_2H_5OH$
Always count the atoms on each side of the arrow to check there is the same number for each element.

(Note: In this case a symbol equation is required, but always check the question. Sometimes questions ask for word equations.)

d

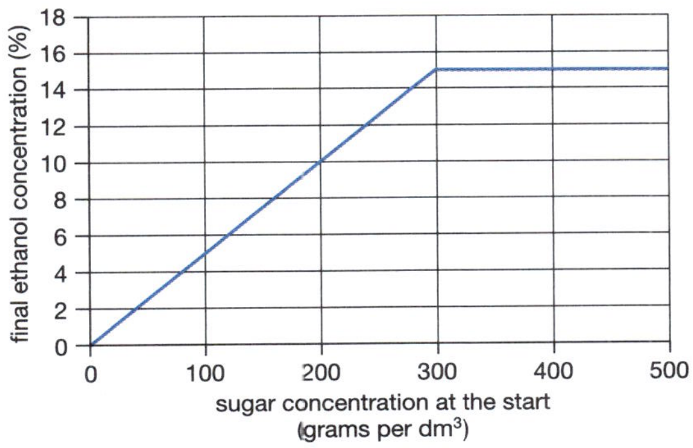

The graph above shows the connection between the sugar concentration at the start and the percentage of ethanol in the final mixture. Explain why the graph reaches a plateau. [3]

The more sugar present at the start, the higher the percentage of ethanol in the final solution until the ethanol concentration reaches 15%. No further increase is possible because the yeast cells that ferment the sugar are destroyed.

e How are higher ethanol concentrations obtained? [1]

More concentrated solutions are obtained by fractional distillation.

GCSE Physics P5 and P6

1 **a** Explain what is meant by a vector quantity and give one example. [2]

A vector quantity has both magnitude and direction. An example would be force.

b The driver of a car travelling at 18 m/s suddenly applies the brakes and reduces the speed of the car to 6.0 m/s in a period of 2.0 seconds.

Use the equations: $v = u + at$ and $s = \frac{1}{2}(u + v)t$ to calculate:

i the acceleration of the car [3]

$v = u + at$
$6.0 = 18 + (a \times 2.0)$
$2.0\,a = 6.0 - 18$
$a = -6.0\ m/s^2$ *(The minus sign shows deceleration.)*

ii the distance travelled by the car during period of 2.0 seconds. [3]

$s = \frac{1}{2}(u + v)t$
$s = \frac{1}{2}(18 + 6.0) \times 2.0$
$s = 12 \times 2.0$
$s = 24\ m$

2 A transformer consists of a primary coil (input coil) and a secondary coil (output coil) wound onto an iron ring.

a Describe what a step-up transformer does to the input voltage. [1]

A step-up transformer changes the input voltage by making it larger.

b Give one domestic example of a device that uses a transformer. [1]

A transformer is used in a mobile phone charger.

c Explain why a constant direct current in the primary coil does not produce any voltage in the secondary coil. [2]

A constant current in the primary coil produces a constant magnetic field.
A voltage will only be induced if the magnetic field linking the coil was to change.

d In terms of the number of turns on the primary and secondary coils, explain the difference between a step-up transformer and a step-down transformer. [2]

In a step-up transformer, the secondary coil has more turns than the primary coil.
In a step-down transformer, the secondary coil has fewer turns than the primary coil.

NOW TRY THIS ANSWERS

Fitness and diet – pages 6 and 7

a aerobic, energy, glucose, anaerobic, oxygen, lactic acid
b 150; millimetres of mercury; stroke, kidney damage; better/low fat diet, regular exercise, not smoking, low or no alcohol intake, not overweight, reduce stress levels
c carbohydrate, growing, very overweight, meat
d carbohydrate–carbohydrase–glucose, protein–protease–amino acids, fat–lipase–fatty acids

Disease and the nervous system – pages 8 and 9

a athletes foot, flu, cholera, dysentery; malaria, scurvy, anaemia, diabetes, red–green colour deficiency; a microorganism that causes disease; acid (hydrochloric); killing mosquitoes; vector
b white blood cells, passive, antigens, pathogen, active, viruses
c true, false, true, true, false, false, true
d cornea–refracts light, iris– controls amount of light into eye, lens–focuses light, retina–reacts to light, optic nerve–carries nerve impulses

Homeostasis, drugs and genes – pages 10 and 11

a to lose heat; temperature, water levels, carbon dioxide levels; insulin; narrowing of the walls of blood vessels; oestrogen and progesterone
b 3.5, 3.08, lower/smaller
c gametes, half, 23, four, genetic, enzymes
d environmental: scar; genetic: ear lobe shape, eye colour; cystic fibrosis inherited; sperm; brown; blue; heterozygote

Ecosystems, respiration and photosynthesis – pages 12 and 13

a fish–gills, amphibians–moist skin, reptiles–dry scales, birds–feathers, mammals–fur
b Ecosystem: living things and where they live; Community: plants and animals; Habitat: where they live; smaller, weed killer/pesticides/fertilisers
c carbon dioxide, oxygen, light, chlorophyll, starch, it is soluble
d false, true, false, true, true

Competition, adaptations and survival – pages 14 and 15

a light, water, minerals, survive, competition, ecological niche
b predator, prey, predator, prey, parasites, hosts, mutualism
c mainly binocular–narrow–predator, mainly monocular–wide–prey, insulate, spread
d survive and breed, water, wind, pollen, insects, pollination

Evolution, natural selection and extinction – pages 16 and 17

a layer f, layer a, evolution
b variation/differences, compete, adapted, breed, inherited, Natural Selection

c burning fossil fuel–carbon dioxide–global warming, old fridges–CFCs– ozone depletion, burning fossil fuel–sulfur dioxide–acid rain, indicator, air pollution
d overfishing, laws, protected habitats, grey squirrels, habitat destruction, hunting, captive breeding

Carbon chemistry 1 – pages 18 and 19

a Potato: cell walls destroyed, absorbs heat energy, changes chemically, flavour improves, gets softer; Meat: proteins denatured, absorbs heat energy, changes chemically, flavour improves, gets softer; Sodium hydrogen carbonate: releases carbon dioxide, decomposes, changes chemically
b Oxidation: a reaction with oxygen; Emulsify: disperse one substance in another; Emulsifier: stops emulsions separating; Hydrophilic: water loving; Antioxidant: stops food reacting with O_2; Hydrophobic: water hating – attracted to oil; Immiscible: cannot be mixed
c intelligent, neither, active, active, active, neither, active, intelligent
d organic acid and alcohol; ester; organic acid; ester; alcohol; ester; ester

Carbon chemistry 2 – pages 20 and 21

a short, long, either, long, short, long
b Covalent bonds – link non-metal atoms, broken by cracking; Alkene – used to make polymers; Cracking – decomposition of alkanes; Alkane – broken by cracking, found in oil; Hydrocarbon – alkane or alkene, found in oil; Catalyst – promotes cracking; High temperature – promotes cracking; Liquid paraffin – broken by cracking, found in oil, a long-chain alkane; Intermolecular forces – overcome by boiling
c ethane, methane, propene, propane, butane
d polystyrene, polyethene, polybutene, polyethene, polypropene, PVC

Carbon chemistry 3 – pages 22 and 23

a parachute rope; bullet-proof vest, safety helmets; fire fighters' uniform, bullet-proof vests, safety helmets; run-flat tyres; fire fighters' uniform; glass workers' gloves
b The true statements are: Recycling codes can be used to identify plastics; some polymers release toxic fumes when burned; most polymers are made from oil products; microbes decompose biodegradable polymers
c carbon dioxide + water; CO_2; carbon monoxide + water; CO; carbon + water; C
d exothermic, exothermic, exothermic, endothermic, exothermic, endothermic, exothermic, exothermic, exothermic, endothermic, endothermic

Rocks and metals 1 – pages 24 and 25

a coloured chemical; drops of one liquid suspended in another; glows in the dark; sticks pigments to surfaces; its colour depends on the temperature; particles of one thing dispersed in another; hardens oil paints
b granite, limestone/marble, limestone, marble/granite, limestone/marble, marble, limestone
c both, basalt, basalt, basalt, granite, granite, granite
d consequence, cause, consequence, cause, cause, consequence, consequence

Rocks and metals 2 – pages 26 and 27

a anode, cathode, cathode, anode, cathode, anode, cathode, electrolyte
b iron, iron, aluminium, iron, both, both, iron, both, aluminium, iron
c decrease, increase, increase, increase, increase, decrease, increase, decrease, increase, increase
d source of the first atmosphere; made by photosynthesis, essential for respiration; oxidised to N_2 and H_2O, in the first atmosphere; condensed to form oceans, in the first atmosphere; an inert gas; dissolved in the first oceans, in the first atmosphere, an increasing percentage of the air

Rocks and metals 3 – pages 28 and 29

a slower, slower, faster, slower, slower, neither, faster
b 40 s, 100 cm^3 of H_2; 210 s, 50 cm^3 of H_2; 210 s, 100 cm^3 of H_2
c surface area, frequently, faster, collisions, used up, little
d 60, 6, 10, 40

Homes and insulation – pages 30 and 31

a false, true, true, false
b insulator, convection, close together, radiation

Waves and signals – pages 32 and 33

a electromagnetic, longer, vibrate, oven
b true, false, false, true
c Second, third and fourth statements ticked

Light waves and seismic waves – pages 34 and 35

a m/s, m, Hz, m
b true, false, true, false
c ozone, cancer, sunburn, blocks

Solar power and generating electricity – pages 36 and 37

a electrical, does not, Sun
b A generator produces an alternating current; To induce a current in a wire you have to move it in a magnetic field; In a dynamo the magnet rotates near a stationary coil; Rotating the coil of a dynamo faster increases the frequency of the current.

Fuels and nuclear radiations – pages 38 and 39

a Renewable: straw, manure; Non-renewable: coal, uranium, crude oil

b

			C	E	L	L	S
	E		A				
	T		N	B	O	M	B
	A		C				
	T		E	T	S	A	W
	U		R				
	M						

c cells, cancer, paper, aluminium, lead, sterilise

Earth and space – pages 40 and 41

a field, Sun, two planets

b Moon, Mars, Sun, Pluto, Stars, Galaxies

c true, true, false, false

d true, false, true, true

DNA, diffusion and circulation – pages 42 and 43

a nucleus – genetic information, cell membrane – controls entry and exit of chemicals, cytoplasm – for chemical reactions, four, complementary base pairs

b true, true, false, true, true, false, true

c diffuses, lower, oxygen, higher, diffuse, alveoli, large surface area/good blood supply/wall only one cell thick

d 1. Pulmonary artery 2. Aorta 3. Bicuspid valve 4. Left ventricle 5. Tricuspid valve 6. Right atrium; left ventricle, all around the body

Growth and reproduction – pages 44 and 45

a division, identical/two, diploid/same, gases/waste, multicellular, chromosomes, ends/poles

b egg and sperm, 46, body cell, gametes

c 1. Nucleus 2. Cytoplasm 3. Cell wall 4. Membrane 5. Choroplast 6. Cell sap 7. Nucleus 8. Cytoplasm 9. Membrane

d about 10–13 years, 9 cm/year, 8 cm/year, 17, 19, the head

Hormone and gene control – pages 46 and 47

a true, false, true, true, false

b Characteristics ticked: grow quickly, produce large quantities of milk, breed easily, usually produce twins, well behaved and docile

c genetic modification, genes, organism, weeds, crop, insulin, diabetes

d asexual, identical, identical, conditions, pathogen/disease, nucleus, egg cell, nucleus, body

Plant processes – pages 48 and 49

a waterproof, chloroplasts, guard, mesophyll, palisade, food/glucose, stomata, chloroplasts, diffusion

b Diffusion

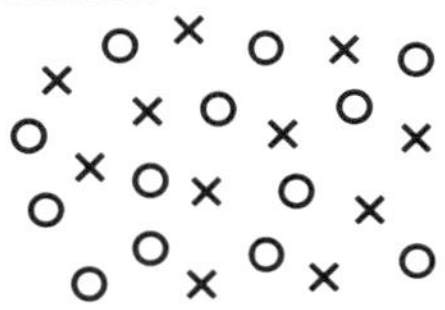

Equal distributions

Osmosis

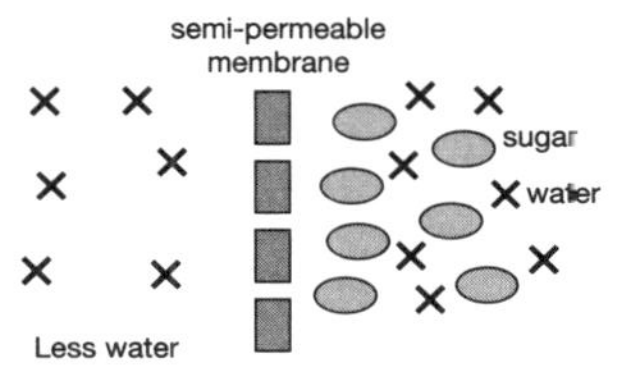

c water, water, minerals, food, glucose, temperature, light, wind, humidity, stomata, water, diffusion

d nitrogen–nitrates–proteins, phosphorus–phosphates–root growth, potassium–potassium compounds–flower formation, magnesium–magnesium compounds–chlorophyll

Biomass, farming and decay – pages 50 and 51

a oak tree, sunlight, pyramid B

b true, false, false, false, false, true

c bacteria, fungi, low/high, sewage, earthworm/maggot/woodlice, decay, preserve, decaying

d 1 photosynthesis, 2 respiration, 3 burning, 4 respiration, 5 decay

The periodic table 1 – pages 52 and 53

a Proton: in the nucleus, number different for every element, mass 1, positive; Neutron: in the nucleus, neutral, mass 1; Electron: negative, around the outside of an atom, mass almost zero

b 2.3, 2.5, 2.8, 2.8.2, 2.8.7, 2.8.8.2, 2.8.3, 2.8.5

c K_2O, $CaCl_2$, NaI, $Ca(OH)_2$, CaO, K_2S, $Ca(NO_3)_2$, Na_2SO_4, MgI_2, Li_2O

d check dot and cross diagrams

The periodic table 2 – pages 54 and 55

a group 1, period 2; group 7, period 3; group 1, period 4; group 7, period 2; group 8, period 3; group 1, period 3; group 8, period 2; group 8, period 1

b The true statements are: Group 1 metals fizz in water, Na displaces H from water, KOH is an acid, Na is oxidised when it reacts

c Chlorine: sterilises water, green gas, makes white salts, used in some polymers, has seven electrons in its outer shell, most reactive; Bromine: makes white salts, brown liquid, only displaces iodine, has seven electrons in its outer shell; Iodine: grey solid, makes white salts, sterilises wounds, has seven electrons in its outer shell

d bromine, Br_2, potassium bromide + iodine, $2KBr + I_2$, sodium chloride + iodine, $KCl + I_2$

The periodic table 3 – pages 56 and 57

a ions, negative cathode, molecules, positive anode, electrons, water

b cathode, cathode, cathode, anode, anode, cathode, anode, anode, anode, anode

c conductor, grey, catalyst in Haber process; green, precipitated by alkali; orange, precipitated by alkali; green, decomposes on heating, releases CO_2 on heating

d Lustrous – mirror; Electrical conductor – wiring; Tensile strength – lift cables; High melting point – light bulb filament; Strong – bridges; Hard – nails; Dense – weights; Thermal conductor – saucepan

Chemical economics 1 – pages 58 and 59

a HCl; KOH; $NaNO_3$; CuO; $CaCO_3$; CuO, $CuCO_3$, NaOH; pH 8; pH 1

b OH^- ion solution and H^+ ion solution; carbonate and H^+ ion solution; magnesium and H^+ ion solution; magnesium, carbonate or copper oxide, and H^+ ion solution

c $2Mg + O_2 \rightarrow 2MgO$ (48 g); $Mg + Cl_2 \rightarrow MgCl_2$ (48 g); $Mg + 2HCl \rightarrow MgCl_2 + H_2$ (12 g); $Mg + 2HNO_3 \rightarrow Mg(NO_3)_2 + H_2$ (48 g); $Mg + H_2SO_4 \rightarrow MgSO_4 + H_2$ (12 g)

d theoretical yield = 44 g, % yield = 50; theoretical yield = 80 g, % yield = 20; theoretical yield = 32 g, % yield = 100; theoretical yield = 20 g, % yield = 75; theoretical yield = 28 g, % yield = 50

Chemical economics 2 – pages 60 and 61

a 82%, 47%, 35%, 21%, 28%

b increase, decrease, increase, increase, neither

c profitability, percentage yield, profitability, percentage yield, neither, profitability

d Solvent – what things dissolve in; Hydrophobic – repels water molecules; Bleach – removes coloured stains; Enzymes – digest food stains; Hydrophilic – attracts water molecules; Detergent – soluble salt, made by neutralising an acid; Brightener – makes whites look whiter; Rinse agent – makes water drain off; Solute – the material that dissolves; Insoluble – will not dissolve

Chemical economics 3 – pages 62 and 63

a continuous, batch, continuous, batch, batch, continuous

b graphite, diamond, graphite, graphite, diamond, graphite, diamond, diamond, diamond

c fullerene, nanotubule, nanotubule, nanotubule, fullerene, both, fullerene, fullerene

d Lead – pipes; Pesticide – farm sprays; Minerals – rocks; Organic waste – households; Sulfates – acid rain; Nitrates – fertiliser

Understanding motion – pages 64 and 65

a m/s, 10 km, Yes

b false, true, true, true

c

			D	E	E	P	S
T	N	E	I	D	A	R	G
	T						
	I						
	M						
V	E	L	O	C	I	T	Y
D	I	S	T	A	N	C	E

Force, work, energy and power – pages 66 and 67

- **a** false, true, true, true
- **b** No work is done on an object if it remains stationary; Power is measured in watts; Work is measured in joules; A car travelling faster has greater kinetic energy
- **c** 6.0, braking, thinking, stopping

Falling and theme park rides – pages 68 and 69

- **a** true, false, true, false
- **b** J, decreases, mass, heat

Sparks and electrostatics – pages 70 and 71

- **a** First and fourth statements ticked
- **b** spark, air, dangerous, temperature
- **c**

S	P	R	A	Y			T
	T						N
P	L	A	S	E	R		I
A			T				A
D				I			P
D					C		
L	C	H	A	R	G	E	
E	A	T	T	R	A	C	T

Safe electricals – pages 72 and 73

- **a** complete, less, dimmer
- **b** true, false, true, true
- **c**

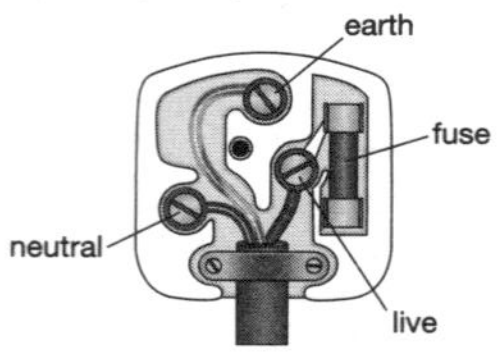

Ultrasound and radiation – pages 74 and 75

- **a** What is the unit of frequency? (hertz); Ultrasound can be used to find the speed of what in the body? (blood); What type of wave is ultrasound? (longitudinal); What type of stones can ultrasound break down? (kidney)
- **b**

				I			
		G		O		S	
		A		N		T	
		M		I		E	
	X	M		S	C	R	
T	R	A	C	E	R	I	
	A		L			L	
	Y	L				E	

Nuclear physics – pages 76 and 77

- **a** First, third and fourth statements ticked
- **b** tracer, pass, increase
- **c** false, true, true, true

Bones, joints and circulation – pages 78 and 79

- **a** chitin, outside, cartilage, bone, inside, living, marrow, blood vessels, cartilage, bone, calcium, phosphorus
- **b** soft bones/lack of calcium, bones, muscle to bone, elbow, knee, shoulder, hip, contract, relax, antagonistic
- **c** double/closed, four, atria, ventricles, arteries, veins, capillaries; fish, Amoeba/Hydra
- **d** coronary, pulse, wrist, ear, temple, heart muscle contraction/heart beat, electric current, increase, adrenalin

The heart and respiration – pages 80 and 81

- **a** one, right, left, oxygen, coronary
- **b** plasma; haemoglobin; reduces; helps; A, B, AB, O; any group; O
- **c** breathing, respiration, oxygen, contract, out, up, contracts, down, increase, decrease
- **d** asbestosis – industrial, cystic fibrosis – inherited, lung cancer – smoking, bronchitis – microorgansims, asthma – allergy

Organs and growth – pages 82 and 83

- **a** excretion, liver, filtered, urine, water, salt, urea, less, selective reabsorption, dialysis
- **b** 1 epidermis, 2 dermis, 3 blood capillary, 4 hair follicle, 5 sweat gland, 6 sweat pore
- **c** false, true, true, false, true, false, false
- **d** heart/kidney/joints/lens, rejection, donor, blood/bone marrow/one kidney, power

Microorganisms, fermentation and biofuels – pages 84 and 85

- **a** false, true, true, false, true, false, true, true, false
- **b** bacteria – tuberculosis, fungi – athletes foot, virus – influenza, protozoan – malaria; a microorganism that carries disease, infectious
- **c** anaerobic, oxygen, asexual, warm, die, less, glucose
- **d** methane, biogas, burning, less carbon dioxide, no particulates, more energy

Soil and life in water – pages 86 and 87

- **a** 1 living organism, 2 humus, 3 soil particles, 4 air and water
- **b** true, false, true, false, true, true, true
- **c** water, phytoplankton, zooplankton, sunlight, sugars, producers, light, minerals, warm, zooplankton, spring (or autumn)
- **d** sewage and fertiliser run off, rapid growth of algae and plankton, algae and plankton die, oxygen used up, animals die; higher, lower

Enzymes and genetic engineering – pages 88 and 89

- **a** substrates, enzymes, carbohydrases, lipases, proteases, reactions, dissolve, digestion, protease/ lipase/carbohydrase/ invertase, glucose/sucrose/fructose/ galactose/maltose/lactose
- **b** false, true, true, true, false, true
- **c** wanted gene identified, gene removed from DNA, DNA in another organism cut open, new gene inserted into the DNA, gene works in transgenic organism, transgenic organism cloned; restriction, ligase
- **d** DNA, rapidly, insulin, resistant, killed, light, water, minerals, faster

How much? Part 1 – pages 90 and 91

- **a** 2, 2, 2, 4, 0.25, 20 g, 20 g, 9 g, 34 g
- **b** MgO, CaO, CO_2, CH_4, SO_2, NH_3, C_2H_6, H_2O
- **c** $2O^{2-} \rightarrow O_2 + 4e^-$, $Al^{3+} + 3e^- \rightarrow Al$; $2I^- \rightarrow I_2 + 2e^-$, $Pb^{2+} + 2e^- \rightarrow Pb$; $2Cl^- \rightarrow Cl_2 + 2e^-$, $K^+ + e^- \rightarrow K$; $4OH^- \rightarrow 2H_2O + O_2 + 4e^-$, $2H^+ + 2e^- \rightarrow H_2$

- **d** negative, positive, negative, positive, negative, positive, negative, positive

How much? Part 2 – pages 92 and 93

- **a** 2, 1, 4, 0.2, 0.5, 20, 126, 7.3, 70, 196
- **b** 0.5 M, 1 M, 1 M, 1 M, 0.25 M, 0.4 M, 0.5 M, 0.005 M
- **c** 2, 0.5, 0.25, 1, 2, 2, 12, 6, 1.2, 48, 24
- **d** sulfur dioxide, oxygen, vanadium oxide, 450, 1, sulfur trioxide, concentrated, 98%

How much? Part 3 – pages 94 and 95

- **a** strong, strong, either, weak, weak, either, strong, either
- **b** silver iodide$_{(s)}$ + sodium nitrate$_{(aq)}$; $AgI_{(s)}$; barium sulfate $_{(s)}$ + sodium nitrate$_{(aq)}$; $BaSO_{4(s)}$; lead iodide$_{(s)}$ + sodium nitrate $_{(aq)}$; $2I^-_{(aq)} \rightarrow PbI_{2(s)}$
- **c** burning hydrogen, both, both, fuel cell, both, fuel cell, fuel cell, fuel cell
- **d** oxidation, reduction, oxidation, reduction, reduction, oxidation, oxidation, oxidation

Chemistry out there 1 – pages 96 and 97

- **a** Methanol: CH_3OH; Butanol: C_4H_9OH; Ethene: dehydrated ethanol; Ethanol: found in wine, hydrated ethene; Propanol: C_3H_7OH
- **b** The true statements are: Electrolysis decomposes salty water, H_2, Cl_2 and NaOH are made from salt, Cl_2 and NaOH react with each other, Cl_2 is produced at the anode(+), O_2 is released by electrolysis of dilute salt solutions.
- **c** chlorine, fluorine, carbon, inert, broke, chlorine, long, ozone
- **d** ozone, CFC, chloride ion, chlorine free radical, oxygen free radical, hydrocarbon, HFC

Chemistry out there 2 – pages 98 and 99

- **a** found in many rocks, makes water acidic, lathers with any water, causes permanent hardness, makes scum with hard water, causes temporary hardness
- **b** The true statements are: Carbonate ions precipitate calcium, Acid breaks down limescale, Washing soda removes any hardness, Boiling decomposes hydrogen carbonates
- **c** alkali; made from fats; decolourises bromine, contains C=C bonds; hydrolysis of fats; used to saturate oils; mixture of fats and oils
- **d** aspirin; aspirin, ibuprofen; paracetamol; aspirin; paracetamol; paracetamol

Space for reflection 1 – pages 100 and 101

- **a** gravitational, attractive, planet
- **b** Third statement only ticked
- **c** true, true, true, true
- **d** What is the spreading of a wave called? (diffraction); What causes low frequency radio waves to be reflected? (ionosphere); What absorbs high frequency radio waves? (rain)

Space for reflection 2 – pages 102 and 103

a false, true, true, true
b The bending of light – refraction; The spreading of light – diffraction; The splitting of light into different colours – dispersion; Different materials have different values of refractive index
c towards, longer, real, inverted

Electricity for gadgets 1 – pages 104 and 105

a the same, increases, divided
b First and third statements ticked
c A generator produces an alternating voltage; To induce a current in a wire you have to move it in a magnetic field; The mains frequency is 50 Hz; Rotating the coil of a generator faster increases the frequency and voltage
d Where might you find a step-down transformer? (a laptop); What is the name for the output coil of a transformer? (secondary) What type of current is needed for a transformer to work? (AC)

Electricity for gadgets 2 – pages 106 and 107

a Second and third statements ticked
b true, true, true
c All statements ticked

ANSWERS TO EXAM-STYLE QUESTIONS

Biology B1 and B2

1 a i Diastolic and systolic
ii Millimetres of mercury
b i To lose heat/prevent overheating
ii It evaporates/diffuses
c Glucose incompletely broken down; glucose goes to lactic acid (+energy); waste taken to liver in blood
d i Homeostasis
ii It corrects against change/returns to normal
2 a Any one from: pitfall traps/nets – to sample; mark and recapture; calculate the estimated population using formula
b Siberian chipmunk; bank voles/field mice
c It has binocular vision/claws/strong teeth/camouflage
d It has no natural predators; there is plenty of food for it
e Darwin's theory: variation in individuals; the fittest will survive and breed

Chemistry C1 and C2

1 a Detergent b Emulsions
c The oil and water would form separate layers
d The hydrophilic ends of the molecules attract water and the hydrophobic ends attract oil e Mayonnaise
2 a Fine particles of solid pigment are dispersed in the oil b Solvent
c Solvent evaporates, the oil forms a film and oxidises to form a tough protective skin

d They change colour depending on the temperature

Physics P1 and P2

1 a Some of the energy is lost as heat (due to friction) b Efficiency = 48 %
2 a The wavelength is the distance between two neighbouring peaks
b They are transverse waves and can travel through a vacuum
c True, false, true d Speed = 2.0 m/s
3 a A photocell transforms light into electrical energy
b It produces a direct current
c Advantage: Long life/no polluting waste/does not require fuel/no cables Disadvantage: Cannot use it when it gets dark
d Increase its surface area; increase the intensity of light
4 a Venus, Earth, Jupiter and Uranus
b Mercury is closer to the Sun; it experiences a greater gravitational force than Mars which is further away from the Sun
c Astronauts for manned space travel would require food and oxygen

Additional Biology B3 and B4

1 a Chromosomes, genes, DNA
b Correct statements: DNA is arranged in a double helix; DNA controls the synthesis of proteins
c Unzip to form single strands; reform by complementary base pairs, using bases A–T and G–C
d i Suspect 2 is the culprit – the bands are identical
ii 1 isolation, 2 fragmentation, 3 separation (by electrophoresis), 4 comparison with a reference/suspect
2 a Root hairs, osmosis, semi-permeable
b i B ii C iii A
c i Uptake of all minerals is increased by mycorrhiza
ii No diseases. No mycorrhiza so less mineral uptake
d By active uptake, by selective carriers which use energy

Additional Chemistry C3 and C4

1 a Separate molecules of CO_2 and a giant lattice of Mg^{2+} and O^{2-} ions should be shown
b Ionic
c The electron shells of magnesium and oxygen should be shown before and after the reaction
d i It has weak intermolecular forces
ii The carbon and oxygen are linked by strong covalent bonds
e The carbon must be shown sharing two pairs of electrons with each oxygen
2 a Burette; Measuring cylinder
b Nitric acid, ammonium hydroxide
c 35%
d The extra nitrate would cause an algal bloom, which would block the light to other plants, cause decay and reduce the water's oxygen concentration, killing animal life

Additional Physics P3 and P4

1 a Average speed = 16.7 m/s
b i The braking distance is the distance travelled by the car from the moment the brakes are applied until the car stops
ii Reaction time = 0.5 s
iii stopping distance = 30 m
iv The braking distance will increase if the speed is greater or the road is slippery (e.g. ice)
2 a i and ii

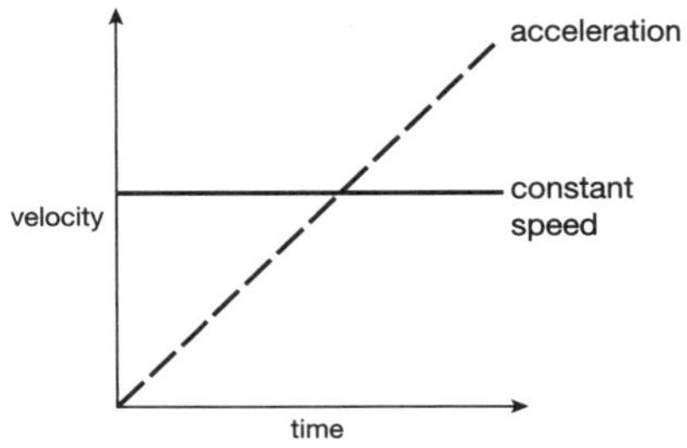

b The gradient is equal to acceleration
c Deceleration = 16 m/s^2
3 a Cell b Filament lamp
c Resistance = 30 Ω
d The total resistance of the circuit increases, so the current in the lamp decreases and the lamp will be dimmer
4 a Similarity: both are electromagnetic waves/transverse waves/can be polarised
Difference: gamma rays have shorter wavelength (or higher frequency)
b Several gamma ray sources are pointed towards the cancerous cells in the patient; the energy of the gamma rays destroys the cancerous cells
c Helium particles are emitted from radioactive nuclei; they are positive and consist of two protons and two neutrons
d The proton number decreases by two; the mass number decreases by four

GCSE Biology B5 and B6

1 a Two boxes ticked: closed, double
b i Arrow drawn from vena cava to right ventricle to leave heart; re-enters in pulmonary vein into left atrium to left ventricle to leave heart
ii Flaps drawn between atria and ventricles or at base of blood vessels leaving heart
iii To prevent backflow of blood
c i Blood pressure in the ventricles will be similar but pressure should be higher in the left ventricle, to force blood all around the body. Therefore, blood leaving the left ventricle will be at a lower pressure. The blood will mix between the left and right ventricles, so blood leaving the heart to go around the body will have less oxygen. The baby's cells/muscles will be short of oxygen and have less energy
ii Rejection of tissues so the transplant fails. Long-term use of immunosuppressive drugs will affect the immune system

2 a Fat, protein

b The stains will not be removed; enzymes denatured

c Enzymes are specific in their pH requirements and usually require neutral conditions

d Protease digests proteins, lipase digests fats. Protease produces amino acids and lipase produces fatty acids. These dissolve in water and leave the shirt

e Immobilised lactase – converts lactose into glucose and galactose. Immobilised enzymes are combined with other chemicals (alginate)

GCSE Chemistry C5 and C6

1 a $S_{(s)} + O_{2(g)} \rightarrow SO_{2(g)}$

b $2SO_{2(g)} + O_{2(g)} \rightleftharpoons 2SO_{3(g)}$

c V_2O_5 catalyst, around 450 °C, atmospheric pressure

d A lower temperature would increase the equilibrium yield of SO_3 but would not be economic because the reaction rate would be too slow

2 a Hydrated iron(III) oxide

b Iron is oxidised because it loses electrons to form Fe^{3+} ions and oxygen is reduced because it accepts them

c Coating the iron prevents contact with oxygen and water

d Zinc protects the iron even when it does not cover it completely, because it is more reactive; if the layer of tin is scratched it makes the iron rust faster than unprotected iron because the tin is less reactive

GCSE Physics P5 and P6

1 a The force is the gravitational force due to the Earth

b 1 day (24 hours)

c The satellite has acceleration towards the Earth's centre and a centripetal force that is also directed towards the Earth's centre

d They are used for communications

2 a Refraction is the bending of a wave or light at an interface

b The incidence angle in glass must be greater than the critical angle for glass; the ray must travel from glass towards the air/glass interface

c Correct refracted ray and weak reflection shown

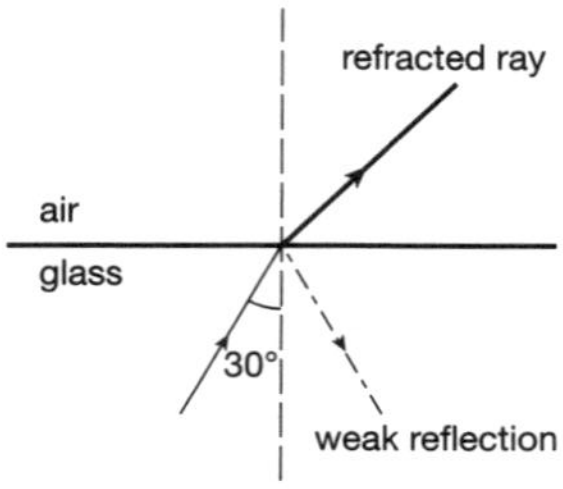

3 a The resistance of the component remains constant, e.g. filament lamp (or diode)

b i Correct shape of curve; graph goes through the origin

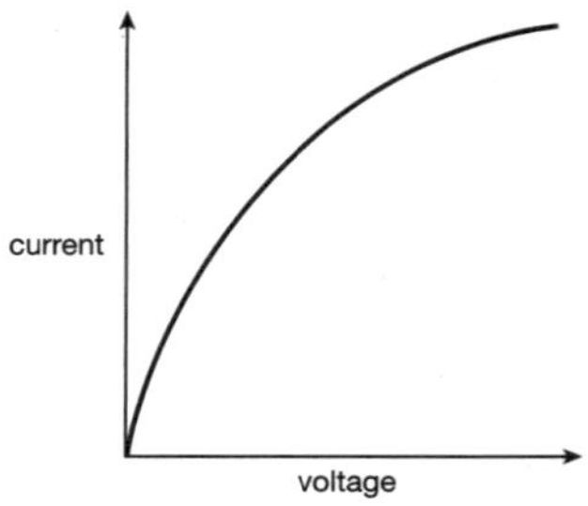

ii Read off the current for that particular voltage from the graph; use the equation:

$$\text{resistance} = \frac{\text{voltage}}{\text{current}}$$

to calculate the resistance

iii The resistance of the lamp increases as the filament gets hotter and the electrons collide more frequently with the vibrating atoms

4 a A signal that only has two possible values – high (1) or low (0)

b Correct column for the output

A	B	output
0	0	0
0	1	1
1	0	1
1	1	1

A	B	C	D	E
0	0	1	0	1
0	1	1	1	0
1	0	0	0	1
1	1	0	0	1